Computer Science
Résumés
and
Job-Finding Guide

Phil B. Bartlett

BARRON'S

About the Author

The author during the past eight years has reviewed more than 60,000 job candidate résumés. During his business career, he was personally involved in the hiring of more than 500 employees, three of whom rose to top corporate senior management ranks of Fortune 500 and equivalent services companies. He served as a senior corporate officer in three technology companies, one in document processing, one in telecommunications, and one in data processing. He was the CEO of a successful start-up company that grew from zero employees to today's base of several thousand. He has a B.A. degree from the University of Iowa and today, in addition to writing, serves as a management consultant and management recruiter.

Note: Users of this book should be aware that web addresses often change. Every attempt has been made to provide you with the most current Internet and e-mail addresses available. However, the nature of the Internet makes it virtually impossible to keep abreast of address changes that may occur past the date of publication.

All inquiries should be addressed to:
Barron's Educational Series, Inc.
250 Wireless Boulevard
Hauppauge, New York 11788
www.barronseduc.com

Library of Congress Catalog Card No.: 2004046201

International Standard Book No.: 0-7641-2907-4

Library of Congress Cataloging-in-Publication Data

Bartlett, Phil B.
    Computer science resumes and job-finding guide / Phil B. Bartlett.
        p. cm.
    Includes index.
    ISBN 0-7641-2907-4
        1. Computer science—Vocational guidance. 2. Computer industry—Employment. 3. Résumés (Employment)   I. Title.
QA76.25.B38 2005
004'.023—dc22
                                                                    2004046201

PRINTED IN THE UNITED STATES OF AMERICA

9 8 7 6 5 4 3 2 1

Table of Contents

Introduction

Successful job hunting today in the computer science field has caused frustration and disappointment for countless numbers of IT (information technology) job hunters. For many, the abundance of web job-posting sites, internet search engine alternatives, and numerous publications related to the job-hunting process collectively are somewhat overwhelming and sometimes misleading.

In the past, networking contacts had always been the primary source of IT jobs. Today, although still a viable source for use, networking is taking second place to employer and web job-posting sites that exist.

Internet job hunting is the most frequently used source for IT job hunting today by a large margin. This is due to its convenience of use and the large number of sites that are dedicated to job posting.

From the perspective of IT job hunters, use of the web exclusively presents two problems. The primary one is that, for every new job posted in the major metropolitan areas of the United States, often as many as several hundred applicants may apply. A second significant problem is the total time required online to locate a significant number of jobs of interest for job candidates.

This occurs today because most job web-posting sites do not currently have available filters that identify only the job titles of interest to each candidate. This deficiency will probably change over the next several years, but today when candidates search for a specific job title on most of the sites with the largest number of jobs posted, their key word searches frequently identify scores of jobs for each query when in reality there are only a few jobs that are applicable to each candidate's qualifications.

The overall objective of this book is to provide IT job hunters the tools and process alternatives to help them become more effective and successful in job hunting by focusing upon job hunting as a process containing five critical components. The following components represent the primary content of this book, which is designed to help IT job candidates successfully pursue their job-hunting activities:

Résumé writing
Locating the best IT job opportunities
Résumé distribution
Getting interviews
Winning in interviews

This book discusses these five critical components of job hunting and will provide readers with ideas, techniques, and specific directions regarding alternatives for

1. Assessing their skills and experience consistent with what employers want to know today.
2. Locating an adequate quantity of jobs to pursue considering their geographical preferences.
3. Developing each candidate's employer prospect list so that the candidate will not experience as much competition as he or she is likely to encounter using most web job-posting sites.
4. Reviewing the alternative sources for IT employment that exist today.
5. Identifying the best available alternatives for employer research for use in initiating employer contacts and in preparing for personal interviews.
6. Refining techniques for use in self-marketing that assist candidates in getting job interviews.
7. Providing assistance in preparing for personal interviews that supports effective performance and techniques for gaining commitment for further consideration beyond screening and initial interviews.

1. Today's IT Job Market

The Objective of This Chapter

This chapter will provide readers with awareness and understanding of the forecasted growth of primary IT job categories between now and 2010. It also analyzes the types of jobs that are available today. This information can be useful for additional IT education considerations as well as career direction for new and entry-level employees. The section on newer and evolving IT employment opportunities will challenge experienced IT professionals to revisit their job experience to be certain that their personal résumés best represent their skills and total qualifications related to the changes that IT employment is undergoing today. The goal for many employees will be to achieve skills and experience that is not as vulnerable to outsourcing outside of the United States.

IT JOB PROJECTIONS 2005 TO 2010

For those estimated 200,000 some IT professionals currently unemployed, the IT profession may not seem to represent a good career employment opportunity. Current IT U.S. employment as forecasted by the U.S. Department of Labor, Bureau of Labor Statistics is estimated to total 2.8 million jobs. By the year 2010, the U.S. IT job base is forecast to grow 43% to the annual employment level in excess of 4 million IT jobs.

This is the approximate job growth expected to occur in these job categories:

Computer software applications engineers	360,000
Computer software systems engineers	220,000
Computer systems analysts	260,000
Network and computer systems administrators	180,000
Database administrators	60,000
Computer programmers	50,000
Computer support specialists	430,000

This forecasted job growth is possibly the most valid data available today because the U.S. Bureau of Labor Statistics has detailed data available on current IT employment by job category by industry designation. Many sources may question the validity of this forecasted data owing to the reduction in staff by many larger companies and the outsourcing of thousands of entry-level and mid-level IT programming jobs offshore.

Even though most forecasting organizations do not consider job growth in the many thousands of new, small- and medium-sized organizations in the United States, the Department of Labor does. The infoUSA corporation's database of public and private organizations of 50 to 499 employees contains company data available for some 458,000 plus organizations within the United States as of this writing. Organizations of this size are likely to provide a significant percentage of the projected IT job growth between today and 2010. Small- and medium-sized companies and organizations today are believed to employ more than one half of the total employed U.S. workforce.

THE BEST IT JOB OPPORTUNITIES TODAY

During 2004, the author reviewed approximately 70,000 IT jobs posted in several of the web job-posting sites that listed the largest number of currently available jobs. These data provide more specific and comprehensive detail than the Bureau of Labor Statistics. Although it is subject to change somewhat over the months, it provides a good indicator of the IT hiring trends that exist.

The Top 20 IT Jobs Most Often Listed in 70,000 Web Job Postings During 2004

Job Category	Total Jobs Posted
Computer software engineers (applications and systems)	11,640
Information security engineers and specialists	5,109
C, C++ developers and programmers	4,601
Technical and software applications project managers	4,172
Computer programmer/analysts	3,607
Database engineers and developers	3,019
IT management	2,905
Network development engineers	2,898
Java/J2EE developers and engineers	2,774
Web developers and engineers	2,504
Oracle developers	2,394
Linux developers	2,241
Unix developers and administrators	1,735
Computer systems analysts	1,678
Quality assurance, engineers, analysts, and testers	1,630
Network and computer systems administrators	1,590
.NET developers (including ASP.NET and VB.NET)	1,570
Oracle database administrators	1,569
Database administrators (other than Oracle)	1,436
Network systems and data communications analysts	1,339

This sampling of today's IT jobs coupled with the Bureau of Labor Statistics forecasts are indicators of the types of computer science jobs available today and those that will be available during the next several years. These data can be helpful for making career plans and decisions to further IT education and change jobs.

Another important aspect of today's U.S. IT jobs is their skill requirements. The following chart summarizes the top IT skill requirements contained in the sampling of the 70,000 jobs reviewed.

**Primary Skill Requirements for Top IT Jobs
(based upon sampling of 70,000 web-posted IT jobs during 2004)***

Skill	Frequency of Listing	Skill	Frequency of Listing
SQL	11,200	Weblogic	2,615
Security	10,870	Data modeling	2,585
Technical Support	9,950	SAS	2,235
Java Language	9,500	Oracle 8i, 9i, 11i	2,120
Project Management	8,350	Wireless	2,050
Unix	8,100	AIX	2,035
Windows 2000	7,570	Cisco	1,970
Knowledge Management, Business Analysis	7,380	ASP.NET	1,870
C language	6,940	Sybase	1,865
C++ language	6,665	Unix/Linux	1,690
XML language	6,640	Firewall	1,670
J2EE language	6,585	Crystal reports	1,610
Consulting	6,530	STF	1,590
Quality Assurance	5,580	IIS	1,585
HTML language	5,230	COBOL	1,580
SQL Server	5,215	EDL	1,515
.NET	5,110	SDLC	1,480
Rational	4,700	Siebel	1,320
Assembly language	4,670	VB.NET	1,270
SAP	4,445	Embedded Software	1,240
Oracle SQL	4,160	ERP	1,240
Unix Script	4,120	DNS	1,235
Security clearance	4,080	CRM	1,220
PERL	3,845	TS/SCI	1,190
MS SQL	3,415	GUI	1,165
Solaris	3,240	SOAP	1,060
Visual Basic	3,215	Apache	920
Active Server	3,210	LDAP	885
Java Script	3,180	DHTML	870
WebSphere	3,095	HTTP	860
DB2	3,080	VPN	850
Linux	2,940	Servlets	790
JSP	2,935	Algorithms	780
ASP	2,920	FTP	750
TCP/IP	2,840	XSLT	700
Windows NT	2,825	ATM	690
People Soft	2,745	API	660
PL/SQL	2,695	JMS	645
Shell Script	2,630	CSS	640
		HP-UX	610

Skill	Frequency of Listing	Skill	Frequency of Listing
XSL	570	SCI	400
JCL	520	T-SQL	400
CORBA	490	Frame Relay	390
UDB	485	ADO	340
OOD	470	Clear Case	330
SMTP	465	CGI	320
SNMP	460	NFS	280
Data Mining	460	CTI	270
ADO.NET	450	ISS	225
PHP	450	PIX	220
DTS	445	IOS	210
CVS	440	ksh	210
MySQL	440	MATLAB	200

* Most IT web-posted jobs require a range of five to ten of the skills listed.

These data substantiate the growth of IT jobs associated with the development and administration of activities associated with the web, data communications networks, relational databases, and information and data security needs. It also supports the apparent growth of Linux as an operating system.

Software writing (programming) is the one area where the Bureau of Labor Statistics growth projections are in doubt. If we consider the current rate of outsourcing of this job category outside of the United States, it is feasible that this area will show negative growth between today and 2010. The number of programming jobs outsourced by large U.S. technology and IT consulting organizations is forecasted to exceed 400,000 jobs or greater by numerous sources during the next several years.

This loss of jobs will occur as a result of the competitive advantage and profit improvement aspects associated with the outsourcing. A significant amount of software writing/programming job opportunities may exist in the older legacy systems area. A recent study commissioned by the IT consulting firm E5 Systems in conjunction with Bain Capital indicated that as much as 80% of $1.7 trillion spent on IT each year goes toward maintaining old installed systems. This estimate indicates that today there is still a large need for software writing associated with modifying and updating these older legacy-type systems.

This opportunity should not be overlooked in job search, especially for those experienced in the COBOL and FORTRAN disciplines.

In addition to the top 20 web-posted IT jobs listed earlier in this chapter, there are thirty additional job classifications based upon the sampling of 70,000 jobs that also indicate potential alternatives for those considering job change or those new to IT employment. This data is also an indicator of the growth of several of the newer technology and software related job growth opportunities that are evolving.

The Top 30 Secondary IT Jobs Most Frequently Listed in 70,000 Web Job Postings During 2004

Job Category	Total Jobs Posted
Applications programmers	1,273
SQL analysts and administrators	1,250
Sun Solaris engineers and developers	1,047
Computer programmers	907
Web analysts	874
Embedded software engineers	837
Cisco network engineers	745
Programmer/analysts	702
Computer support specialists (tech and help desk)	674
Web administrators	657
Perl developers and engineers	649
PeopleSoft developers and analysts	643
Algorithm engineers	616
Wireless engineers and developers	602
Java consultants	507
Technical writers	480
SAS analysts	446
Computer operators	309
Operations research analysts	292
Encryption engineers	287
SAP developers and administrators	276
WebSphere developers	274
DB2 database administrators	239
COBOL programmers	233
CRM administrators	215
PHP	193
MySQL	175
Delphi programmers and analysts	162
FORTRAN engineers	153
VoIP engineers and developers	103

NEW AND EVOLVING IT EMPLOYMENT OPPORTUNITIES

During the past year, the fastest growing job segment within IT has been jobs associated with information and data security relative to computer networks and the internet. The increased use of wireless systems will also contribute to making computer network security one of the leading IT job growth opportunities for several years.

Three additional areas of high potential job growth included in this secondary listing are wireless, CRM (customer relationship management), and VoIP (voice over internet protocol). In wireless, there is sizable job growth opportunity within the telecommunications industry today and for the next several years. VoIP is evolving today, and significant IT job-growth-related opportunities will continue to grow rapidly. For those with relevant skills, this is a possibility. Much of this work may be done through IT consulting work.

CRM application developers is a rapidly growing area of job growth. This industry is forecasted to grow by two of the leading IT industry research firms to annual revenues of between $75 billion and $77 billion by year end 2007. Job candidates who have significant application development experience within the sales, marketing, finance, supply chain, and customer relations disciplines will find employment opportunities. There are also employment opportunities for those who have data mining, knowledge management, and call center software expertise.

Most CRM applications will be related to the web, relational database, and network development and engineering areas. Wireless applications also will become more prevalent.

Several of the leading CRM companies specialize in software for specific industries and functional disciplines, which is important for candidates with similar experience. Many CRM companies are relatively new, and there is some degree of risk in employment with many of these companies. Nevertheless it is overall one of the higher-growth technology opportunities and will continue to grow for at least the next 10 years.

THE CHANGING IT JOB MARKET

Today there is justifiably significant concern among unemployed and currently employed programmers in large technology, IT consulting firms, financial services, and other large industrial companies where a large number of employees are basically doing similar software development and programming work. This concern arises because of the thousands of programmers and other IT employees who have lost their jobs as a result of outsourcing outside of the United States. The outsourcing also affects a certain amount of planned job growth by these organizations and others that have not yet outsourced jobs.

Peter Drucker, the renowned management consultant and author, states in a January 12, 2004, interview in *Fortune* that India currently has 150 million people for whom English is a primary language. India's total base of people who are college educated in the technology disciplines during the next several years may be equal to that same portion of the U.S. population. Because India is concentrating on the technology area for job development, IT job candidates can expect to see continuing significant competition from jobs moving to India for the next several years.

To be somewhat insulated from this exodus of jobs in the software writing and engineering disciplines, current employees must seriously consider broadening their areas of expertise and work experience. This will mean additional education, job rotation, and experience in working with newer evolving disciplines for many.

Another factor that may cause further job dislocation in the software area during the next 10 years, is current ongoing efforts to simplify software code writing. One of the former founders of Intel Corporation has been working on this for several years. If and when this materializes and quality computer code can be produced as a result, current non-IT employees who have a detailed understanding of functional applications within their industries as well as the uniqueness of their industry and company business practices can become significant factors in the software-writing discipline.

The problem today for many software writers without similar expertise is that they do not have the in-depth understanding of how software changes and improvements can contribute significant value-added type improvements to their organizations. If they are not able to develop this understanding, the careers of many will become vulnerable to outsourcing or staff reductions. This situation again builds a strong case for job rotation or the building of additional skills and experience within other IT disciplines.

For example, programmers and software engineers who have good functional application expertise within specific industries and who also have experience with networks, databases, and the web will be less likely to have their careers jeopardized. For some time, it has been obvious that individuals who are specialized in one IT function in large companies where large numbers of other employees do similar work are much more vulnerable to job cuts and outsourcing unless their skills are at the top level of their profession.

Because software writing and engineering is currently the largest area of employment within the IT job sector, what does the changing forces in the IT job market mean to those currently in software and those entering this job market?

It means that in the process of updating your résumé you must list your technical skills and emphasize your development of items such as industry- and functional-knowledge-specific application experience and knowledge.

In addition, employees with interpersonal skills, communications skills, team participation and leadership skills, problem analysis and solving skills, and project participation and management skills should aggressively market them along with their technical skills.

Candidates who have contributed to significant accomplishments that helped solve significant problems or added significant value to their organizations should highlight these accomplishments in their résumés. In some cases, the employer will see these soft-type skills as being just as important as the candidates' technical skills inventories.

The author recently reviewed more than 1,200 IT job applicant résumés and found that less than 14 percent of these résumés listed these softer skills in their résumés. Less than 10% listed verbal, written, and interpersonal skills, even though today more than 30% of all IT employers list one or more of these skills as a requirement in their web-posted job descriptions.

The rate of inclusion of these skills as being desirable has increased above the 30% level to 50% and higher for jobs in the IT consulting, management consulting, and application services provider job postings.

Approximately 14% of the 1,200 résumés reviewed listed the following soft-type skills:

Interpersonal skills (includes oral and written communication)	50%
Analytical, problem solving	20%
Team building/leadership	15%
Project management	8%
Industry-specific knowledge	5%
Other miscellaneous	2%

Chapter 5 includes a detailed listing of the skills desired by employers and their frequency of occurrence in the 70,000 web-posted IT jobs reviewed. The trend for inclusion of soft-type skills has increased significantly during the past 10 years, but today they still appear in less than 5% of all résumés submitted for consideration for all occupations. The author, while reviewing more than 50,000 résumés during the past 8 years, saw the frequency increase from less than 2% of all résumés eight years ago to as high as 14% for IT résumés today. The reason for this significant increase is that employers recognize the relationship of good soft skills to employees' job success and contribution to their work group. Today some of the more progressive companies value soft skills as highly as 50% of total job responsibilities and performance. Candidates who have good to excellent soft-type skills as well as some of the skills covered in the section entitled "Employer Ranking of Most Desired Nontechnical Skills" in Chapter 5 need to update their résumés and emphasize these skills in their job application efforts. The type of work that requires these types of skills is less likely to be outsourced outside of the United States.

For many current employees, additional education, job rotation, and experience in other primary IT disciplines will not guarantee lack of vulnerability to job outsourcing but, as a minimum, will strengthen their marketability in the IT job market. For example, if you have expertise in C/C++, Java, or Java2EE, you may want to become Cisco network certified, which could provide triple-dimension-type skills—programming, database, and networks. If this type of portfolio will not enhance your potential value in your current employment, you may want to consider contacting the smaller- and medium-sized organizations in the 100 to 999 employee range, of which there are approximately 170,000 listed in the referenceUSA and Employer Database products of infoUSA covered in the Chapter 9 section entitled "Tailoring Your Job Search."

During the next several years, there will be numerous job opportunities for software engineers who have expertise in the information and data security, VoIP, open source software and wireless communications disciplines. Many IT employees who have the relevant skills in these disciplines, when their development work may be finished in their current organizations, will have employment opportunities within consulting organizations or as individual consultants.

For the next 10 years as a minimum those who have these skills will have significant opportunities to apply their knowledge and expertise in the small- to mid-sized growth organizations that will have needs for these services.

GROWTH OF NONTRADITIONAL IT EMPLOYMENT

As high as 20 percent of IT employment opportunities in the United States today are located in what the author defines as nontraditional employment sources. For the purposes of discussion, these employment opportunities are classified as "defined term"-type opportunities. They are primarily project oriented and have a planned duration of 6 months to as much as 2 years. Dice, Inc. (*dice.com*), a leading technology online job-posting service consistently lists 30,000 to 40,000 technical job listings per month. As many of 40% of these listings are for contract-type (limited-term) employment opportunities.

Although many contract-type projects may be located within corporate or government organizations, the candidate sourcing services will be provided by staffing or contract employment organizations. IT management consulting and application services providers will also be good sources for employment in these limited-duration projects. A profile of some of the staffing, contract employment, IT consulting, and management consulting firms that are most active in IT hiring for these type of projects is included in Chapter 9.

The large IT and management consulting firms doing IT consulting, also annually post a significant number of permanent jobs.

Job candidates with strong industry-specific applications knowledge who have expertise in one or more of the primary disciplines—security, networks, databases, and the web—and who have strong interpersonal skills may find significant job opportunities within the web site job postings of the IT and management consulting firms and the applications services providers. Some of the permanent-type jobs in many of these organizations will at times require extensive travel working on projects outside of the candidates residence area.

HOW AND WHERE MOST IT JOBS ARE FOUND TODAY

The author believes that as much as 80% of all IT jobs today are found by networking and searching for jobs on company and independent job- and résumé-posting web sites. Estimates exist within the job hunting industry that as many as 70% of all IT jobs today are found through networking.

Richard Nelson Bolles, author of the best-selling job-hunting book *What Color Is Your Parachute,* in his book *Job-Hunting on the Internet* believes that as many as 45 out of every 100 IT jobs today are found through internet-search-related activities. Whether these estimates are entirely representative today is debatable, but Bolles' research as well as other industry estimates support the advice that networking and web résumé- and job-posting sites should receive a job candidate's primary attention and effort in any job search efforts.

The author believes that networking estimates related to job-finding success are somewhat suspect today. This is especially true for an estimated 200,000 or so IT professionals who are currently unemployed or working part-time.

Networking

Networking today is possibly still the best source for IT job hunting for most job candidates. In the past it has been widely reported to be responsible for as much as 70% of IT job placements. This estimate may be accurate for job candidates who have top-level technical skills and job experience that is in demand today.

For the majority of IT job hunters, most specifically those who have experienced significant periods of unemployment, these estimates are not valid. If you have skills and experience in demand and you have good networking sources who respect you and know your capabilities within your targeted job geography, networking is still possibly your best source for IT job hunting. However, total dependence upon networking is risky for most IT job seekers.

The best possible network source is a former work associate or employer who has a good current knowledge of the local IT employment market where you want to work and who understands and respects your experience and skills. Other than this situation, participation in local IT associations is often a good potential source of learning about the availability of jobs that are not yet advertised or posted on the web. IT networking organizations today operate in larger metropolitan areas such as Manhattan and Chicago and are another potential source for contacts.

The author has talked with several job candidates who spent quite a bit of time concentrating on network-related job-hunting activities but did not identify enough specific opportunities relevant to their skills, experience, and job and geographic preferences that resulted in interviews. This point underlines the inherent risk in pursuing only a few potential sources for jobs.

As a guideline, if candidates are not able to schedule a minimum of three interviews for every 100 contacts made, including network resultant contacts, web sites where their résumés are posted, and web sites where they have applied for individual job-listing consideration, then they would be wise to consider alternative methods of contact. The data in Chapters 8 through 10 can be helpful for anyone who falls in this category.

If candidates decide to change their job-hunting strategy, they should first review the material in Chapter 6 to be certain that their résumés do the best possible job of representing their job experience and their technical and soft skills.

Web Job-Posting Sites

In *Job-Hunting on the Internet,* Richard Nelson Bolles indicates a near 45 percent success rate for IT job seekers using the internet job-posting services. The primary problem with these services is that unless your skills and experience are in high demand, you will often be competing with as many as several hundred applicants for a newly posted job, which can put you at somewhat of a disadvantage. In addition, organizations that use web job-posting services have complained that as many as 70 percent of applicants who post their résumés do not meet the qualifications listed in the posted job description.

For many IT job seekers, online résumé posting or responding to online posted jobs may not work as well as might be desired. Chapter 8 further explains why and in what situations responding to web-posted jobs may not be the best method of locating appropriate job opportunities for many new job candidates. This situation probably has merit for those who are currently unemployed or who are looking for initial employment within the IT job sector.

Chapter 8 lists the web job-posting sites that posted the largest number of IT jobs during 2004. This information is important in the IT job search because job candidates need to spend their time focusing upon the sites that regularly have the largest number of IT jobs. Several of the web job-posting services repeated the same job as many as three times during the course of 30 days. The same job may also be posted on more than one site. It is a good idea to make a copy of the posted job description for every job for which you post your résumé for consideration. Also keeping a summary type log is wise because recalling where you have posted your résumé and for what job becomes increasingly difficult as the number of jobs you have responded to increases.

If you have specialized IT job interests regarding local, state, and federal jobs as well as jobs classified by industries, occupation, or specific educational disciplines, you should locate one of the latest publications that contains the details regarding the web job-posting sites for specialized interests. You should not, however, review anything older than a 2003 or 2004 publication because in the author's review more than 50 percent of the directories changed in one year's time. This happens as a result of the newness and rapid change that many of the web posting sites are experiencing.

The sites listed in Chapter 8 had the most IT job postings during 2004, but this information is subject to change annually. An excellent publication for special interest job sites is the Public Library Association, 2002–2003 edition of the *Guide To Internet Job Searching* published by VGM Career Books. The authors, Margaret Riley Diker and Frances E. Roehm, have prepared the most comprehensive and current source directory that the author has seen for job and career search information sources on the internet.

Today, owing to the rapidly changing IT job market, everyone pursuing or in the IT profession should have a written, annually updated career plan and personal résumé on their PC. Also they should have a formalized job-finding strategy to follow when needed.

The career plan can be a one-page summary-type document that recognizes change within the profession and outlines the personal skill and experience improvement plan necessary for continuing relevance and employment several years into the future. Suggestions for assistance with these items is included in Chapters 4, 5, and 7. The plan should consider such things as an individual's annual job performance, changes in technology that have relevance to the individual's job responsibilities, and education or other job experience's that can help the individual become more valuable to the current employer.

TODAY'S LEADING U.S. IT JOB MARKETS

For those candidates who apply to IT jobs posted by the web job-posting services, there are several important correlations as to where the majority of computer science jobs are today. This is meaningful for job hunters if they are to be effective in their online search efforts and still expend the least time possible.

The U.S. Department of Labor, Bureau of Labor Statistics has compiled IT job data by major metropolitan area through the year 2002. The author believes that this is the most valid data of this type available because it is based upon the submissions of employers. The primary value of this data is that it indicates where the majority of IT jobs are today in the United States. This is where IT job hunters will probably find the most opportunities during the next several years. This opportunity is a result of job growth and also a function or employee turnover due to retirement, job change, and employment terminations.

The Bureau of Labor Statistics (BLS) reports that, at the end of 2002, approximately 2.8 million computer-science-related jobs existed in the United States. This IT job base is forecasted by the BLS to grow to 4 million IT jobs by year-end 2010. Of these million jobs, approximately 50 percent of them exist in 24 Standard Metropolitan Statistical Areas (SMSAs) in the United States. These SMSAs are used for the purposes of census, job, wage, and other economic data.

The following is the most current data that the BLS has released.

Metropolitan Area	Total Computer Jobs by Year End 2002
Washington, D.C.-Northeastern Virginia area	166,160
Chicago	98,810
New York City metropolitan area	93,750
Los Angeles-Long Beach	84,628
Boston	79,460
Atlanta	73,540
Dallas	72,520

Metropolitan Area	Total Computer Jobs by Year End 2002
Seattle-Bellevue-Everett	65,120
San Jose	64,440
Philadelphia	58,100
Minneapolis-St. Paul	54,750
Houston	45,950
Detroit	45,480
Denver	44,360
San Francisco	41,040
Baltimore	37,390
Orange County, CA	37,180
Raleigh-Durham	34,530
San Diego	34,510
St. Louis	34,180
Austin	31,996
Middlesex-Somerset-Hunterdon, NJ	30,680
Oakland	30,560
Newark	26,610

During 2004, the author reviewed the job location for approximately 70,000 computer science web-posted jobs from several of the largest posting sites. The results were that 64% of the new jobs reviewed were located within the 24 U.S. SMSAs with the largest IT employee populations as tracked by the Bureau of Labor Statistics. This is compared to these 24 metropolitan areas representing 50% of the existing IT jobs, as tracked by the Bureau of Labor Statistics.

Although some degree of change exists, there is still a strong enough correlation to be meaningful for IT job hunters. For those job hunters for whom these data are not meaningful, "IT Job-Posting Sites with the Most Jobs" reviewed in Chapter 8 as well as the other sources for job prospecting will be helpful.

Results of the 2004 sampling of 70,000 IT postings by metropolitan area shows the following results.

Metropolitan Area	Share of 70,000 New IT 2004 Job Listings
Washington, DC-Northeastern Virginia-Baltimore area	7,945
New York City-Long Island metropolitan area	6,372
Los Angeles metropolitan area	5,429
North Central New Jersey	4,129
San Jose	2,844
San Francisco-Oakland	2,819
Seattle-Bellevue-Everett	2,062
Boston	1,980
Philadelphia	1,735
Chicago	1,674
Atlanta	1,424
Dallas	1,311
Minneapolis-St. Paul	972

Metropolitan Area	Share of 70,000 New IT 2004 Job Listings
San Diego	885
Denver	775
Austin	591
Houston	527
St. Louis	486
Raleigh-Durham	441
Detroit	413

As a point of interest in comparison, Dice, Inc. (*dice.com*), during 2003 and 2004, consistently listed these metropolitan areas as the leading monthly technology job markets.

Metropolitan Area City	Monthly Job Range
New York City	3,700–5,900
Washington, DC	1,800–4,500
San Francisco	3,000–3,600
Los Angeles	1,800–2,600
Chicago	1,300–1,800

There is some degree of correlation between these data and the author's analysis of the leading U.S. job markets. The *dice.com* database includes all technology jobs, while the author's analysis included only IT jobs.

Also noteworthy for IT job hunters is the results of the 70,000 sampling of web-posted jobs for the following metropolitan areas.

Metropolitan Area	Share of 70,000 New IT 2004 Job Listings
Ft. Lauderdale	502
Tampa	489
Cincinnati	485
Charlotte	404
Miami	403
Phoenix	398
Milwaukee	358
Kansas City	354
Cleveland-Akron	339

By including these nine metropolitan areas, the new job sampling indicates that 40 metropolitan areas within the United States represent more than 70% of total IT job hiring each year in the United States. Considering turnover as well as incremental jobs, this analysis is understandable. Annual turnover resulting from such things as retirement, health problems, resignations to take other jobs, and terminations of employment for other reasons means that as much as 15% of the total IT job base will turn over each year for these types of reasons.

Consequently, companies in large metropolitan areas such as New York, Los Angeles, Chicago, and Boston will always be looking for several thousand employees each month. The significant IT hiring that exists today in the Washington, DC-Baltimore-Northeastern Virginia-Maryland periphery areas will show a lower turnover rate owing to federal government expansion hiring and the fact that annual employee turnover will not be as high as the other large metropolitan area.

The thing to remember is that these are indicators of where most of the IT jobs are today based only upon a limited sample of the online jobs postings of several of the larger web job-posting services. There is certain to be some degree of replication, but the sampling is statistically large enough to be valid. The author also reviewed 10,000 IT job listings during mid-2003, and the results were quite similar. The only major difference was the movement in positions of total jobs for some cities. For example, the San Francisco area in mid-2003 showed less than 25 percent of the total listings that it shows during early 2004.

For those who are entering the IT job market for the first time and for those who are now employed, looking for new affiliations, and willing to consider relocation, this type of data can serve as a guideline defining where to target job search activities so as not to waste a significant amount of time.

Overall, 2004 hiring activity in the majority of the major metropolitan areas showed a significant increase over 2003. The employment areas that remain soft are programming and software writing in the large technology companies and software development in the larger IT consulting firms, financial services companies, and large industrial corporations where most of the outsourcing of jobs outside of the United States has occurred.

2. The IT Job-Winning Process

The Objective of This Chapter

This chapter provides a summary type overview of the five critical components of the IT job winning process. Each of these subjects will be covered much more comprehensively in later chapters. For readers in any portion of the IT job search process, this chapter's purpose is to provide thought stimulation regarding each job candidates strategy and progress in the job-finding process, regardless of whether the candidate is just beginning or far into the process.

Another objective of covering all of these important job-hunting components early is to challenge candidates current search methods as well as to provide exposure to the potential value of new ideas and approaches that have not been considered by the readers.

For many candidates, the job-winning process today will be the equivalent of a full-time job. The amount of time needed is particularly difficult for many who have full-time jobs but are interested in changing affiliations. This means a lot of evening and weekend effort. For those who are unemployed or new to the IT job market, a significant amount of self-discipline is required daily to generate an adequate level of activities relevant to a successful job search. The author believes that, whatever your level of experience or skill, this publication will provide helpful information that can help you to be successful in your job search. There are approaches and techniques herein to accommodate almost everyone's preferences.

Every relevant part of the IT job search is covered somewhere in this book. In addition, this book offers several techniques and ideas that the author has not seen in any other job-hunting-type publications to date. The important thing is that you find an approach or technique that works for you.

THE FIVE CRITICAL COMPONENTS OF IT JOB WINNING

To be successful in IT job hunting today, most job hunters need to be effective in all five of these important activities.

1. Writing the résumé
2. Locating the best IT job opportunities

3. Distributing the résumé
4. Getting interviews
5. Winning in interviews

Writing the Résumé

Your résumé is the experienced IT professional's career report card and the first-time job seeker's summary of potential for success in the IT job market. Some individuals in the job search business tend to discount the importance of one's résumé in the job search process.

The quality of a job candidate's résumé is often the primary reason that a potentially qualified candidate for an IT job does not receive proper consideration. What is being communicated here is, that if you are at the top of your profession in jobs skills and academic achievement, of course you will receive some degree of employer interest even if your résumé does not comprehensively define your capabilities and potential value.

If you are serious about locating the best job opportunities possible, your résumé must comprehensively define your skills, employment history, and total qualifications. Otherwise, you simply will not receive the degree of employer interest that your experience, skills, and accomplishments justify. This situation has occurred time and again when accomplishments, value provided, soft skills, and industry- and application-specific content have not been included or properly developed in résumés.

In the author's experience, the biggest contributor to poorly developed résumés is lack of time spent in preparing the résumé and an inadequate explanation of how the candidate's skills and capabilities benefited the previous employer. The worst culprit in this situation is the one-page résumé. This author has reviewed hundreds of these résumés, which tend to belittle the skills and potential of job candidates to prospective employers. This subject will be covered in detail in Chapter 6.

Since 1996, the author has reviewed more than 50,000 résumés of applicants wanting to obtain jobs with annual incomes ranging from $50,000 to as much as $300,000. In 90% or more of these résumés, the author believes that the candidates did not properly present their skills, experience, and accomplishments. Most had spelling and grammar errors, used action words improperly, and did an inadequate job of properly describing the candidate's work experience, responsibilities, and significant accomplishments. Many that were mailed were of poor quality appearance, fonts that were hard to read and the author trying to apply action words to make them read more impressively. In hundreds of cases, the end result was a poorly written résumé that did not make sense.

Keep in mind that the résumé represents the work output of years of work for job candidates who were frequently at the annual income level of $80,000 to $120,000. In the author's opinion, the résumé is also a primary reason why thousands of IT job applicants who have posted their résumés to scores of web-posted job listings are not receiving the type of employer interest they would like to receive.

Most job applicants are not professional résumé writers. Also, the author believes that too many job candidates have relied on résumé-writing guides that have provided them with improper or inadequate advice.

Using action words is one of the suggestions that often contributes to an end product that does not do the job candidate justice. Many résumé-writing guides advocate the use of as many as 100 action words; however, there may at the most be 30 to 35 words that have some degree of relevance for potential inclusion in an IT job candidate's résumé.

Another suggestion of questionable value is the use of a functional résumé instead of a chronological résumé, which lists the current or most recent job first. Functional résumés are often hard to follow and are confusing for the reader, making it difficult for them to understand career job progression and responsibilities. Even for candidates who are new to the IT job market or in search for their first job, the use of the functional format is still questionable. Because they lack job experience, new college graduates normally use different component formats and order of presentation, which is fine.

New and recent college graduates are the only candidates who can justify using one-page résumés. Any IT job candidate who has had two or more jobs and has had more than 3 years of on-the-job experience in most cases will reduce his or her chances of employer interest by using a one-page résumé.

During the past 8 years, the author has seen hundreds of résumés that obviously came from candidates receiving outplacement support, where the outplacement advisors recommended using one-page résumés. Most of these individuals were above the annual income level of $80,000 per year and in most cases significantly diminished their chances for potential employer interest unless their record of significant accomplishment was exceptionally strong.

In contrast, the résumés of PhD scientists who have done advanced chemistry and material science work use three or four pages to explain the work and accomplishments of these scientists properly and may include attachments of several additional pages detailing things like patents received, articles and work papers written, speeches given, and honorary-type achievements accomplished. The majority of these individuals were in the $80,000 to $110,000 annual income range and in most cases had between 7 and 12 years of work experience. If this is typical within these disciplines, why should it be any different for a computer science professional with similar levels of experience and income levels? It certainly goes beyond the logic of a one-page résumé. And if applicants have good skills and experience, why should they undermine their potential value?

Another frequently common mistake made is use of action words to add more content to a résumé because a candidate is in a hurry to get it completed. This addition of filler does more harm than good. For anyone in that situation most frequently there has not been enough thought given to the planning of the content to be used in the résumé.

As mentioned earlier, employers are saying that as many as 70% of candidate responses to web-posted jobs do not meet the specifications for the job listing. As an IT professional, your résumé must be comprehensive, present your skills and experience in a proper format, and be relevant to the posted job description. If not, your résumé will not get attention when compared to others that achieve these conditions.

Chapters 5 and 6 will help you construct the best possible résumé based upon your personal situation. The process provided in these two chapters will help you relate your background to situational examples that will help you avoid mistakes that will place your résumé at the bottom of the piles of résumés that recruiters and employers receive in response to web-posted jobs.

For applicants to complete their best possible résumé, they should first assess their technical skills, experience, soft skills, and any accomplishments that have benefited the employers by solving significant problems or adding significant value to the organization's business processes. These accomplishments should include contributions made as a participant on a team or project group. Any specific industry experience as well as functional application knowledge should be developed, as should relevant knowledge in multiple IT job functions.

For example, if you decided to market yourself using a self-promotional campaign, to research small- and medium-sized companies of 100 to 500 employees within your preferred work geography, and to make the initial contacts through a query letter without including your résumé, how would you present yourself in the letter? What would be a statement of the services that you would offer prospective employers for consideration? This type of marketing is not done often enough by IT candidates in their job-hunting activities. It is so much easier to web-post your résumé or apply to web-posted jobs. This type of creative marketing takes more time and effort in research and implementation to do it professionally. These are some of the things candidates need to evaluate.

The February 14, 2004, issue of *Fortune* states that U.S. companies have sent over one half million tech jobs overseas in the past couple of years. All IT professionals today need a well-thought-out and developed strategy to avoid getting trapped into this outsourcing situation, especially if they possess basic or immediate level programming and software writing skills. Open source software is another potential threat to the employment of many. If an employee is among those whose future employment may be threatened by the proliferation of open source software, what can he or she do to turn this possible threat around and benefit from it?

The vast majority of IT job hunters do not use soft skills as a potential benefit in their résumés. As was mentioned in Chapter 1, less than 15% of more than 1,200 IT professional's résumés reviewed during 2004 included any mention of soft skills. This observation stands in contrast to a detailed review of more than 10,000 web-posted IT job descriptions where more than 30% of the employers had included one or more soft skills as being a desirable skill requirement.

The type of personal skills included in the soft-skills category are interpersonal skills, which covers the entire range of communication skills (verbal, written, presentation, and listening), team and group participation skills, customer or other end user relationship building, training and end user instructional ability, project management and problem solving skills, to name a few of the most frequently mentioned skills.

In summary, a significant improvement opportunity exists for the résumés of the majority of computer science job applicants. Most résumés reviewed tend to focus primarily upon the listing of technical skills and work experience. Most résumés can improve significantly by addressing soft skills, functional application knowledge, industry-specific knowledge, and the overall category of significant problem solving and value contribution to the business practices of the employing organization. Examples of how to do this will be reviewed in Chapter 6.

Locating the Best Job Opportunities

If you have not been satisfied with your previous job search results or if you are just beginning your search, reviewing Chapters 8 and 9 could be helpful. Possibly some new job sources reviewed in this chapter can provide you with some additional alternative sources of jobs that you have not yet considered.

After reviewing the potential sources of jobs in Chapter 8, completing the recommended employment strategy document could prove to be helpful, regardless of where you are in your personal job search process. This strategy, in essence, becomes your job search action plan.

The listing of the most active IT job posting sites in Chapter 8 will help you avoid significant wasted internet time. Because you will find some degree of duplication for jobs of interest, it is a good idea to keep a log to avoid posting more than once for the same job. The only exception would be if you posted a different résumé version for testing purposes.

It is estimated that the web posting sites listed in Chapter 8 at this date will post more than 90% of the total IT jobs posted by the web job-posting services. This estimate does not include much of the IT job posting for the government and corporate web sites. Keep in mind that you are most likely to receive interest from those postings where your résumé most closely matches the skills and experience requirements of the job specification.

It is important to remember that dependence on web job-posting services alone is risky because of the fact that the listing sources may receive as many as several hundred responses to a posting. Because of the number of responses for most of the jobs, it is easy for most résumés to be lost with the masses without the possibility for any feedback. You will also want to respond quickly to any posting that appears to fit your employment background and skills.

Another important factor to remember is that jobs that are attractive to you are in most cases attractive to scores of other job candidates. Considering this, you should check the posting services you are using once or twice a week for new listings and respond rapidly to any postings of interest to you. Waiting a week or two for most good opportunities is too long because, in many cases, candidates of interest will already have been selected. In addition to web job postings and postings in your local media sources, most public libraries as well as college and university libraries have company directories, which are good sources for identifying companies to contact in the geographic areas of interest to you.

If you are not identifying enough potential organizations to contact, see the section entitled "Tailoring Your Job Search" in Chapter 9 where the public and private company database of infoUSA is discussed. In any major metropolitan area, this database will identify hundreds of potential organizations to contact regarding potential employment. This database includes contact information for more than 13 million organizations throughout the United States.

You may find the infoUSA database available through your state employment assistance office or in local colleges, universities, or larger public libraries. This excellent database is available under the name referenceUSA in college and university libraries and under the name Employer Database in state employment assistance offices. The primary advantage of using this database is that you can tailor your search to a defined geographical area, size of company (annual revenue or employees), and industry SIC code designation (Standard Industrial Classification).

If you are not receiving the desired results from posting your résumé on the web or responding to the web job-posting services or corporate web sites, sending query letters to small- and medium-sized companies that you have selected for contact from this database may provide positive results. Many of the small- and medium-sized companies in this database do not use online job-posting services so you will not experience any significant degree of competition for many jobs that you find.

Different techniques for use of query letters for contacting potential employers rather than sending out résumés is covered in Chapter 10.

Résumé Distribution

Because no single source in the United States catalogs more than 30% of the currently available IT jobs at any given time, it is wise to cover most of the primary sources. The largest IT web job-posting services may list a maximum of 30,000 to 40,000 IT jobs at any given time; however, there may be as many as 200,000 IT jobs available across the United States on a continuing basis from all web posting services. When you consider that the total IT U.S. job base of 2.8 million jobs is projected by the Bureau of Labor Statistics to be growing at a rate of approximately 140,000 jobs annually and then factor in 15% average annual turnover for IT jobs and factor out the jobs that are duplicated posted in the same and like services, there are realistically likely to be 100,000 IT jobs available each month.

The problem is that no one single source is aware of where the jobs are. This is why many job hunters committed to serious jobs search must work multiple sources before they are able to secure jobs. This is also why job candidates need to have their résumé on file in retained and contingency executive search firms of which there are several thousand that handle IT job placements.

The government today is another excellent source of thousands of annual IT job openings that many applicants often choose not to pursue because of the procedural aspects of applying. Chapter 9 provides data regarding government IT job potential, as well as the available online sources for locating and posting résumés for consideration for these jobs. When properly researched and understood, government IT job opportunities in many U.S. localities may compare more favorably to those available in the commercial sector. This is definitely a factor when considering the employment stability factor. It is also doubtful that any significant amount of government IT work will be outsourced outside of the United States. The only exception to this would possibly be the government's inability to hire the IT employees that are needed to complete the work that needs to be done.

For candidates to maximize their potential job opportunities, they must have a plan for résumé distribution. For example, mass mailings of résumés to potential hiring sources is often a waste of time and money. The reasons are many. Many résumés are poorly written, contain more than one spelling error, use inappropriate formats, have a mediocre to poor appearance from a print quality perspective, and are directed to the wrong individual or company, among other problems. The author has seen this mistake occur in hundreds of situations. The end results of these mistakes and many others is that they often diminish consideration of the job candidate.

The unfortunate end result in many of these situations is that job candidates who have good qualifications often do not receive the consideration they deserve because of poorly prepared résumés. Chapter 10 discusses résumé distribution strategies that can help improve a job candidate's potential for employment consideration.

Getting Interviews

It is amazing to see in bookstores and libraries the number of publications that are focused primarily upon such subjects as résumé writing, sample résumés, cover letter writing, and interviewing. Even though each of these subjects is an important aspect of job hunting, to be successful in their job searches candidates must apply a basic process effectively for each key component of the job search process.

Possibly the most critical aspect of job finding that is rarely covered in most job-finding publications is how to go about getting interviews. Basically, you are nowhere in the job-finding process until you are able to secure a significant number of personal interviews. Other than winning the job, getting quality interviews is possibly the most difficult challenge that most IT job candidates face.

In the job-hunting process, subjects such as résumé quality, insufficient identification of jobs where a candidate's qualifications meet the hiring organization's needs, inadequate distribution of résumés, distribution of résumés to sources of questionable value, insufficient effort in posting résumés on the web or applying for web-posted jobs, and poor targeting of potential employment sources to contact, can all hurt a job candidate's chances to schedule an adequate number of personal interviews.

At this juncture in the job-hunting process, if the candidates have not eliminated themselves from interview consideration as a result of one or more of the previously listed choices they have made, the most challenging part remains. How do candidates get a sufficient number of personal interviews for jobs in which they are interested? What type of personal performance do they need to exhibit during these interviews to be given further consideration for potential hiring and to move further through the interviewing process?

Enhancing one's chances of securing job interviews is a function of research, analysis, and a large number of other activities directed toward the jobs that the candidates have identified as being appropriate for their skills and experience. The problem for most applicants is that they do not move quickly enough with quality actions for newly posted jobs on the web job-posting services. Candidates need to look at the job-posting sites they have chosen to use daily, or as a minimum every 2 or 3 days, to be certain they respond quickly to all postings that appear to be a good match.

Getting interviews is comparatively difficult for most job candidates. The exception may be those individuals who, via their résumés, appear to have the best array of skills and successful experience. However, if you are new to the IT profession, have been unemployed for any significant period of time, want to change careers, or have had IT employment for 20 years or more and are at the higher end of the income range for your job category, securing a significant number of interviews may take more effort over a longer period of time.

The job search will often also require a higher quality effort that is more smartly focused than is a general posting of résumés to online posting services. In many cases, if candidates are to achieve the type of success they desire, they must employ some innovative techniques. Some of these techniques are outlined in Chapter 10.

Candidates who have put forth a significant job search effort and who have not been successful in obtaining job interviews should consider reengineering every part of their job-finding process. They need to identify the areas where there is significant opportunity for improvement that can help improve their results.

First, candidates must realistically assess their skills and experience from a value provided perspective. Candidates who have been job searching for several months and have not achieved the desired results need to consider changing their strategies. This means reviewing the material in Chapters 4 through 11 to identify the specific areas of the process that will most effectively improve job search results.

This type of exercise takes self-discipline and commitment to complete a meaningful assessment and then to put forth the effort necessary to improve results.

Candidates must follow up this type of reengineering assessment by experimenting with techniques they have not yet tried. For some, the problem may simply be one of improving the quality of activities through better and more effective efforts. For others who are frustrated and discouraged, it will take a change in attitude and a willingness and determination to try some new approaches and techniques to break through some of the barriers.

Self-marketing is not an easy thing for anyone, and it is possible that thousands of job hunters who are frustrated and discouraged have become their own worst enemies by letting rationalization and the wrong type of attitude take over. Frankly, most of us are not too effective in situations where we believe that we have applied a lot of relevant effort to something such as job searching and have not experienced any degree of success with the results. It is basic human nature to want to avoid things that we have put considerable effort into and have not achieved the results we wanted.

The author does not intend to overcomplicate job search. He believes that thousands of job hunters have not achieved the success they desire primarily because they have used the wrong approach and have applied a great deal of effort toward activities that, when critically analyzed, did not have much chance of succeeding.

Most IT job hunters have consulted publications and many other sources for advice that did not provide them with effective advice.

During the past year, the author has reviewed more than one hundred job-hunting/finding-type publications that focus on one or more of the important process components associated with successful job finding. Out of all these publications, only four or five represented the quality and relevance necessary to help job hunters be successful in today's job search activities. The author believes that these things are more critical in the IT job market today than in the general job search market. As mentioned earlier, the author does not see the necessary level of sophistication in the majority of résumés from IT job candidates.

Job candidates may want to consider some creative and different approaches. If you have strengthened your personal résumé to the maximum degree possible and have done a good job of identifying both the web job-posting sites that you believe offer you the best potential and other prospective companies, you may want to look at other types of contact and ideas outlined in Chapters 7 and 10 as well as the Tailoring Your Job Search section of Chapter 9 can be helpful.

The use of query letters and résumés specifically tailored to individual companies and industries is not normally advocated, but their use could prove beneficial.

If you decide to test tailoring of your search, the quality of your research is important. Also important is the strategy, techniques, and tactics that you use in efforts to schedule personal interviews. In responding to online job postings, you will not have a lot of time in most situations to research the companies. You will have much more time to research organizations in which you are trying to create interest in yourself but that have not posted jobs.

Every candidate who is serious about the job search needs to be able to optimize the most important aspects of the five critical components of job winning discussed in this chapter. Some of the more fortunate candidates are quickly successful in their job search endeavors. For most, however, they must implement the highest possible quality process for the primary job search components, and they must do so several more times throughout their IT careers.

Winning in Interviews

After you are successful in securing interviews, either in person or over the telephone, you must engage in proper research and preparation. Being ill prepared is a primary reason why many candidates do not succeed in moving beyond the initial interview. This is unfortunate, especially when in many situations the candidate is qualified to be seriously considered for the job. The better the job a candidate does in researching a company to understand their needs and type of work, the more confident a candidate will usually be during the interview.

Chapter 11 provides advice and some ideas regarding preparation for and personal performance during interviews that can help you win. Winning in every interview is gaining a commitment to proceed on to the next step leading to a formal job offer.

Other than lack of proper preparation for the interview, a significant number of job opportunities are lost during interviews because job candidates display questionable judgment during the interview. There are many reasons why candidates lose a good job opportunity during interviews. Sometimes candidates do not show proper respect for the hiring companies' internal procedures, which in some cases may require several additional interviews.

Candidates also lose out because they ask too many questions regarding the company and job during the interview or inquire about the salary opportunity and other benefits such as vacation at an inappropriate time. In initial interviews, candidates should be totally focused upon convincing the interviewers that they are well qualified for the job, answering any skill- and experience-related questions of the interviewer to their satisfaction, and learning if they will be considered further for the job and what the next step will be.

Candidates get into trouble primarily because they are uneasy during the interview. They are often overanxious and concerned about whether they are doing well. At times, this manifests itself by asking too many questions which will often make the interviewer think that the candidate may be hiding something. Questions regarding salary and benefits should come at the end of the process as should anything of a personal nature. The initial focus and discussion should be on convincing the interviewer that the candidate is well qualified and capable of achieving what they need to accomplish.

In medium-sized to large-sized companies, their process may entail several interviews with several people, and candidates should view every step as an opportunity. Usually only in smaller companies where a senior official does the interviewing will things move rapidly. If you are interviewing in a company with several hundred to more than a thousand employees and the interviewer shows impatience and is anxious to move quickly, this is not a good sign and can indicate that significant problems exist within the company.

There exists a tendency within the IT profession to oversimplify the job-hunting process and treat it too lightly. In the author's opinion, this has contributed to conditions within the industry where many candidates have had far too many jobs, many of short duration. If a candidate possesses this type of outlook and is not willing to show patience and to employ a comprehensive process in the key aspects of job search, in many cases they are relegating themselves to lower quality, temporary or short-duration contract-type employment, which may better suit some candidates if this is their outlook.

Asking questions during interviews shows interest, but asking too many questions often prevents the interviewers from covering all the matters that are important to them. This may also create doubt about the candidate's qualifications. If candidates research the company and job properly, their primary questions should be used to better understand items of importance from the perspective of the interviewers. This is important in order for the candidate to respond properly to any items that are of primary importance.

The key thing to keep in mind in all initial interviews is that, in most cases, they would not have scheduled you for an interview unless they thought that your qualifications warranted it. Also your objective is to win and gain the next step commitment. Remember that, in most situations, you will be competing with several other candidates. If you believe that the job is a good opportunity for you, you want to do everything possible to be the final candidate and have the ultimate right of acceptance or refusal of an offer.

Taking the posture at the outset that you are evaluating the company is a judgment mistake. Even if you are, you do not want to give that impression by your actions. The goal should always be to move forward in the process. Your presence, attitude, enthusiasm, and verbal communication are also important parts of successful interviewing that are further discussed in Chapter 11.

At the end of an initial interview, candidates need to try to close for a commitment to move further. If this cannot be accomplished beyond the we-will-let-you-know-type closing, candidates should try to determine their status so as not to waste further time and hang on to any type of unrealistic further expectations. If the interview was an initial screening interview conducted by someone other than the ultimate hiring manager, it is a reasonable request to ask frankly whether the individual interviewing thinks that there will be any further consideration. In doing this, candidates want to be certain that their verbal manner is friendly and does not appear overly aggressive or denote impatience. If candidates are still uncertain after asking this type of thing, it may be a good opportunity to ask something to the effect of, "Is there anything that I can do or any type of assignment that I could complete to address any potential concerns that you have regarding my qualifications for further consideration?" If you do not get any type of a reaction in a situation where you have doubt, in most cases what you sense is probably correct, and the end result is that you will not be considered further. You might also say, "You seemed to indicate that my qualifications are good, is there anything of a personal nature that concerns you, things such as my manner or communications skills? If there is anything of this nature that is a concern, please be frank because I realize that it is important how you think I might fit into your organization."

This type of probe at the conclusion of the interview at times will open up the interviewer to voice some concerns, especially if the inquiry is done in a pleasant manner and is discussed in terms of the organization's chemistry.

At times, this type of query may also open up discussion of some concerns regarding a candidate's qualifications that the interviewer was not previously comfortable in discussing. If this should occur, this opens up the possibility of the question, what can I do to prove to you that this should not be an item for concern? This is the type of situation where requesting some type of assignment might be appropriate.

Keep in mind that today, in many cases, you have expended a significant amount of effort prior to achieving the initial in-person interviews. If you have researched the organization and believe that it represents a good potential employment opportunity for you, you want to do everything possible to try to move forward in every job interview. Everything that you have done prior, does not really matter now unless you are able to gain a commitment to move ahead. This is the point where many candidates lose opportunity.

It is frustrating and disappointing to have gone on several interviews for good opportunities and not win. If this occurs, you have to assume that your résumé was adequate but how you handled yourself during the interview was the problem.

In those situations where your performance needs to be changed significantly to be effective, you need to remember that in some interviews the interviewers are particularly vague on purpose to see how the candidates handle themselves. In these situations, you must sell yourself by presenting your skills as a potentially valuable solution based upon your knowledge of the company, the job description, and any of its challenges discussed in the interview. If you have not completed proper research, this will be difficult, if not impossible, in most situations.

In any interview where you are unable to acquire significant information regarding the organization and are not able to obtain a detailed job description and have made the effort, you should mention this at a proper time early in the interview. You should also suggest that with this information you might be better able to explain how your skills and experience could benefit the organization.

Chapter 11 will go into much more detail regarding techniques that can help you perform effectively in personal interviews. The author believes that this subject is possibly the most critical one in the job-hunting process. This observation based on the fact that, when the author reviewed more than 100 job-finding-related publications, this most important subject is the one that receives the least mention, which is somewhat ironic when you consider its importance.

3. Skill Requirements for Today's Top IT Jobs

> ## The Objective of This Chapter
>
> This chapter identifies the top IT jobs that employers are trying to fill today. Also included is a brief review of the newer and emerging IT jobs.

The skill profiles provided in the last section of this chapter can be useful for candidates in their job search when reviewing the online job postings. Many of these job skill profiles represent stand-alone jobs. But more importantly, many of the most frequently posted job skills are requirements for several of the leading jobs.

Another important point in candidates' jobs searches is the requirement for good written and oral communications skills, which are now mentioned as desirable in more than 30% of web-posted job specifications. The critical importance of communications skills is highlighted by the fact that during a 2004 review of more than 1,200 IT job candidates' résumés, these skills were listed in less than 5% of the résumés reviewed. This and other items of importance infrequently listed in candidates résumés are discussed in Chapter 6.

LISTING OF TODAY'S TOP IT JOBS

This listing is the result of the author's 2004 review of approximately 70,000 IT job postings on the online posting services. The data were also compared to the 2003–2004 job skill profiles of Dice, Inc. (*dice.com*). *Dice.com* is one of the leading technology job-posting sites, which during 2003 and 2004 has consistently posted 30,000 to 40,000 technology jobs each month.

Online IT Job Postings Consistently in the 8,000 to 15,000 Job Range Monthly

- C,C++ Developers, Programmers
- Oracle Developers and Database Administrators
- SQL Software Engineers
- Unix Developers, Administrators

- Windows NT, 2000, XP Programmers
- Java Developers, Programmers
- Java/J2EE Developers and Engineers
- Programmer/Analysts
- Network Security and Web Security Engineers
- Software Engineers, Applications and Systems

Online IT Job Postings Consistently in the 4,000 to 8,000 Job Range Monthly

- Project Managers
- Web Developers, Administrators
- ASP/ASP.NET Programmers
- Database Engineers, Architects
- Computer Systems Analysts
- Network Engineers, Administrators
- IBM DB2, WebSphere, AIX Engineers

Online IT Job Postings Consistently in the 1,000 to 4,000 Job Range Monthly

- Perl, Other Scripting Programmers
- Linux Developers
- Systems Administrators
- .NET Developers
- Wireless Engineers, Developers
- Embedded Software Engineers
- IT Management
- Cold Fusion Engineers

NEWER AND EMERGING IT JOB OPPORTUNITIES

High Growth Industries for IT Jobs Today

Gartner, Inc., forecasts that government, healthcare, and education will be the higher growth industries for IT jobs between 2004 and 2007. These industries are forecasted at an average annual composite job growth rate of 12%. Much of the federal job growth will be for contract work or limited-duration-type projects contracted with outside IT consulting and technology contractors that specialize in government contract work. A significant portion of these jobs will require security clearances. The last section of Chapter 8 and the government section of Chapter 9 provide more detail regarding job growth in these sectors.

VoIP Engineers, Developers

The March 1, 2004, issue of *Information Week* reported the results of a survey of 300 business and technology executives, which indicated that more than 80% said that their companies are using, testing, or planning to deploy VoIP technology.

Web, Network, and Database Security Engineers

The need for web, network, and database security engineers currently is greatest for organizations concerned with global intellectual property protection and knowledge management database content security. Many of the related developed initiatives are handled by IT consulting and applications-services-provider-type organizations. This means that many of the incremental new jobs will be for a limited duration on a contract or project basis. The residual permanent jobs will be for systems administration and related maintenance functions. Some degree of permanent jobs will exist in small- and medium-sized organizations where candidates have the ability and experience to handle security development and skills required of other IT job classifications.

Embedded Software Engineers, Programmers

Jobs for embedded software engineers and programmers will continue to increase and will provide significant opportunities to candidates with strong embedded software experience. These opportunities will occur primarily in companies that manufacture PDAs (personal digital assistants), digital gaming devices, mobile phones, palm top, and hand-held devices as well as organizations with embedded web and database applications needs.

Linux Open Source Engineers, Programmers

Thousands of organizations are currently considering switching to or migrating toward the Linux alternative. Good employment opportunities are available for candidates with Red Hat Linux, Unix operating system (Unix, AIX, Sun Solaris, HP-UX, IRIX), C++, Perl shell scripting, Java front end GUI and Windows NT, 2000 skills and experience. In addition, candidates who also have MySQL open source experience will have additional potential value.

Wireless Engineers, Developers

Every month more wireless-related jobs are appearing. It is expected that this trend will continue for the next several years. This situation will present good employment opportunities for candidates with good WIFI protocol, IP telephony, network communications, embedded systems, and C/C++ programming experience and skills.

Scientific Programmers, Engineers

Although jobs for scientific programmers and engineers have existed for quite a few years, today more and more companies such as IBM, GE, and Microsoft are benefiting from global communication of R&D and other technological development work. This is also occurring in the drug and gene research development work of pharmaceutical and other medical research institutions. This work has and will continue to result in increased demand for knowledge workers who have IT, math, and other physical science discipline experience and software engineering skills.

Customer Relationship Management Programmers

This rapidly growing software development discipline is forecasted to grow to the annual revenue level of $75 billion to $77 billion by year-end 2007. Several of the current industry leaders are IBM, Siebel, SAP, PeopleSoft, and Oracle. Several of the Big Five management consulting firms also have CRM practices. Several newer small companies that have entered this market have shown some degree of early success are E-piphany, Pivotal, Salesforce.com, and WhisperWire.

The largest potential revenue growth area within CRM today is software that focuses on sales, marketing, and the supply chain, which are all primarily focused upon business relationships with external customers. Maintaining excellent customer service is associated with the quality and timeliness of the administration of these items and has a critical relationship to annual revenue growth.

Specialized software for the finance, accounting, procurement, engineering, human resource, and manufacturing functions has existed for many years as have software modules for the administration and management of employee-benefit-related programs within organizations. Sales, marketing, and the supply chain have a much stronger relationship to external customer service and relations. The sales, marketing, and supply chain disciplines for the most part had been left behind in value and level of sophistication compared to other key functional software until the last several years.

Sales force automation software, which focuses upon customer/prospect contact and sales lead management, has existed for more than 20 years and is the forerunner of today's more sophisticated CRM software, which incorporates data mining and other intelligent-type software that helps manage the most important portions of the sales, marketing, and customer-service-related process.

Software engineers and programmers who have industry-specific application development experience will find job opportunities in several places. It can be found in the thirty plus CRM companies that are developing new software components. Engineers and programmers with operations research math and algorithm skills and experience may also find good opportunities within CRM companies.

Also existing will be project-related contract job opportunities for IT professionals who have previous successful experience with the implementation of CRM software in larger organizations.

Digital-Programming-Related Opportunities

Digital-programming-related jobs have existed within the movie and entertainment industry for some time. The newer jobs requiring this skill have appeared during the past several years within advertising and marketing promotion-type organizations. The need for these type of skills has been incremental to the more traditional computer graphics, multimedia, and CAD-CAM-type skills required of graphic artists and other graphics specialists.

Project Managers

Job opportunity in this discipline increased significantly during 2004. A significant percentage of these jobs can be classified as project contracts or defined-term jobs where IT consulting firms and technology contractors have formal contracts for the project.

Examples of these types of contracts include COBOL-based legacy-systems undergoing conversion to newer languages; security systems development for database, web, and network systems; and retail industry systems conversions requiring high volume transactions processing expertise.

Some of the present project management needs are focused on Linux, Java, and Oracle initiatives, which are all currently in high demand. Many networking projects requiring voice and data communications knowledge and the capability to manage the development of high-volume, fault-tolerant networks are in demand. Project managers for systems engineering/architecture projects are also needed. These positions require knowledge and expertise in database development, hardware platforms, and programming knowledge related to the most popular software languages as well as legacy software that is undergoing conversion.

INFLUENCE OF THE INTERNET ON IT JOBS

For subjects such as knowledge management, marketing, data mining, and application of intelligent analytical type software, many new IT-related job opportunities will continue to develop during the next 10 years. Because applications are better defined for these types of data management categories, new descriptions for IT jobs will continue to evolve. These types of initiatives can be classified as the application of more creative and sophisticated computer science capabilities.

Consistent with these developments, many IT professionals proficient in these types of capabilities will become consultants or will choose to start small businesses of their own. Today the U.S. Department of Labor reports that there are approximately 3 million IT employees in the United States as reported by their employers. There are an estimated additional 1.5 million individuals self-employed as consultants or individual business proprietors in the IT profession who are not included in the government data.

As with the previously discussed CRM software, the web will continue to evolve as a cost-effective method to provide companies with valuable data for developing their market potential as well as for developing more intelligent databases of potential customers for their products and services.

This type of activity is currently undergoing what might properly be defined as the learning phase for most organizations that use the web for marketing purposes. Many IT professionals will continue to apply creativity to develop new opportunity areas for businesses focused upon web-related application.

Software writers and systems engineers who gain successful experience working with the newer type of intelligent software applications will have significant opportunity to enhance their career opportunity during the next 10 years. The author believes that skilled software engineers and other IT technologists who have industry-specific knowledge of key applications within the R&D, engineering, marketing, sales, manufacturing, and supply chain disciplines will have significant competitive career employment advantages for at least the next 10 years. The ability to work effectively with the web and other communications technologies that are evolving is also an important aspect of any type of continued employment.

In addition, IT professionals who have education or significant experience working within the physical sciences will have additional advantages. Companies sharing internet, intranet, and extranet data across the United States and globally today are receiving significant benefit from shared technology work. General Electric, Microsoft, and IBM, for example, are today benefiting from this worldwide shared technological expertise.

Today the global sharing of knowledge over the web is making significant contributions possible in several important professions. Some of the most noteworthy at this time are medicine, R&D, pharmaceutical drug development, genealogy, complicated surgical procedures, IT technology and software development, and manufacturing/engineering-related processes. Certainly many more examples exist, but these are several of the web-hosted disciplines that offer important potential career opportunities to IT professionals with relevant skills and experience.

These and the previously discussed newer and emerging IT job opportunities are examples of some of the types of job opportunities that exist and are developing and that can make the future employment of many IT professionals less vulnerable to things such as outsourcing.

In conclusion, what is happening in the IT profession is the emergence of more creative and important value-related activities and functions, which have been made possible by the developments within IT technology during the past 10 years. What we are beginning to see is the emergence within the IT profession of new concepts that will continue to place more value on other employee skills in addition to their technical capabilities.

The internet and its related applications possibilities has served as a new force that has possibly resulted in the development of more worldwide employment and business opportunities than any other single factor during the last 10 years.

SUMMARY SKILL PROFILES FOR TODAY'S TOP IT JOBS

During 2004, the author analyzed approximately 1,200 employer job specifications for IT jobs to determine the jobs and related skills that were in highest demand at the time. This survey resulted in the identification of IT skills that were most frequently required for the top IT jobs. It also resulted in the identification of skills that were frequently required and those that were occasionally required for the various jobs.

In reviewing and using this data, it is important to remember that not all skills listed are required by most employers. Only those skills listed as most frequently required showed up on the majority of online job descriptions posted for that specific IT job classification. For each job category, a minimum of 30 job descriptions were reviewed. Those skills listed in the occasionally required portion showed up only a few times on the job specifications.

Also in using this data to prospect for potential jobs, it is important to remember that similar job skill requirements showed up often in several different job classifications, which may present some additional prospects for candidates to consider in their job-hunting activities. The following is a listing of 40 top IT jobs and the associated skills frequently required during 2004.

C++ ENGINEER, PROGRAMMER

Skills Frequently Required
C++ (most frequently required)
Unix (most frequently required)
Java (most frequently required)
Web technology: HTML, XHTML, CSS, JavaScript, DOM
Programming Languages: C++, C, Perl
Data Communications Protocols: TC/IP, IPX, Frame Relay, SNMP
Windows NT, 2000
Oracle
DB2
Linux
Oral and written communication skills

Skills Occasionally Required

MySQL	ksh
UML	Embedded software
JMS	JNI (Java interface)
Rational Rose	ERwin

ORACLE DATABASE ADMINISTRATOR

Skills Frequently Required

Oracle 8i, 9i, 11i (CRM) (most frequently required)

PL/SQL back end DB server experience and SQL queries (most frequently required)

Operating Systems: Unix, Linux, Sun Solaris, AIX

Cold Fusion

XML

Unix Shell and Perl scripting

C++, Java, MS SQL Server

Reporting Tools: Oracle Developer, forms and reports

Verbal and written communication skills

Skills Occasionally Required

SAS	CRM business process and practices knowledge
TS/SCI	Oracle Clinical
ASP	Oracle DBJ Expert Data Architect, Data Modeleru
CGI	Data Modeleru data warehouse, ERwin, UML
Front end GUI	XMD
Process modeling	DB2

JAVA DEVELOPER, PROGRAMMER

Skills Frequently Required

Java, JSP, Java Beans, Java Servlets (most frequently required)

XML code (most frequently required)

Operating Systems: Linux, Unix, AIX, Sun Solaris, Windows NT, 2000

Database: Oracle, MS Access, MySQL, SQL Server, DB2

Programming Languages: Perl, C, C++, HTML, DHTML, VB Script, Visual Basic, MS Access, SQL, PL/SQL

Web: CGI, Flash, Cold Fusion, PHP, CSS, JavaScript

Protocols: HTTP, LDAP

Technology: struts, J2EE

Servers: Apache, Tomcat, BEA Weblogic, JBoss, WebSphere, SQL Server, DB2

Verbal and written communication skills

Skills Occasionally Required

VB.NET	Crystal Reports
Servlets	Rational Rose
Data modeling	

SQL DATABASE ADMINISTRATOR

Skills Frequently Required

SQL (most frequently required)
PL/SQL (most frequently required)
Oracle 8i, 9i (most frequently required)
Unix (most frequently required)
Perl and Unix Shell scripting
Java, C, C++, .NET
Sun Solaris, Windows NT, 2000
Programming: VB, PowerBuilder, C, PL/SQL
Database: MS SQL Server, SQL Server, T-SQL
Verbal and written communication skills

Skills Occasionally Required

Data modeling/mining software	OLAP
JavaScript, VB Script	Cold Fusion
XML, HTML, XSL	MS Access, Excel
Oracle, DB2	ERwin
ADO	UML
ISS	ASP
DTS	

UNIX ADMINISTRATOR

Skills Frequently Required

Unix environment knowledge (most frequently required)
C++ (most frequently required)
Unix Shell scripting (most frequently required)
TCP/IP (most frequently required)
Sun Solaris (most frequently required)
AIX, HP-UX, Linux
Unix in SAP environment
Java, Windows NT, 2000, XP
Perl and Korn Shell scripting
Verbal and written communication skills

Skills Occasionally Required

Database: Oracle, MS SQL, MS Access	JMS
UML	Veritas Cluster
XML, SOAP, web services	VPN (virtual private network)
SNMP	Security
Visual Basic, C, J2EE, DB2	Crystal Reports

Applications/Utilities: Checkpoint, Firewall, SNTP, DNS, FTP
Web Servers: Apache, iPlanet, WebSphere, Oracle

PROGRAMMER/ANALYST

Skills Frequently Required
C, C++ (most frequently required)
Unix (most frequently required)
SQL/PL/SQL (most frequently required)
Operating Systems: Windows NT, 2000, Linux, Sun Solaris
Database: Oracle SQL, MS SQL Server
Languages: Java, JavaScript, C#, COBOL, Oracle 6i, 8i, 11i
Verbal and written communication skills

Skills Occasionally Required
Internet: ASP, ASP.NET, HTML, XML, FrontPage
Additional Database: MS Access, SQL Server, T-SQL, DB2

Active Server, Active X	MySQL
MS Word, Excel,	php
Visual Basic, VB Script	SAS
Weblogic	Citrix
TCP/IP	ADO
Perl, Unix Shell scripting	

JAVA/J2EE DEVELOPER

Skills Frequently Required
Java/J2EE (most frequently required)
Operating Systems: Linux, IRIX, Windows NT, 2000, Sun Solaris
Programming Language: Java, J2EE, JavaScript, XML/XSL, C, C++, C#,
VB Script, DHTML, SQL, Perl
Database: Oracle 8i, 9i, MS SQL, SQL Server, DB
Unix Shell script
IBM WebSphere
BEA Weblogic
Writing and verbal communication skills

Skills Occasionally Required
Additional Software: J2SE, Java Servlets, ASP.NET, ASP, Visual C++

JSP, Enterprise Java Beans	TCP/IP
Java Virtual Machine	ISS
GUI	JMS
HTML	CMP
Struts, servlets	Crystal Reports
PL/SQL	Rational Unified Process, Rational Rose
J2EE security architecture	Rational Requisite Pro

SOFTWARE ENGINEER APPLICATIONS, SYSTEMS

Skills Frequently Required
C, C++ (most frequently required)
Java (most frequently required)

J2EE (most frequently required)
Visual Basic, Visual C++ (most frequently required)
XML (most frequently required)
Operating Systems: Unix, Linux, Sun Solaris, IRIX, Windows NT, 2000
Database: Oracle, SQL, SQL Server, DB2
TCP/IP
Unix and Linux kernel
ASP, ASP.NET
Data mining from legacy systems
Verbal and written communication skills

Skills Occasionally Required

Perl, Korn, CGI, Unix shell scripts   JBoss
QA   VB Script
WebSphere, Weblogic   JSP, Java Beans
Communications Protocols: IP, RIP, OSPF   LabView
Tomcat, Apache servers
ISS
Checkpoint Firewall
ADO (Active X Data Objects)
RDO (Remote Data Objects)
ETL
ERwin
Code debugging
Embedded software
UML modeling, OOA, OOD
Rational Unified Process
SNMP
GUI
Cold Fusion
Crystal Reports
Certifications: CCNA CISSP

SECURITY ENGINEER

Skills Frequently Required

TCP/IP (most frequently required)
Windows NT, 2000 (most frequently required)
LDAP, LDAP Compliant Directory Services (most frequently required)
Firewalls, Cisco systems (most frequently required)
Security Software: VPN, encryption, cryptography, ISS, ASA, Cisco PIX
IOS Checkpoint, Net Screen, Sidewinder
Networking: IP, ATM, Frame Relay, RIP, DSL, SNMP, wireless LAN, cellular, ISDN
Protocols: VPN, IPSEC, L2TP, PPTP, SOAP
Operating Systems: Windows NT, 2000, XP, Unix, Linux, Solaris, AIX
Source Code: Java, Java Enterprise, Script & Beans, C, C++, C#, ASP, ASP .NET

Database: Basic SQL, LDAP
Web Page Design: HTML, JSP, ASP
Web Servers: IIS, Apache
Web Security Tools: Rational Unified Process, Oblix, getAcess, Clear Trust, Secure Way
Security Clearance: TS/SCI (DITSCAP) NIACAP, DCID 6/3
Certifications: CISSP
Verbal and written communication skills

Skills Occasionally Required

MS Access, Java, J2EE	Oracle Security Engineer
Wireless technology	IP
WebSphere, Weblogic	PL/SQL
Vision MS Excel	Perl Shell scripting
URL filters	VLAN'S
Antivirus	

WEB DEVELOPER

Skills Frequently Required

Java, Java Script, Java Beans, JSP (most frequently required)
XML, HTML, DHTML (most frequently required)
SQL, SQL Server (most frequently required)
Operating Systems: Linux, Unix, AIX, Solaris, Windows NT, 2000
Programming Languages: Java, JSP, Java Beans, J2EE, Java Servlets, Oracle 8i, 9i, VB Script, ATP, VB .NET, Visual Basic
Database: Oracle, MS Access, MySQL, SQL Server 2000
Web Development Language: HTML, CGI, XML, Flash, Cold Fusion, PHP, JavaScripts, CSS
Protocols: HTTP, LDAP
Servers: Apache, Tomcat, BEA Weblogic, JBoss, WebSphere, DB2, Oracle
Scripting Frameworks: ASP, ASP .NET, ASP .IIS, Cold Fusion, PHP, VB Script, CGI Script
SQL queries
C, C++, C#
Verbal and written communication skills

Skills Occasionally Required

CORBA/COM
FrontPage
Source Control: SOAP, LDAP
Apache administration

DATABASE ADMINISTRATOR

Skills Frequently Required

Java (most frequently required)
SQL (most frequently required)

Oracle database administration (most frequently required)
Oracle 8i, 9i (most frequently required)
XML (most frequently required)
Unix, Sun, Perl Shell scripting
Operating Systems: Windows NT, 2000, Unix, AIX, COBOL
Database: DB2, DB2 Connect, UDB. DB2v7.2, SQL Server, Oracle, MS SQL Server 2000
Programming Languages: Visual Basic, JavaScript, C, C++, HTML PL/SQL, Embedded SQL
OLAP
Verbal and written communication skills

Skills Occasionally Required

Database security software
Data modeling experience using UML
Cold Fusion
Case tools
COBOL
Unix C++ Server
Data mining software
QA testing

PROJECT MANAGER

Skills Frequently Required

Previous successful project management experience (most frequently required)
CRM/ERP software implementation experience
Operating Systems: Linux, Windows NT, 2000, Unix, HP-UX, Solaris, AIX
Database: TIS/XA, DB2, Oracle, SQL, PL/SQL, MS SQL Server
Networking: Frame Relay, VPN'S, VLANS
Programming Language: C++, HTML, XML, COBOL, Perl, Java, Unix shell script
Project Management Software: MS Project, Visio, Documentum
Modeling: Rational Unified Process, Oracle
Verbal, written, communication, and interpersonal skills

Skills Occasionally Required

PMP	DSL	VPN Deployment	802.11a/b/g
VoIP	JSP	ATM	BEA Weblogic

IT MANAGEMENT

Skills Frequently Required

Organization staffing structure and people management
Excellent writing, verbal, and presentation skills
Operating plan preparation and related financial management
Company business practices and functional applications knowledge

Strategic planning capability

Matching of technology to enterprise objectives and strategy

Working knowledge of key IT job classifications and skill requirements

Experience with and/or working knowledge of these IT responsibilities:
- Network, internet, and database security and disaster recovery
- Database and network development and administration
- Internet and intranet development and connectivity
- Systems engineering
- Project management and application development process

QUALITY ASSURANCE SPECIALIST

Skills Frequently Required

Unix (most frequently required)

SQL server (most frequently required)

Java (most frequently required)

Test Scripts: Rational; Robot, Test Manager, Clear Quest & Clear Case (most frequently required)

Verbal and written communication skills (most frequently required)

C++, C, Windows NT, 2000, XML, HTML

Korn Shell and Perl Script

Embedded Web Applications: API, XML, C, JavaScript, php, HTML

Web Testing: WinRunner, TSL scripts, Test Director

Domain Tools: Load Runner, Mercury Tools

Skills Occasionally Required

GUI

SQL Script, SQL query, FTP

ASP

Sun Solaris

Oracle RAC

J2EE, JSP

MS Excel

Clinical System

Embedded systems

NETWORK ENGINEER

Skills Frequently Required

TCP/IP (most frequently required)

VoIP (most frequently required)

Cisco tools and network solutions configuration experience (most frequently required)

Security (most frequently required): Firewall, Intrusion Detection, Encryption

Operating Systems: Windows NT, 2000, XP, Unix, Solaris, Linux

Database: Oracle 8i, 9i, MySQL, SQL, MS Access, MS SQL

OSI Reference Model and Protocols: TCP/IP, FTP, SMTP, AXP, SNMP,

IP suites
Common Protocols: NTP, WIRE, HTTP, DNS, DHCP, ISDN
Wide Area Technology: Frame Relay, SDLC, HDLC, ATM
Catalyst Switches: OS 6.3 & above
ATM/POS/D53/TI
Verbal, writing, presentation, interpersonal, and teamwork skills

Skills Occasionally Required

OSX server	Juniper Routers
IPX	Checkpoint, Nokia firewall
RIP, OSPF, EIRGP, BGF	Kernel programming
XML, HTML	Fractional TI
php, RTP, RSVP	Unix across LANS and WANS
SQL, MS SQL Server	Oracle for Linux
Oracle 8i, 9i for network administration	Unix/Linux Apache web server

Certifications: MCSE, CCNP, Red Hat Linux, CCSE, CCNA

NETWORK ADMINISTRATOR, ANALYST

Skills Frequently Required

CCNA certification (most frequently required)
Active Directory (most frequently required)
Java Web Servers: Weblogic, JBoss, Tomcat (most frequently required)
Network Protocols: TCP/IP, IPX/SPX, FTP, SNMP, SIP, H.323
Security and security intrusion detection software
Verbal and written communication skills
Windows NT, 2000, XP, Unix, Solaris

Skills Occasionally Required

NIDS, HIDS	Catalyst switches
Oracle 8i, 9i, SQL, MS SQL Server	VPN, IIS
Novell, Ethernet, Token Ring	Scripting skill
Cisco Routers, IP Routing	Kernel programming
LAN, WAN client server	MCSE, CCNP, CCIP certifications

NETWORK/DATABASE SECURITY ENGINEER

Skills Frequently Required

TCP/IP (most frequently required)
LDAP servers (most frequently required)
Firewalls: Cisco products (most frequently required) Checkpoint, Net Screen Sidewinder
Operating Systems: Windows NT, 2000, Unix, Solaris, AIX, Linux Red Hat
Wireless technology
Intrusion detection
Verbal and written communication skills

Skills Occasionally Required

Oracle Security Engineer	Perl Shell scripting
IP	PL/SQL

EMBEDDED SOFTWARE ENGINEER

Skills Frequently Required

Operating Systems: Windows NT, 2000, Linux, Unix, Solaris
Languages: C, C++, Assembly, Pascal, VP, Java, HTML, ADO, MATLAB, C#
Protocols/Standards: TCP/IP, FTP, VPN, IEEE, Telnet
Telecommunications: VoIP, H.323, TCP/IP, ATM, TI
Wireless: IS-136, GTSI GSR
Test Scripts: Unix, Perl Shell
DSPC (Digital Signal Processing System Design)
Verbal, written, and presentation communication skills

Skills Occasionally Required

UML, XML, SQL	CSCI embedded testing
Encryption/decryption	Rational Clear Case, Rose (modeling)
J2ME	

WIRELESS ENGINEER, DEVELOPER

Skills Frequently Required

WIFI Protocols including applications protocols (most frequently required)
Embedded systems experience (most frequently required)
Embedded: C/C++, RTOS/Bluetooth, VxWorks, QNX, ThreadX, Embedded Linux
Programming Languages: C, C++, Java, J2EE, JSP, servlets
TCP/IP, IPX, OSI Model
Communications: Cisco wireless (Aironet), RIP, EIGRP, 802.11 a/g network protocol, 802.11 a/b/g (Bluetooth)
Operating Systems: Unix, Linux, Windows NT, 2000
Verbal and written communication skills

Skills Occasionally Required

WML, HDML
UWB (ultra wide band)
QA for wireless
Perl Shell scripts
SQL
UML
VoIP
Java on Unix platform
Application servers: BEA Weblogic, ATG
Certifications: CISP, GIAC

COLD FUSION ENGINEER

Skills Frequently Required

Cold Fusion skill and experience (most frequently required) 4.5 and above

Operating Systems: Unix, Solaris, Windows NT, 2000, XP Professional

Languages: SQL, HTML, XML, CSS, Java, JavaScript, Perl, ASP, C, C++, DHTML

Web Applications: Cold Fusion, IIS, MS SQL Server, SQL Server, CSS, XML, HTML, JavaScript, ASP, JSP, php, VB.NET

Database: SQL server, Oracle, MS Access

Wireless Application Protocol: WML

Verbal and written communication skills

Skills Occasionally Required

Oracle PL/SQL, 8i, 9i, MS SQL		Embedded SQL and HTML
WebSphere	J2EE	Cold Fusion Fuse Box

LINUX ENGINEER, DEVELOPER

Skills Frequently Required

Red Hat Linux (most frequently required)

Sun Solaris (most frequently required)

Perl scripting (most frequently required)

C++ (most frequently required)

Operating Systems: Unix, IRIX, AIX, HP-UX, Windows NT, 2000

Servers: Apache, Tomcat, Veritas Cluster

Languages: Java, Java front end GUI, C, FORTRAN, Assembly

Verbal and written communication skills

Team participation skills

Skills Occasionally Required

Unix Shell scripts

Firewalls: Nokia, Checkpoint

Oracle 8i, 9i

HTML

Cisco applications

ksh scripting

Embedded Linux

DVD Playback

Version Control Language, CVS

Bourne Shells

LDAP

VoIP

MySQL

Relational database connectivity

DATABASE WAREHOUSE ARCHITECT

Skills Frequently Required
Operating Systems: Unix, Solaris, HP-UX, Windows NT, 2000
Programming Languages: SQL, PL/SQL, C, UML, XML, Linux Red Hat
Database: Oracle 8i, 9i, SQL Server 2000
Tools: ERwin, Rational Rose, Crystal Reports
Design: SMP technology architecture
Scripting: Perl, Korn, and Bourne scripts; Unix; Sun Shell scripts; PL/SQL scripting
Verbal and written communications skills

Skills Occasionally Required
MS Word, Excel, Access, MS SQL Query
MySQL
OLAP
C Shell scripting

SYSTEMS ADMINISTRATORS

Skills Frequently Required
Windows NT, 2000 (most frequently required)
Unix (most frequently required)
Linux
MS SQL Server 2000
File Structures: TCP/IP, SNA, DNS, NFS
Verbal and written communication skills

Skills Occasionally Required
Network security, firewalls
Scripting languages
Citrix
Server Environment: Dream Weaver, Front Page, Cold Fusion, Apache, Tomcat
BES (Blackberry enterprise server)
HP Open View
Active Directory Exchange
IIS (internet information server)
Certification: MCSE

IT CONSULTANT

Skills Frequently Required
Strong verbal, writing, presentation, interpersonal, and negotiation skills (most frequently required)
Project management leadership and experience
Software systems engineering including operations research experience
Skills and experience within high-demand newer initiatives: Linux open source, wireless, VoIP, security, relational database, networking, and the web

Skills Occasionally Required
Integration of CRM software with back end legacy ERP systems
Industry-specific functional application knowledge
Conversion of COBOL-based legacy systems
System conversion and integration initiative experience
Data mining experience

CUSTOMER SUPPORT, HELP DESK SPECIALIST

Frequently Required Skills
Operating Systems: Windows NT, 2000, Unix, Linux, AIX, Solaris
Network Protocols: TCP/IP, IPX/SPX, FTP
Software: MS Office (Word, Excel, Access, PowerPoint), Adobe
Acrobat, Tivoli, Oracle
Scripting: Unix, Korn, Bourne, Shell
Hardware and software training ability
Hardware and software troubleshooting capability
Network testing tool and security system knowledge
Verbal and written communication skills

SYSTEMS ANALYST

Skills Frequently Required
SQL (most frequently required)
Unix (most frequently required)
Windows NT, 2000
Languages: Visual Basic, DB2, Java, JavaScript, J2EE, HTML, C++, SQL,
XML
Oracle 8i, 9i
Quality assurance
Unix, Perl, and Korn Shell scripts
Verbal and written communication skills

Skills Occasionally Required

WebSphere, Oracle PL/SQL JPL	UML
Linux, IRIX	ERwin
Rational Tools, Crystal Reports	Servlets, applets

COMPUTER GRAPHICS DEVELOPER

Skills Frequently Required
C, C++ (most frequently required)
Graphics Software: PowerPoint, Lightwave, Flash MX, Adobe;
Photoshop, Presentation Manager, Acrobat, Illustrator, Quark X Press,
Dream Weaver, Corel Draw, Maya
Writing and verbal communication skills

Skills Occasionally Required

Unix, Linux	JavaScript
ASP	DHTML, HTML, XML
SQL Server	XSLT
Perl Script	Object-oriented design

APPLICATION DEVELOPER, PROGRAMMER

Skills Frequently Required

Operating Systems: Unix, Windows NT, 2000, Linux
Database: Oracle, DB2, MS Access
Software: Oracle 9i, SQL Server 2000, ERwin, Rational Rose, MATLAB
Development Tools: Interdev, Net Beans, IDE, Visio
Programming Languages: . NET, VB .NET, ASP .NET, ASP, JSP, CSS, JavaScript, COBOL, PL/SQL, C, C++, VB, HTML, Java, VB Script, SQL, XML, MS SQL
Writing and verbal communication skills

Skills Occasionally Required

Unix Scripts	Crystal Reports
BEA Weblogic	C#
J2EE	

AIX ADMINISTRATOR, PROGRAMMER

Skills Frequently Required

AIX (most frequently required)
Sun Solaris (most frequently required)
SQL (most frequently required)
Java, Java iPlanet, DB2
Oracle, WebSphere
C, C++, TCP/IP
Verbal and written communication skills

Skills Occasionally Required

Korn Shell scripting	LDAP direct server
Tivoli storage management	Data mining
CGI web utilities	Perl scripting

SCIENTIFIC ENGINEER, PROGRAMMER

Skills Frequently Required

C, C++ (most frequently required)
Java (most frequently required)
Operating Systems: Unix, Linux, Windows NT, 2000
SQL, SQL Server, PL/SQL
MS Excel
ISIS
MATLAB, algorithm development
Verbal and written communication skills

Skills Occasionally Required

Java XML, MS Access, Visual Basic, Perl	SQL Chem Draw, Python, LISP
Weblogic, Apache server	VPN VoIP level 3 services
Verilog/VHDL&FPGA architecture	ATM frame relay

VISUAL BASIC DEVELOPER, PROGRAMMER

Skills Frequently Required

Visual Basic, VB.NET (most frequently required)
Oracle 8i, 9i & higher (most frequently required)
ASP, ASP .NET (most frequently required)
XML, HTML
Written and verbal communication skills

Skills Occasionally Required

Unix Shell scripting, JavaScript	MS Access, Excel
Languages: C, C++, C#, PL/SQL, J2EE	Security
ADO, ADO.NET	LDAP
JSP	Crystal Reports
DB2	

TECHNICAL SUPPORT SPECIALIST

Skills Frequently Required

Unix, Windows NT, 2000
MS Office; Word, Excel, Outlook
SQL, PL/SQL, SQL Server
Java, Oracle 8i, 9i, Visual Basic
XML, HTML
Web Servers: IIS, Weblogic, Tomcat
Written and verbal communication skill

SAP CRM ADMINISTRATOR, ANALYST

Skills Frequently Required

SAP Software Modules (most frequently required): BW, R/3, APO,
Basis, ABAP
Previous SAP implementation experience
Operating Systems: Linux, Solaris, AIX, Windows NT, 2000
Database: Oracle 8i, 9i, Net 8, DB2, SQL Server
TCP/IP, XML, LDAP
Shell scripting
Verbal, written, and interpersonal skills

Skills Occasionally Required

ASAP methodology	Veritas
Citrix servers	Load Runner testing tools
SAP project manager	LABWARE

SAS ENGINEER, PROGRAMMER

Skills Frequently Required
SAS software modules (most frequently required)
Unix (most frequently required)
SQL database (most frequently required)
Operating Systems: Windows NT, 2000, XP, all Unix versions
Database: Oracle, MS Access, DB2
Programming Languages: SQL, PASCAL, HTML
Scripting: JavaScript, Unix Shell, CGI, Perl and Korn Shell
Statistical software: SPSS, MATLAB
Servers: MS SQL, Visual Basic
Verbal and written communication skill

Skills Occasionally Required
VBS   MS Excel

PEOPLESOFT ADMINISTRATOR

Skills Frequently Required
PeopleSoft Software modules (most frequently required)
Interface Development: SQL, Application Engine, COBOL
Unix, XML, HTML
CSS
Java, JavaScript, JSP
CGI
BEA Weblogic
Oracle 8i and above
Prior PeopleSoft CRM implementation experience
Verbal and written communication skills

WEBSPHERE DEVELOPER

Skills Frequently Required
WebSphere experience (most frequently required)
Operating Systems: Unix, AIX, Linux Red Hat, Sun Solaris, Windows
NT, 2000
Web Services: Perl, php, XML, SOAP, DB2
Verbal and written communication skills

Skills Occasionally Required
BEA Weblogic
Apache server
MySQL

TECHNICAL WRITER

Skills Frequently Required

Excellent writing and verbal communication skills (most frequently required)
MS Office (Word, Excel, and Outlook)
HTML files creation
Windows 2000, XP
Adobe (Acrobat and Frame Maker)
Testing, training, and documentation experience
Instructional systems design

Skills Occasionally Required

PowerPoint	Web development content tools
JavaScript	Robo HELP
Interleaf Publishing System	

VOIP ENGINEER, DEVELOPER

Skills Frequently Required

VoIP Protocols: H.323, SIP, MGCP, SCCP
SNMP (most frequently required)
SQL Server (most frequently required)
Cisco products and services (most frequently required)
Unix/Linux (most frequently required)
Network Protocols: Ethernet, Token Ring, Frame Relay, TI, ISDN, ATM, STP, VLAN, WIFI
Operating Systems: Windows NT, 2000, XP, Unix, Linux, Cisco IOS
Languages: C, C++, Java, VB .NET, Assembly, Pascal, HTML, JavaScript, SQL Server, Unix Shell
Applications: MS Office, Project, MATLAB, IIS, SQL server, Crystal Reports, Mercury tools, WinRunner
Network security, encryption, PIX firewalls
TCP/IP
CTI applications
Written and verbal communication skills

Skills Occasionally Required

J2EE, Java coding
Voice XML
Avaya voice mail
Octel Aria voice mail
CT Media
Inter Net Merge

.NET DEVELOPER

Skills Frequently Required
SQL Server (most frequently required)
MS .NET (most frequently required)
VB .NET (most frequently required)
XML (most frequently required)
MS Server 2000 (most frequently required)
Languages: Visual C#, VB, JavaScript, VB Script, SQL, C, C++, C#, JDL
Internet: SOAP, HTML, DHTML, DOM, CSS, ADO.NET
Database: Oracle 9i, 8i, IBM DB2, MS Access
Test Tools: Rational Visual, WinRunner
Applications Servers: IIS, Apache
ASP .NET, ASP
Visual Studio .NET
Verbal and written communication skills

Skills Occasionally Required
.NET Framework
PL/SQL
Perl
php
Unix, Linux
Crystal Reports

VISUAL BASIC .NET DEVELOPER

Skills Frequently Required
MS VB .NET (most frequently required)
SQL Server (most frequently required)
ASP, ASP .NET
Visual Basic, C++, XML
Written and verbal communication skills

Skills Occasionally Required
Java, J2EE	C#
MS SQL Server	HTML
Security	ISS
LDAP	Windows NT, 2000
.NET Framework	DB2

4. For Those Having Difficulty Finding IT Jobs

> ## The Objective of This Chapter
>
> This chapter provides tools to help IT job candidates who are having difficulty with the key components of job hunting. It provides candidates with a problem/alternative solutions type of approach to use for assessment of their personal situation in the job hunting process.

The primary value of the data in this chapter is to help job candidates better understand what problems they are having in job hunting. This is the first step in improving job search results. After candidates focus upon the problem, they move ahead to try to understand what may be causing the difficulties. After they understand what part(s) of the job hunting process is holding them back, they should move to the section of this publication designed to help remove the barriers that they have been facing.

Improved effectiveness is only possible when candidates are willing to make an objective critical assessment of their job hunting efforts. To achieve significant improvement, this type of evaluation goes beyond such simplistic conclusions as "I think that they thought I am too old," "my salary was too high for them," "I don't believe that the interviewer liked me," "I didn't do well in the interview," or "I can't get any responses to my résumé postings or online applications." For candidates who are having difficulty, these excuses are unacceptable because subscribing to them places candidates in the wrong frame of mind and thwarts the attitude necessary for success.

Meaningful, constructive analysis must go much deeper and be more specific than these excuses.

WHY YOU NEED A JOB-FINDING STRATEGY

The first step toward improving job-finding results is completing an assessment of completed activities and effort. The primary value of this assessment is that it can help job candidates implement a series of improvements that are more meaningful and relevant than what they have previously been doing.

The content in Chapters 9 through 11 should be the basis for the content of a revised or a totally new strategy. After reviewing the content in this chapter and Chapters 9 through 11, many candidates will conclude that they really did not have a meaningful job-finding strategy.

Job candidates often lose perspective regarding the importance of a relevant, quality, comprehensive job-finding effort. If you are unemployed or are in need of a new job for whatever the reason, your priority and full-time job in many cases is finding a job and the subject must be attacked accordingly. Part-time effort or concentrating upon comfortable, non-threatening activities that don't test your resourcefulness and determination in most cases will not help you win.

Most of this chapter presents situations that are commonly encountered by IT job candidates. Comparing these situations and some potential solutions to those experienced by IT job candidates who are not achieving the desired job search results can help them better understand what they have been doing wrong. This understanding must occur if they are to implement the type of improvements that will make them more effective.

Those readers who are interested in improving their job-hunting results should remember that they must make a self-critical, frank assessment of their job search efforts and be realistic and hard on themselves. Without this effort, it is doubtful that they will be able to improve their situations significantly.

When you have an in-depth understanding of your problems, your efforts and primary focus should be placed upon new and renewed effort to overcome your previous difficulties.

The following listing of typical problems and potential alternative solutions can help you better understand what you need to do to improve your personal effectiveness in your job search.

15 PROBLEM ANALYSIS/POTENTIAL ALTERNATIVE SOLUTIONS

Problem # 1 Situation—Online Job Posting, No Interest Received

I have posted my résumé on most of the leading web sites that list IT jobs and have responded to scores of individual job postings during the past 90 days, but no one has shown any interest.

Problem # 1 Potential Alternative Solutions

Hiring sources for web-posted jobs feed back that as much as 70% of the responses that they receive do not meet the job description or specifications that are posted.

Are you certain that your qualifications have been a good match for each of your postings? A 50 to 60% match is not good enough in most cases to be considered unless you have all of the skills and experience required for the most critical items.

If you saved copies of the posted jobs, you should review them for compliance with what you wrote in your résumé. Candidates often try to put qualifications in cover letters or messages that should have been in their résumés. If you find yourself writing lengthy dialogue, you may be doing this.

In any of the situations where you applied, were you able to identify the employer? If so, did you request a more detailed job description? If not, you should ask in your posting if they could email you a more comprehensive job description. If you ask this ten times, you may get a response in two or three. In those cases when you do receive a response, you may find after review that the posting was a waste of time in a number of situations.

In any situation where you are able to identify the employer, you quickly should research the company via the search engines to see if you can learn of any events or developments that can help you tailor your cover message or résumé to the prospective hirer.

Where you are able to identify the employer, it is also a good idea to call the IT department for any job of interest and ask to talk with someone who understands the requirements for the posted job. It does not hurt to try, and after you do this several times, you will probably get better at it and will be successful in gaining information that can help you get considered. If you get rejected or rebuffed in this eight of ten times, do not be concerned. Maybe the next ten times you will improve your effectiveness and get valuable additional information four out of ten times.

Remember that to be successful you must turn yourself into a marketer of you. Nobody will do this for you, and after you have developed a quality résumé that best represents your qualifications and have identified the best sources of IT jobs meeting your personal preferences, your ability to market yourself to get interviews and in those interviews to market yourself to win are the most critical points in being successful. None of the other things matter including the amount of effort expended.

If you have identified the company and are unable to obtain information from them, stop by the company. In the reception area, you will usually find internal media that can be helpful, and in larger public companies you may find their annual report. These types of things can help you make more professional contact than the others with whom you are competing. Remember that you need to act quickly if there is a job that fits your qualifications and interests you. Waiting days to respond after you become aware of the opportunity loses any potential advantage you may have gained from your research.

Also remember that even if you improve the quality of your applications for web-posted jobs and still are not achieving improved results, you may be competing against several hundred applicants after a job has been posted for several days. If you do not achieve improved results and you believe that this may be occurring, you may be better served trying other approaches such as the one covered in the last section of Chapter 9.

As you are reviewing your past work activities, try using a format similar to the following one to assist with your analysis. When people have difficulty completing something such as this, they frequently learn something about the problems they have been having.

Hierarchy of Relevant Skills and Job Experience

- Relevant Technical Skills (rank your skills of significance)
  - High-Level Skills (best in industry type skills in high demand)
  - Mid-Level Skills (proficient in the skill, have skills similar to the majority of employees doing the type of work)
  - Entry-Level Skills (first IT job having just completed formal education or technical school courses or changing careers with no prior IT work experience of significance)
- Summary of Nontechnical Skills (industry, application, team, problem solving, other soft skills)
- Expertise and Experience Summary Description
- Primary Strategies Used For Job Finding

Try to keep this exercise to one page. Using a few of the right words in a summary often means much more relative to one's skills and their related accomplishments.

Problem # 2 Situation—Participated in Several Interviews, Unable to Move Forward

During the past several months I have participated in several interviews with IT officials in companies that have hiring needs for which I believe I have been qualified, but I did not achieve a final interview in any of these situations.

Problem # 2 Potential Alternative Solutions

Call one or two of the people who interviewed you and who impressed you most with their knowledge of IT and the discipline for which you interviewed. Tell them you were impressed with their knowledge and ask them for their help. If there has been a significant time lapse, you may need to refresh their memories because they may have interviewed a large number of candidates especially if they were recruiting for more than one job. This type of question can be most effective at the end of an interview after it is obvious that there will not be further interest in you.

Clues to this lack of interest are found in statements like "We will let you know or someone will get back to you" or "I have to talk with several more people and then we will let you know." When interviewers say things like this, it is a good time to try to get a more definitive reaction. In this situation, in a pleasant voice and manner, say, "I don't believe that I was successful in convincing you to consider me further." If this type of statement does not draw out a more definite reaction or a conclusive rejection, then ask, "What would I have to do to convince you that I am a candidate qualified to be considered further? I am willing to put in some effort to do this."

At this point the interviewer may be willing to help you with how you can better present yourself in other interviews. In some situations, the interviewer may simply say that they made a mistake, and that you really don't have the necessary qualifications. This response can happen in some situations and is factual at times. However, in most situations the interviewer would not have brought you in for an interview unless he or she thought that you may be qualified for the job.

For those situations you follow up after the interview date, even if you have to start with a voice message, be honest and tell them that you are having difficulty getting a job, that you have been on several interviews, and that you would appreciate any sincere, critical feedback or any suggestions that they could make regarding where you need to improve in interviews.

Problem # 3 Situation—Unable to Find Opportunities in Desired Geography

I prefer to limit my job search to a specific geographic area. The majority of jobs that are listed in the online job-posting sites don't appear to be a good match for my experience and skill. What options do I have to increase potential employment opportunities?

Problem # 3 Potential Alternative Solutions

First, you should review the listing of job-finding alternative sources listed in Chapter 9 to determine if any of the sources that you have not considered could help. You should also use query letters in conjunction with the process outlined in the section entitled "Tailoring Your Job Search" section at the end of Chapter 9.

It would also be appropriate to review the employment strategies data in Chapter 7 to determine if any of these situations apply to your personal situation.

The other primary suggestion relates to your use of potential network sources within your targeted geographic area. You could team with anyone you respect in your job-hunting network to compare experiences and share strategy information and ideas. Each of you could test different approaches and ideas and share that experience. Sometimes the experience of two individuals working together is more valuable than the two individuals working alone.

The other networking possibility is participation in local IT associations or any self-help network groups that may exist in your locality. These types of sources are often good for exchange of information regarding potential job opportunities that have recently developed.

If none of these suggestions are that helpful, you might consider sending query letters to senior IT management in thirty to forty local companies in the one hundred to several hundred employee range that you identify from a database such as referenceUSA, an infoUSA product. If this database is not available in any of your area libraries, you may find it through a nearby state employment job-hunting assistance office. A significant number of colleges and universities have this product available. A half day of work with this product will identify scores of potential organizations to contact within a 50-mile radius or less of your base point. Another potential value of query letters is that if you have strong experience within a certain type of industry, you will be able to identify all of those possibilities that exist within your targeted area.

In query letter mailings, the quality of the letter is critical. It should never be more than one page and test sending them out without including a copy of your résumé. Tailoring your query letter to a brief summary of your objectives, experience, and skills overview as well as a listing of key points showing that you have done a thorough job of researching the company or organization is important. An example of an effective query letter is included in Chapter 10.

It is a good idea to follow up phone calls within a week of sending the letters. As a minimum, the IT managers contacted may have knowledge of other jobs available in other area companies. You may also be able to gain access to some of their personal IT management networks. Even if they do not foresee any jobs becoming available in the near future, things always change, and it is a good idea to ask anyone with whom you talk if you can follow up with them in a few months.

If you are not having any success after you have tried and tested numerous approaches and your personal situation places you immediately available for work, it would be a good idea to check with any area staffing companies or application services providers to determine if they have any positions available for short-term project or contract work. Occasionally these type assignments can work into extended assignments, and they look much better on your résumé than months of not working.

Problem # 4 Situation—Several Months of Job Search, No Results

You have spent considerable effort over the months and still believe you are at ground zero. You occasionally have concerns regarding one or more item such as your age, employment status, weight, years of experience, and higher income requirements. What is recommended for job candidates in situations similar to these?

Problem # 4 Potential Alternative Solutions

If you frequently have thoughts similar to those listed here, you are not alone; thousands of IT job candidates do. One or more of these situations, when factual, are some of the most challenging to deal with in job hunting, and if several exist, they tend to collectively undermine the attitude and emotions of job hunters through frequent frustration, especially when the job hunter has been working diligently to find another position.

In most cases, candidates in these situations have significant marketing problems, and what they have been doing obviously has not been successful. If they are still committed to additional effort, changes in approach and strategy are needed, or their situations will probably not improve. Any new fresh approaches that are tried require an accompanying change in attitude because if candidates move into new approaches focused upon the previously listed concerns, many will be defeated before they try any new approaches.

If you have achieved several personal interviews, you need to understand why you were not able to go further. You need to focus on your personal effectiveness in presenting yourself, how you answered key questions, and why you believe you were unable to go further. In this assessment-type exercise, you must be objective and, in some cases, hard on yourself because no one really knows you better than yourself. At times it is somewhat difficult and painful for all of us to be self-critical especially when things are not going well employment-wise.

In the interview situation, many candidates often fail in this critical portion of job hunting because they simply don't ask things like "What would I have to do to prove to you that I am qualified for further consideration?" This type of query forces a response from the interviewer, and nothing ventured, nothing gained. If an employer is willing to discuss this subject, candidates must be ready to propose an assignment of some type that will show capabilities.

If you need employment, even going as far as part-time work or offering to work several days on a project free of charge is not a bad idea in some situations. If this type of thing is difficult for a candidate to handle pride-wise that is not the right type of attitude in these situations. How you handle such an offer is important, and your manner is critical. In discussing things such as this, there is a small difference between projecting self-confidence and sounding desperate. It always needs to be presented in a pleasant, confident manner.

If you are able to get into a discussion like this but your proposal to work several days free of charge to demonstrate your capability is not well received, try this, especially if your research has placed you in a busy, progressive organization. Today new employees hired by many organizations initially work under a probationary policy for the first 90 days of employment. It is known that hiring mistakes occur as much as 20% of the time or greater in most companies, even for the best management. With this information, you can confidently say, "You have none of this type of risk in what I am proposing and I am willing to invest my time to prove my potential value. What can it hurt?" If the hirer at this point is still apprehensive, ask if some part-time work over several weeks would be a better alternative for them?

During the dot com meltdown of several years ago, some IT employees who were laid off proposed working for free for defined periods of time in order to gain what they perceived to be valuable experience. This proposal may seem extreme to most job candidates, but it also indicates the type of thing that some candidates may be competing against in tight job markets. Of course in situations such as this, financial affordability may be an issue for some candidates.

The point here is that if candidates are not able to get themselves into some type of actual work situation in those stable and vibrant companies that they have researched, and they have been out of work for a significant period of time, they must pursue things such as this if improved résumés and better and higher quality contact strategies have been implemented and have not provided the desired results.

Pursuing short-term or limited-duration projects is possibly the best alternative at this point. At this juncture, considering relocation to geographic areas where IT jobs are more plentiful is possibly their only other alternative unless they have determined skills-wise that additional education relative to other IT disciplines is needed to be more viable.

Problem # 5 Situation—Difficulty Achieving Job with Desired Income Level

The problem that many applicants face is that the pay difference for tenured employees with 20 or more years of experience and relatively new hires with 5 years or less in many employment situations is greater than many employers are willing to pay. For example, a 20-years-of-experience employee may be at the $100,000 per year level, while the fewer-than-5-years employee is at the $65,000 annual income level. The problem in situations such as this is that, often in new employment situations, the experienced applicants must prove that they are worth the potential income difference in skills and potential value to the organization. This is not an easy task for most applicants. Some employers can take a hard stance and conclude that someone with 20 years of experience should have at least double the skills and potential value as one with fewer than 5 years of job experience. This type of situation is difficult for many applicants to overcome.

Problem # 5 Potential Alternative Solutions

Candidates who are not willing to consider significant annual salary discrepancy compared to what they have been earning should try to negotiate. In some situations, this type of approach may work. If consideration for merit salary increase is annual and your potential offer is in a range that makes employment difficult but possible, try to gain agreement for a salary increase special merit review after 6 months of employment, which would be justified by contributions of significant value beyond the basic responsibilities of the job.

Another possible alternative to try to get over the salary differential hurdle is to suggest that you spend a day or two in the department to understand fully the responsibilities and what needs to be accomplished. Suggest that, after doing this, you will write the hiring manager a formal proposal regarding what you would be able to accomplish beyond the basic responsibilities of the job description. Of course, this should only be proposed in situations where the applicant is confident that he or she has the necessary ability to accomplish what is proposed.

If a candidate is pursuing employment in progressive, growth-type companies that are in the small- to medium-sized range, one hundred to several hundred employees, some candidates have the type of skills and job experience that may enable them to propose combining responsibilities normally handled by two different jobs.

If a candidate has this type of skill and experience and has handled similar IT needs previously, a proposal such as this could gain interest in some companies. Smaller growth companies are currently in need of this type of experience. The potential benefit to these companies is that they obtain the necessary experience to deal with some of the challenges that they realize they face as well as the possibility of avoiding the need to hire an additional employee for some period into the future. This situation, if well received, could justify consideration of a higher starting salary than the organization had planned to pay.

Problem # 6 Situation—Programming Skill for Older Legacy Systems

My software writing/programming skills are primarily based upon the older legacy-type systems and I am not having much success finding very many job situations posted on the web-posting services where this type of experience is needed.

Problem # 6 Potential Alternative Solutions

You should reassess your job-finding strategy and your résumé, consulting the components within Chapter 6 to be certain that you are not missing significant job opportunities because of the way in which you have presented your skills and experience. This is particularly critical for web posting of your résumé.

As mentioned earlier, a study commissioned by an IT services company indicated that as much as 80% of annual IT expenditures are still associated with the older, legacy-type systems. Whether or not this is accurate is unknown, but as a minimum it is a significant indicator. For some reason, if your résumé is posted in a majority of the most active IT web job-posting services, your résumé is not gaining the attention that it should. You should consider further developing and including things such as specific industry and functional applications expertise, as well as a summary description of projects in which you played a significant role working with legacy systems.

Also if you have not included a listing of any of the soft skills you have that are discussed in Chapter 5, you should incorporate them. In your preferred geographic area, you may find that a lot of the work involving the older legacy-type systems is being contracted out to IT consulting and applications services providers which, if you have not explored these possibilities, should be another part of your contact work.

Problem # 7 Situation—Little Interest After Job Posting to Most Major Online Sites

I have posted my résumé in most of the major job-listing sites and have responded to a significant number of jobs posted in the job-posting sites where I believe my qualifications fit the job specifications. I have also distributed my résumé to a significant number of local companies. From all of this effort, I have received very little interest, and basically I am at a loss for what to do now.

Problem # 7 Potential Alternative Solutions

You should reassess your job-finding strategy as well as your résumé, reviewing the components portion of Chapter 6. Many applicants have significant opportunity to strengthen their résumés in addition to their technical skills by expanding one or more of the following items: specific industry knowledge, functional applications experience, significant accomplishments and achievements, and project and team experience and in the nontechnical skills areas as outlined in Chapter 5.

After completing this type of evaluation, you should be able to develop additional components for alternative résumés where you can target selected companies within individual industries. You also may want to post two or three alternative résumés in the résumé-posting sites to see if you receive any greater interest than before.

It would also be a good idea to test the use of query letters to companies identified in the small- and medium-sized category using the company selection criteria outlined in the Chapter 9 section entitled "Tailoring Your Job Search."

You might also try significantly raising your total level of contacts made, which should increase the level of interest received when compared to previous efforts. The main thing that appears to need work in this situation is the quality of your résumé, and if you can make any of the additions previously mentioned, this should help generate more interest.

If your skills and experience are relevant and your résumé is strengthened, you should be receiving somewhere between five to ten positive responses for every hundred contacts, which includes résumé postings, responses to web-posted jobs, and query letters to individual companies that you have researched.

Do not overlook the IT and management consulting firms, applications services providers, staffing and contract employment firms, and executive search firms as potential sources of jobs to consider for contact. If you have not contacted a significant number of the sources listed in the preceding paragraph, you should make this a priority to determine if your results show any improvement compared to the online job-posting services.

Problem # 8 Situation—Difficulty Moving Beyond Initial Interview

Many job candidates who are successful in gaining personal interviews have difficulty moving beyond the first interview. Are their interviewing skills the problem, or should they have other concerns?

Problem # 8 Potential Alternative Solutions

Their interviewing skills may be the problem, but their lack of effectively trying to gain commitment to move farther in the hiring process also may be occurring in many situations.

If an organization has scheduled an interview with you and you meet with an IT official, in most cases there had to be significant interest in your qualifications. Occasionally, however, organizations schedule interviews to gain an understanding of the level of talent that is available in their geographic area. These are exploratory-type interviews. However, if you have been on several interviews, this probably is not a primary reason why you are not able to move forward.

You need to ask yourself three basic questions regarding preparation for interviews and your performance during the interview. You should be your own best critic, but you also may be able to gain valuable feedback to these questions by following up with individuals who interviewed you. In some cases, you may also find that the job has not yet been filled which may still represent an opportunity for you.

The three basic questions follow:

1. Prior to going on the interview, did you do some research to understand what the hiring company needs you to do? In addition, if you did some prior research, what did you learn about the company that helped you market yourself during the interview?

   In any interview situation where you are not able to do this research, you lose some advantage that could have helped you sell yourself better.

Always try to obtain detailed job specifications prior to the interview, and if the hiring company has annual reports, reviewing the latest one can help you present yourself more effectively during the interview. If the organization does not have an annual report, stop by their employment office or main reception area several days prior to the interview to pick up any internal publications that are available. If this is not possible, most local newspapers today have online databases of their articles that usually go back a couple of years; these articles can be another potential source of information. The U.S. Securities and Exchange Commission has public companies annual, quarterly and 10k reports in their Edgar database which can be accessed at sec.gov.

2. During the interview, how well did you present what you can provide the company relative to what they need to have accomplished by the holder of the job for which you are interviewing?

In most interview situations that do not go well for the candidate, this type of discussion rarely occurs. Most candidates are never able to get this type of a discussion going. In many interviews where the candidates are successful and move forward, they are able to get the interviewer at ease and willing to discuss the challenges and sometimes the problems associated with the job and what the incumbents need to accomplish.

Those candidates who can get this type of conversation opened up have the opportunity to communicate how their skills and experience can solve the problems or contribute the type of performance that is needed in the job. Unless candidates are able to achieve this sort of thing in interviews, they will, in most cases, not move forward in the process.

Prior research on the company can help open up this type of discussion. You can also ask the interviewer, "From your perspective, what are the critical portions of this job that will help the organization or department move forward?"

In any situations, the more that you can get the interviewer to open up and discuss things such as this and present your relevant capabilities effectively, the better chance you have of moving ahead in the interviewing process. These are the types of questions you should ask in the interview. Do not ask things in the posted job listing or detailed job specification or mention anything regarding your personal concerns or interests.

3. During the interview, were you able to communicate your capabilities effectively relative to the employer's needs, and were you able to provide the employer with any examples of relevant value that you have the potential to provide them in addition to what they need achieved in the job?

Again in this situation, unless you are able to get things such as this opened up in the interview, sometimes initiated by you, when the interviewer does not, you stand a good chance or not moving beyond the first interview.

The interviewer expects you to be able to perform what you résumé lists as skills and experience, and there is a good chance in most situations that your résumé is a good match for their perceived needs. If you can get into discussions that show effective skills and experience relative to what they need, your chances of moving forward are much better.

If you are successful in getting the interviewer to discuss the company's needs relative to your skills but you sense doubt on the interviewer's part during the interview, before you lose a good opportunity, propose that the company put you to the test—to test you on some work. This may not be feasible in some situations, but far too many job opportunities are lost because candidates do not effectively market themselves in interviews. This is unfortunate when in many situations the candidate has the right skill set and experience to do the job. In other words, if you are close to winning, ask what you can do extra that can help you win.

In some situations, candidates are often being judged by some interviewers on items that don't have much to do with their IT skills and experience. Things such as verbal communication skills, personality, and good listening skills are extremely important relative to working on project teams, groups, and with end users. At times, candidates also get judged on some of the more superficial things such as appearance, nervousness or anxiety, eye contact, posture, and general mannerisms.

The author is not too sure how this last group of things can detract from the work results of a skilled employee, but candidates often are judged on these things. All candidates need to understand this in their interview preparation.

Problem # 9 Situation—Close to Winning Jobs, Unable to Finalize

Candidates who are close to closing out job opportunities but are unable to conclude any frequently find this situation particularly frustrating. They must be doing most things in the interviews correctly, and they must have most of the necessary skills required for serious hiring consideration, or they would not move to the end of the hiring process. What happens? In some situations, another candidate appears whom they simply like better or believe has better qualifications.

Some companies like to go into the final hiring steps with two qualified candidates in case one happens to drop out from consideration. This situation often occurs when working with retained search organizations because, in order to satisfy clients who pay their fees, they need to provide several qualified candidates in most hiring situations.

Also in some situations, companies decide to fill the position internally. If candidates can learn why they have not gotten the job and these types of reasons are the ones given, then these candidates could not have done anything differently. Things like this happen, and job hunters must move forward. From the job candidate's perspective, this is why it is always wise to generate enough job-hunting activity to have more than one possibility moving forward whenever possible because uncontrollable things happen. Job candidates cannot control all aspects of their job search activity.

Problem # 9 Potential Alternative Solutions

The situations described are all somewhat frustrating and difficult for those who have experienced them. It is also difficult to recommend things that they could have done differently to win the job. The longer a job stays open, the greater the possibility of losing the opportunity to another candidate becomes. Once you are close to the formal job offer that you want, you need to do everything that you can possibly do to help expedite finalization of the offer and accept the job.

In situations like these if you are unable to obtain a firm starting date and are not able to understand why the offer is not forthcoming, tell the employer if you are working that you need to give notice. If you are not employed and you have any other offers pending, you can mention that you need to make a decision.

In discussing a starting date, you need to exercise care. You can say that you prefer the job under discussion but in your situation you need to make plans and cannot let the other job go without a formal commitment. You might also ask if there is anything you can do to help finalize the offer because you are anxious to get started.

If there is some problem that the employer is not willing to discuss with you, bringing the possibility of another offer into the situation is risky. In some cases, you may get the answer that you should go ahead with the other offer, especially if they have some reason for not being willing to commit the job to you after a reasonable delay. If the employer really wants to hire you, when you mention the possibility of another pending opportunity, in some cases they will be willing to explain why the delay in finalization is occurring. Some offers can be delayed for weeks, and this type of follow-up discussion can help clarify the reason for the delay.

Problem # 10 Situation—Effective Handling of Initial Screening Interviews

Many candidates are asked to participate in initial screening-type interviews, which may be conducted by someone other than IT management. In most cases, this individual may be from human resources. In small companies, it may be one of the senior managers from one of the functions that IT supports. When this occurs this is an opportunity to gain significant level management support for a candidate.

Problem #10 Potential Alternative Solutions

If a company uses human resources to conduct initial interviews, it usually indicates either that the employer is screening a lot of candidates or that the candidate is considered a secondary candidate based upon their résumé and IT would like to get an outside opinion before entering into the interview cycle. In some situations, it may be the company's policy to handle initial interviews in this manner.

If human resources or another function official conducts the interview, it is a good idea during the course of the interview to solicit the interviewer's opinion of how IT could better serve other functional needs. In either case, the interview, in most cases, will be subjective, with the objective of getting to know you and, in smaller companies, developing an idea of how they think that you might fit into their company culture.

Any advance research that you do can help you show knowledge of the company in these situations. In interviews of this type, it is often more difficult to keep a discussion going compared to an IT interview where the interviewer is testing your knowledge relative to your experience.

In screening-type interviews, you should be prepared for more open-ended types of questions such as, "Tell me about yourself." Candidates need to be careful with questions such as this and need to direct their answers more to how their skills and experience can help the employer achieve its business objectives.

In the interpersonal skills area, personal strengths related to working effectively with others and in team environments will be of interest to human resource officials. If candidates have user training ability this is also an item that will be of interest to HR officials.

Problem # 11 Situation—Things That Can Defeat Candidates Before They Start

For IT job candidates who are having significant difficulty in their job-hunting activities, especially for those who have been unemployed for significant periods of time, there is a tendency to put the blame for their difficulty elsewhere, which is human nature. In these situations, there is frequently too much rationalization placing blame elsewhere or justifying the logic behind why they are having difficulty getting hired. Unless some type of skill and relevance problem exists, the candidate's attitude is the problem. Unless they are willing to consider significant change of attitude and commitment to renewed and different types of effort, they are not going to be successful in their job hunting.

Problem # 11 Potential Alternative Solutions

This situation is possibly the most difficult one to deal with particularly for IT professionals who have been unemployed for long periods of time.

Often their self-worth and confidence have been severely tested, and it will not be easy for them to move to any new type of behavior that may help them be successful. After all, many of them believe that they have tried basically everything. Their personal frustration is significant, and often it is less painful to subscribe to rationalization because it is extremely difficult for them to deal with the lack of success that they have had in their job-hunting experiences. There is not a simple solution for candidates who have had similar experiences.

The author believes that the majority of unemployed IT job hunters who continue to pursue jobs after long periods of unemployment do not continue to pursue jobs where their skills are inadequate. He believes that the majority of them are more intelligent than that and know whether they have a skills of relevance problem.

The author sees most of their problem as being a function of their personal attitude and the fact that the majority have either made the wrong job-hunting choices or adopted a strategy and methodologies that have not been the right ones. After all it is unrealistic to think that most IT employees can be expected to be highly effective job hunters.

If those IT professionals who are unemployed and have been for a significant period of time are still committed to being successful in getting a job, every chapter in this book will help them. They simply have to be committed to the effort it takes to implement new things and work job hunting a lot smarter and more effectively than they previously have. The author believes that there are a significant number of new concepts and techniques in this book for any IT job hunter to consider using.

It will take significant effort and a strong commitment to persevere without backing into the rationalization syndrome that sometimes sounds like, "Everybody is wrong but me." Hopefully some of the new approaches suggested within this publication can help many of the unemployed be successful in their job hunting. The author is confident that they can help those willing to make the effort.

Problem # 12 Situation—Making Outplacement Work for You

For IT professionals entering outplacement services as a result of job cuts, how the time allowed to each is used is critical. Many outplacement participants, for the most part, found the time spent interesting and somewhat helpful, but many others did not find it that helpful to them in finding employment.

Problem # 12 Potential Alternative Solutions

The problem for many is that, in the final analysis, they did not find the time spent that helpful. In most cases, the problem was the lack of putting together the right job-hunting strategy. Outplacement can assist participants with many things that are helpful, but the participant needs to select the items that can be potentially the most beneficial to him or her. The assigned counselors can help, but the participant needs to tailor the personal program to the items that they believe they can benefit the most. The outplacement section in Chapter 7 goes into more detail regarding effective use of outplacement services as well as some areas of concern for participants.

Problem # 13—Getting More Interviews and Improving Interviewing Effectiveness

I am actively employed, but I am interested in the possibility of job change. I have posted my résumé to a significant number of online job postings during the past year and have participated in two interviews. I believe that I am having too much difficulty in getting interviews, and when I do, I do not believe that I have been effective.

Problem # 13 Potential Alternative Solutions

First, you should review the content of Chapter 6 regarding résumé preparation to be certain that your résumé is the best possible representation of your overall qualifications. Second, you should review the alternative contact sources in Chapter 9 to consider contacting the job sources that you have not contacted, apply to the ones selected to determine if you receive any better reception than you have been. If you do not receive a higher level of interest than previously after reworking your résumé and contacting new potential hiring sources, you should consider putting significant effort into the tailored job search approach outlined in the last section of Chapter 9.

If you have made significant changes to your résumé or have developed any alternative résumés, you should test them by applying to jobs listed on the same online job-posting services that you previously used to see if you achieve any improvement in the degree of interest.

If the degree of interest shown has not improved, then the marketing yourself content of Chapter 10 may prove helpful. If you are successful in achieving a higher level of job interviews, then your focus should move to improving your performance during interviews. Chapter 11 makes a number of suggestions regarding the various problem situations where more effective techniques for use during interviews are suggested.

In addition, if you are successful in increasing the number of interviews, you should place most of your effort in adopting and using those techniques in Chapter 11 that you are comfortable with. If you can successfully increase the number of personal interviews and if you can become more effective in marketing yourself and your personal effectiveness during interviews by gaining experience with some of the techniques suggested, your options for finalizing the desired employment will improve.

If you are able to schedule several more interviews and are still not able to finalize new employment, you should call several of the IT officials who interviewed you and solicit their opinions regarding how you might be more effective in future interviews. You want to do this quickly after it has been determined that you are not being considered further for the job.

You can open the discussion by thanking them for considering you and then asking for suggestions. If they are hesitant to make any suggestions, you should say something to the effect of, "Frankly, I failed to impress you favorably, and it would be helpful to me if you could help me with any specifics as to how I need to improve."

Problem # 14 Situation—Poor Results with Web-Posting Sites, Other Alternatives

My résumé-posting activity has been primarily for jobs posted in the web-posting services and the web sites of the larger employers within my preferred geographic area. I have made some progress and had some interest, but, overall, I believe that I am experiencing a lot of competition for the jobs where my qualifications appear to fit. It seems that there are many other candidates with similar qualifications. What are other alternatives that I can pursue?

Problem # 14 Potential Alternative Solutions

First, you should review all the potential job sources listed in Chapter 9. If you have not applied through any of these sources, try the appropriate ones to determine if your results show any improvement.

You should also consider tailoring your résumé the best you can to any job situations where your personal job experience may show any advantages when compared to other candidates. Things such as industry-specific knowledge, functional applications expertise, and project management can help distinguish you.

Do everything possible to tailor your skills and experience to the uniqueness of their culture and business, which you should be able to identify from prior research.

In addition, you should gain some experience in self-marketing with some of the smaller- and medium-sized companies using the process outlined in the "Tailoring Your Job Search" section of Chapter 9. Sending out 30 to 40 well-written query letters to organizations that you have selected is a good test of an entirely different strategy than what you have previously used. Also your concern regarding the amount of competition that you may be experiencing in your present job-hunting methods will be substantially less in any situations where you are able to generate interest.

Problem # 15 Situation—Able to Get Interviews, Not Performing Well in Them

Your performance after having several job interviews has brought you to the realization that possibly you may be your own worst enemy in the way that you have handled yourself in the interviews because you are not getting any job offers. You don't appear to have difficulty scheduling interviews, which means that your personal qualifications must be good.

Problem # 15 Potential Alternative Solutions

Many job applicants ruin their chances for job offers simply by the manner in which they conduct themselves during interviews. There are a series of common mistakes that need to be avoided. Things such as talking too much, not letting the interviewer ask the questions, offering responses that are too lengthy to the interviewer's questions, and asking too many questions about the job can be answered with a little research or can wait until later.

If an applicant is continually asking questions, interviewers may think that they are hiding something or trying to avoid being asked questions that may reveal weaknesses that are inconsistent with a well-written résumé.

Questions such as, "What does this job pay?" reflect questionable judgement. This and other personal questions should wait until after the hiring company has indicated that they want to go further in considering you. Likewise, simple informational-type questions should be avoided during the interview. If several of the previously mentioned situations occur during the interview, it can appear to an experienced interviewer that a candidate has used questionable personal judgment during the interview.

The candidate should focus on the interview from the interviewer's perspective. The interviewer wants to know whether the candidate is qualified to fulfill the company's needs and whether the candidate is worthy of further consideration.

From the applicant's perspective, the emphasis should be upon convincing the interviewer that the applicant has the proper skills and experience to fulfill the requirements of the job and that the applicant has the necessary skills and personal qualities that provide the potential to make contributions beyond the basic responsibilities of the job that can help the company achieve its objectives. This type of possibility is important to rapidly growing small- and medium-sized companies.

If application of improved interview technique is not helping you to move toward finalization of job offers and you have situations that are of interest to you, the prospective employers must have some question regarding whether you are the right person for the job.

At this point, about the only option left for you is to propose that the company test you in some type of work situation or assignment that is meaningful to the employer or to propose that the employer hire you on a probationary basis for a limited time period so that you can prove yourself.

DEVELOPING AND IMPLEMENTING A WINNING JOB-FINDING STRATEGY

For any IT job candidates that have had difficulty finding the desired job or that have been unemployed for several months or more, a new job-finding strategy is necessary in most situations.

The first step for those interested in improving is critical constructive assessment of what you have previously done. In these situations, the candidates who can benefit the most are those who become their own best critic. For most individuals, no one should understand themselves better than them. For those who cannot objectively do this, significant improvement in job-hunting results is doubtful. The following type of assessment and evaluation needs to occur.

Job-Finding Activities

If you are currently unemployed and not participating in part time employment, have you been putting in the equivalent to an eight hour workday or longer? For the employed, the same question is appropriate regarding evenings and weekends.

If the candidate's job-hunting-related activities have been significant for any period of time longer than a month, and have not been successful, several possibilities may exist.

1. You have applied to a significant number of online postings where your qualifications did not meet the listed specifications.
2. If you have posted your résumé on several online posting services, and individually posted it to one hundred or more online posted job descriptions and have had little or no interest, either your qualifications have not generated interest, your résumé needs significant improvement, or you need to consider contacting additional potential sources of IT jobs that you have not yet contacted.

If any or all of these situations apply, the candidate should review Chapters 5, 6, and 9 for possible improvement considerations. Limited-term contract jobs, projects, and consulting are all areas to consider as potential sources if they have not been worked. If you believe that you may have a skill and experience problem, these alternatives may represent better potential sources for you to pursue.

For candidates who meet the most frequently required skill profiles for top jobs listed in the last section of Chapter 3, two possibilities may exist, either your résumé in its present form is not properly presenting your total qualifications or you are not spending enough time reviewing job postings in all the potential sources. Online job research should focus on one or two IT job classifications and several key word versions of these classifications using advanced search where available. This research requires a great deal of effort because most of the online posting services keyword or advanced search capabilities at this date are not that well refined, and you often get several other job descriptions for each one that is desired.

After completing your assessment, complete a one-page summary of key words that describe the change actions that you intend to implement. Usually three to five items that represent new approaches or strategies should be identified. Chapter 10 content should also be considered in completing your list. The first step on this list for most candidates is an improved résumé or alternative résumés to test. The next step for most is determining where to prospect, including adding new sources. You should also consider including other quality improvements focusing on things such as employer research and self-marketing-related tactics.

In the majority of situations, this simple change of strategy combined with much consistent, quality effort will pay dividends in generating more employer interest.

5. Assessing Your IT and Personal Skills

The Objective of This Chapter

The purpose of this chapter is to develop additional material that will strengthen IT job candidates' résumés. The chapter begins with a discussion of "Ten Rules for Reducing IT Career Vulnerability to Outsourcing and Other Job Loss Situations." An employer ranking of desired nontechnical skills, which add an important dimension to IT job candidates' résumés, follows, but less than 15% of résumés today include these soft skills. A discussion of ten important skills that can help employees achieve sustained career success is followed by self-assessment and skill profile exercises that will help strengthen personal résumés. The desired result of the self-assessment is the completion of a revised résumé that will create more potential hiring interest in IT job candidates than their current résumés generate.

TEN RULES FOR REDUCING IT CAREER VULNERABILITY TO OUTSOURCING AND OTHER JOB LOSS SITUATIONS

RULE # 1—THE EMPLOYER'S FINANCIAL POSITION

Continued good financial health of your employer is an important aspect of career stability. Large public companies report their financial results quarterly and annually to the SEC (Securities and Exchange Commission). You can gain access to these reports through the SEC Edgar web database, *sec.gov*. This database in most cases contains reports for several years. The database also contains the reporting companies' 10k reports, which is another good source for assessment of a companies financial condition.

For job candidates who are evaluating prospective companies, Hoover's online is a good summary source of financial information for large companies as well as for small- and medium-sized companies both public and private. The referenceUSA database of infoUSA, which is available in many college and university libraries as well as large public libraries, provides profiles of more than 13 million U.S. companies and identifies their credit ratings, which is another good source for evaluation of potential employers. This source is also helpful for company contact information when a candidate is considering contacting small- and medium-sized employers in their geographic area of preference in the 50- to 999-employee range.

Another excellent source of media articles on organizations that covers several years of data is available from the Academic Universe database of Lexus-Nexus, which again is available in many college and university libraries. This database often has articles about smaller companies that will also be helpful in preparing for job interviews with companies.

RULE # 2—AVOIDING CERTAIN LARGE COMPANY DILEMMAS

The largest dilemma today is the outsourcing of programmer and other software engineering jobs outside of the United States. It is estimated by some sources that as many as 400,000 U.S. technology jobs have been lost over the last several years to outsourcing offshore.

The outsourcing is primarily occurring in large technology, financial services, and manufacturing-type companies as well as software development and large IT consulting firms. Their primary motive in outsourcing is to reduce costs and improve profits which many companies believe they are forced to do, especially when their competitors are doing it.

It is the author's opinion that IT employees who are most vulnerable to outsourcing today work in large IT organizations where large groups of employees are doing similar work involving programming and software writing. This is where the financial incentives exist.

There is also significant instability in employment in large companies where some of the jobs can properly be classified as specialist-type jobs. An example of this could be web development.

After a web is fully established, the majority of the systems work is focused upon things like maintenance, update, and change revisions. Many IT employees in specialist-type positions are subject to employment-tenure-vulnerability-type situations unless their skills are at the highest level of their profession and there is a continuing need for their skills.

How do IT employees avoid the type of employment vulnerability that is occurring today? The first and best solution is always to be among the best at what you do. This does not guarantee that during your career that you will not be the victim of job cuts, but if you are, you probably will not be unemployed for a very long period as long as your skills are relevant in the IT profession.

Those who believe their IT future is potentially vulnerable may want to consider some of the options recommended in the following rules.

RULE # 3—PURSUING IT JOB ROTATION

For those employees in good standing with consistently good job performance records, it is a good idea to consider moving into different IT jobs and or IT jobs focused upon functional applications that will broaden their experience. This type of career-broadening experience can result in reduced vulnerability to job cuts in the future. When you look at the résumés of senior IT management officials in many companies, you will see that many of them who came up through the IT ranks often had as many as three or four different IT job classifications, some in different disciplines.

It is inferred that job rotation will not help much for employees whose companies are facing significant job cuts, but as a minimum these employees will usually have more potential job alternatives in job hunting than those employees who spent most of their employment in one job classification.

IT technology options that affect jobs have changed significantly during the past several years, and employees who have developed multidiscipline-type expertise and experience and have good performance records are the ones who are least likely to be vulnerable to future lack of employment stability. What is being suggested is that those IT employees who are multitalented have the best opportunity for stable employment.

For example, if you are a software engineer and you have experience and develop a good understanding of applications for things such as security, wireless networks, and the internet and have performed successful work in most of these disciplines, you will be comparatively less vulnerable than a specialist who has worked primarily in only one of these disciplines unless that specialist's skills are at the top level of the profession.

During the 6-year period through 2002 that the author spent in the management recruiting portion of the search business, the author made a significant observation. Employees who had spent a significant number of years in specialized jobs for large corporations had a problem in that these jobs were unique to that corporation and did not exist in the majority of others.

The author believes today that some of the best future IT career stability opportunities for employees will be for those who develop multidiscipline-type experience of the type previously discussed and apply this expertise in the smaller- and medium-sized companies that are successful and growing.

The author further believes that IT jobs in these types of companies (at least until some get quite large) will not be vulnerable to things such as outsourcing outside of the United States. At last count there were close to 388,000 of these U.S. public and private companies in the infoUSA database with between 50 and 999 employees. This is the sector where the author believes that the majority of the job growth projected by the Bureau of Labor Statistics will occur between today and year end 2010. The reason for this is that as they grow, most of these companies have the same IT technology needs of large companies only on a smaller scale.

RULE # 4—THE POTENTIAL VALUE OF MULTIINDUSTRY IT JOB EXPERIENCE

Of course today, there is significant risk in all categories of IT employment; in other words, nothing is guaranteed to anyone for long. If you have job skills that were developed in more than one industry and in more than one IT classification with today's relevant skills, when you are faced with employment change needs, you potential employment value is enhanced.

If you review the job classification employment data by metropolitan statistical employment area, compared to the Bureau of Labor Statistics IT job forecast through 2010, you will find that the potential employment opportunities in most IT job classifications are significantly increased. This is another good reason to consider multiindustry choices during your career.

RULE # 5—MAINTAIN THE BEST POSSIBLE PERFORMANCE RECORD

Be the best that you can be at what you do throughout your career. Even for IT employees who achieve this type of performance, there are certain red flags that should be of concern.

If your job is primarily routine, repetitive, task-oriented work that a large number of employees do in your IT organization, how do you distinguish yourself? This is difficult in any organizations where annual merit performance appraisals do not exist or in organizations where annual performance appraisals are basically checklist-type reviews where significant narrative and dialogue assessment of work value against defined responsibilities does not exist.

If you consistently maintain a top level of performance and you are employed in either of the previous situations, you need to create an annual narrative-type performance report that details your most significant activities and accomplishments achieved during the year. The type of things that should be included are significant problems solved, any improvements or changes that add significant value, and efficiency or cost savings contributions to any of your organization's business processes or applications.

This formal document should be submitted to your manager for review and comment in the absence of a formal annual merit review or in situations where the checklist-type performance review exists. It is also a good idea to have your immediate manager sign to acknowledge the assessment. If your manager is willing to make any favorable comments, this could help when applying for any future jobs in other companies.

This type of review is particularly important to employees in organizations who are realistically the best at what they do in order to guarantee that job performance of significance does not get lost. Effort of this type by the employee shows and supports leadership, and if this appears to be threatening to your manager, then it is possibly time to consider alternative employment.

RULE # 6—FOR THOSE STILL IN COLLEGE OR ADVANCING THEIR IT EDUCATION

For those still enrolled in college computer science courses, or those IT employees considering or taking additional courses, completing dual majors is a good career investment. Or in addition to their computer science primary focus, additional concentration in another IT discipline or additional majors or minors in areas such as finance, math, bioscience, and marketing are good investments. Having this type of combined education will expand your potential for entry-level jobs and, in the case of current IT employees, will help expand your future job opportunities within your current company or outside opportunities that you may choose to pursue.

This is another approach to continuing relevance and value that is wise to consider for those in the IT job disciplines today and in the future.

RULE #7—MULTITASKING AND MULTIFUNCTIONAL IT JOB EXPERIENCE

This rule focuses upon such things as job rotation covered in rule #3 and enhancing your potential employment value by promoting your multi-function or multitasking abilities in your job search activities. During his recent 6 years in the job candidate search business, the author rarely saw this type of experience properly developed and exploited in the hundreds of IT job candidate résumés that he reviewed. During his 2004 review of 1,200 current IT employee résumés, this was rarely seen as well. The possibility existed in many of these résumés, but it was only developed in a few.

In Chapter 10, the possibility of sending query letters to prospective employers is discussed. The multitasking subject focuses upon promoting yourself as an IT job candidate capable of handling two distinct IT functions as job responsibilities concurrently. Some fortunate individuals may have adequate understanding of three or more distinct disciplines. If any of these possibilities exist, that IT professional's potential value is probably greatest in small- and medium-sized companies that need to consider increasing their IT employment. These are the companies primarily in the 50- to 999-employee range covered in Chapter 9.

IT employees with multiple skills and the right interpersonal skills may qualify for managerial or supervisory jobs or for positions where they can concurrently perform two responsibilities for a defined period of time. These individuals are more attractive for the employer because the potential to delay the need to hire an additional employee for several months may exist.

This can also help in establishing an employee's value as they learn the organization's business processes. In other words, many employees who are new to the IT profession or who want to enhance their IT careers may have the opportunity to gain significant career-enhancing multitasking and multifunctional experience in the small- and medium-sized company. Jobs in large companies typically specialize in fixed-task-type responsibilities, which the author believes are primarily the type of jobs where thousands will continue to be outsourced outside the United States annually.

Any individual who has experienced a successful business career working in large corporations as well as with small, financially healthy, fast growing or new start-up companies that have achieved success understands the career value of the risks they took associated with employment in the small company environment as compared to the large company environment.

The problem today is that it is more difficult to locate the opportunities in these smaller-type organizations because the larger organizations do the majority of the online job posting. Chapters 9 and 10 will help those IT job candidates interested in pursuing potential employment in the small- and medium-size company segment.

RULE # 8—EXPLOIT AND DEVELOP YOUR SOFT-SIDE-TYPE SKILLS

This chapter discusses in detail the importance of soft skills in today's more challenging IT job-finding and career-success-related endeavors. The potential importance and value of these attributes is increasing every year. It is important that all IT job hunters be aware of the potential value of having these skills as an asset, which can provide them significant additional benefit in their IT careers.

If an IT job candidate has some of these skills and has not given much thought to their role in achieving success in their IT career thus far, it is a good idea to spend some time thinking about this to determine if these skills can be incorporated into their résumés to strengthen and better help them market their résumé to potential hiring sources.

A good start is to review the soft skill requirements that appear today in approximately 33% of the online IT job listings as desired skills. If applicants do not have the majority of technical skills and experience required by the employers that value these soft skills, they will probably not help applicants that much. In situations where their skills and experience appear to be close to a match, the mention of having certain of these soft skills may help applicants get their résumés selected for consideration often separating them from several hundred other applicants.

RULE # 9—ENHANCING YOUR IT CAREER MARKETABILITY

In the IT job market today, many IT employees are becoming career challenged as early as age 30. This is a reality that dictates that IT employees interested in careers that successfully last between 30 and 40 years will have to consider implementing significantly different career education and experience strategies than those IT employees who began careers between the early 1950s through 1980s.

Whether this means additional formal education in other IT disciplines, certifications, job rotation, multitasking, application expertise, or something else is a subject that every current IT employee needs to consider.

Awareness of the employment opportunities within IT associated with technological change that continues to evolve should be part of every current employee's awareness for career evaluation purposes. Opportunities that have evolved during the past 20 years were primarily focused upon new operating systems, the internet, networks, and relational databases.

Within the past several years, security, wireless technology, open source architecture, grid computing, voice over internet protocol, and simplification of software code writing are a few more things that have appeared. Progress of using the computer for critical R&D activities within the physical science disciplines and healthcare field applications is another area that is developing significant potential for increased employment for IT professionals. Use of the web for application of CRM applications software is one of the largest potential IT job growth areas as more applications are developed and refined that show promise for significant efficiency and productivity improvement within key business practices for various industry applications.

The questions relative to current IT employees are such things as where your best personal opportunities for the future are, where you can benefit most, and the additional skills and education you need to take advantage of these new and evolving opportunities.

The author is of the opinion that several things within the programming and software writing disciplines over the past several years existed that hurt this job classification and is hurting it today. Within this discipline, job hopping for salary increases became too frequent. It was not uncommon for some employees to have many jobs within a period of a few years. Thus, it often became much more of a task-oriented occupation that many thousands of employees could do; this characteristic made it much easier to outsource. The profession will probably be injured further if and when the simplification of writing software code is perfected and can produce quality code. If routine repetitive tasks become too simple where thousands upon thousands are able to do the work to the degree where it loses its sophistication and is not providing value beyond basic routine functions, many jobs that fit this description will be threatened. This is what is occurring today in the outsourcing of IT work outside of the United States.

RULE # 10—DON'T OVERLOOK POTENTIAL OPPORTUNITIES IN IT CONSULTING

Those IT employees who have demonstrated good to excellent skills within specific disciplines but see that their employment future is uncertain where they work today may want to consider IT consulting.

An example is employees who have successful experience in design, development, and implementation of sophisticated web installations. These individuals may have continuing employment opportunities in the maintenance, revision, updating, and other modification aspects of these systems as well as in important application implementation and refinement within their present company affiliations. However, if their alternatives are not challenging enough, consulting may be a better alternative for them.

The previously mentioned estimate wherein as much as 80% of the $1.7 trillion of annual IT expenditures is applied to work associated with the older legacy-type software applications represents an opportunity. This is an example of potential employment opportunities for the unemployed and others with years of experience working with software applications for legacy applications based upon COBOL and FORTRAN programming languages.

The Unix operating system has now been widely used for more than 20 years by financial organizations that do extensive financial analysis for large quantities of daily numbers-crunching work. This is another example of an application that offers employment or consulting opportunities for those who have successful experience with Unix and today want to combine it with Linux for web-related or other open source network applications.

These things need to be considered for consulting-type work. They are potential alternatives that merit the consideration of those who are concerned with future IT employment opportunity.

If you have the right skills, the problem is finding the right match, which today has started to be facilitated by the emergence of the web social networking organizations covered in Chapter 8 under networking.

EMPLOYER RANKING OF THE MOST DESIRED NONTECHNICAL SKILLS

This listing is the result of the author's analysis of approximately 12,000 online job specifications for IT employees posted on the larger web job-posting sites during 2004. As previously mentioned, these skills are either desired or required by one third of total job listings, and they are mentioned in over half the listings when the employer is either an IT or management consulting firm or an IT applications services provider.

In the author's 2004 review of approximately 1,200 résumés of IT applicants, applicants listed one or more of these skills in only approximately 14% of total online résumés posted. This represents an opportunity for candidates who have these skills to promote them in their résumés and their self-marketing efforts for their job-hunting activities.

The employers who listed these skills as necessary or desirable listed an average of two skills per job. When only one skill was mentioned in the job specification, approximately two thirds of the time it was either for communications skills or writing or verbal communication.

Skill Ranking	Frequency Mentioned in Job Specifications
1. Communications (verbal and written)	35%
2. Analytical/problem solving	18%
3. Interpersonal	10%
4. Team participation	9%
5. Leadership	8%
6. Presentation	6%
7. Organization	5%
8. Project management	5%
9. Customer service	4%
10. Negotiation	3%

Communications (Verbal and Written) Skills

Verbal communications was mentioned more frequently than written when one was specified. They both were mentioned most frequently in jobs posted by IT and management consulting firms and applications services providers where frequent interface with clients or end users is important.

Presentation skills were also mentioned frequently by these employers. Overall communications skills are very important in team work environments and large projects where employees are interfacing with each other over long periods of time.

Writing skill was frequently required again for consulting firms in report writing and other types of analytical/problem solving types of responsibilities.

Analytical/Problem Solving Skills

Both skills were mentioned frequently together in job specifications, but they were also mentioned individually. These skills showed up more frequently in QA testing and network and technical support positions. They also appeared in systems software- and architecture-type responsibilities.

Interpersonal Skills

This category of soft skills is the one that is appearing more frequently during the past several years, and its occurrence is more likely to show up in large-project-type work where participation on teams is important. Also many employers are mentioning it today in specifications for a high percentage of management jobs. They emphasize interpersonal skills because all forms of communication—oral, written, and listening—are important for supervisors and managers.

Interpersonal skills also includes respect and consideration of the viewpoints of others as well as the ability to relate with others from various types of backgrounds, ethnically, educationally and skillwise. This capability is more focused upon the personality aspects of human relations in the workplace.

Individuals who are overly self-absorbed or arrogant usually have problems with this skill.

Team Participation Skills

Team participation skills are closely related to communications and interpersonal skills. In work situations, they manifest themselves primarily as a function of participant's attitude, cooperative spirit, and the willingness to show respect for the opinions of others, as well as willingness to work cooperatively with other team and group members toward established goals.

Leadership Skills

All employers want leaders who are consistently capable of doing a good job on their personal work responsibilities and who are a positive influence on an overall work group or department. Leaders not only can be counted on to do good work but will make significant contributions to the overall success of an enterprise, business, or organization. They are continually able to command the respect of the majority of other employees in the organization and maintain a positive attitude and pleasant manner.

Presentation Skills

Presentation skills are particularly important in any type of client or end user work where orientation or employee training is required. These skills include good to excellent verbal communications ability as well as the ability to relate to audiences of varying responsibility and skill levels. This is a skill that is developed by frequency of experience and is a critical item in the marketing and sales work involving clients.

Organization Skills

The ability to handle multiple tasks concurrently and any type of comprehensive planning or project management responsibility requires good personal organization skills. These skills are also important for supervisory and management positions where individuals are responsible for a significant number of employees who report directly to them.

Project Management Skills

IT employees who are capable of accepting the personal responsibility for individual projects and effectively managing them are in demand today in all types of organizations. These skills rank among the highest in the IT occupational category because they represent an important responsibility in every major IT discipline in larger organizations. Project management is the essence of the IT consulting business. Most of the major hardware and software companies as well as most of the major education institutions have courses on this subject. IBM has probably provided courses on this subject as long as any business entity, and their courses are well respected.

Customer Service Skills

The subject of customer service has moved to the forefront with the advent of the internet. Most major retailers and financial-service-type organizations have learned that the quality of customer service, easy access and quick response not only affects customer satisfaction but also is possibly their best marketing tool for the sales of their services and products. Much of the fast-growing CRM revenue has been built upon a similar premise.

Negotiation Skills

In order to have good negotiation skills, employees need to have good communication skills and to be able to relate effectively to others, regardless of their stature in organizations or their personal backgrounds. Effective use of this skill is critical in client consulting work and any type of contractor work in IT because there will always be problems and other matters that often will become points of negotiation.

10 TOP SKILLS IMPORTANT FOR IT JOB AND CAREER SUCCESS

This section describes the details and provides examples of the traits and characteristics of employees that the author has observed at all levels of job responsibility that today represent a good road map for any IT employee who wants to achieve a successful career. Unfortunately for many, their growth potential remains dormant and does not ever get developed.

1. Knowledge

Knowledge is a function of one's basic education, continuing education, and job experience. The important thing about knowledge as it relates to career success is whether or not a personal commitment to continued relevance exists. This factor is particularly relevant in the IT profession at this time due to the fact that the industry is undergoing and will continue to undergo significant change during the next few years.

These projected changes mean that each individual must answer a question: What additional technology courses, certifications, job experience and other type of skill development activities do I need to consider pursuing to continue to provide the expected value to employers?

Experienced IT employees should take a hard look at this question and compare their backgrounds to the jobs and skill profiles in demand today as well as to the newer evolving areas that will effect future employment opportunity. This is also an important question for college students who will soon complete their educations and for those who have recently entered the IT job market.

2. Awareness

Awareness is possibly one of the most important but least discussed subjects today relative to its relationship to an individual's career success. In order to be aware of potential beneficial solutions or needs, everyone must have exposure to things that they do not understand that well. Some individuals find much more safety in the status quo and in reality do not want to become involved or to understand things that could help them maximize their career potential. In these cases, they are either not willing to spend the necessary effort or simply do not want to become involved in any type of activity that may create problems for them or that may foster any type of insecurity on their parts. The end result of this type of behavior in most employees is mediocre performance at best and, over time, the distinct possibility of being left behind in their careers.

What does this mean today to most IT employees? It means that, for continued employment and job success, more than job competence will be required for many. It was discussed earlier that in order not to be vulnerable to outsourcing replacement, experience with different functional and industry-specific applications as well as with the newer technology in the IT discipline will be important for most to continue to provide meaningful value to their employers and at the same time not become vulnerable to job loss.

Two examples of situations that have occurred with occupations other than IT during the past several years will show what is possible for well-educated, comparatively highly paid employees during the first 10 years of their business careers.

During the early 2000s, the author had the opportunity to review more than one hundred résumés of relatively young MBAs, many with degrees from some of the most respected educational institutions. These individuals had held product manager, brand manager, or other types of marketing director or management jobs in consumer retailing or marketing companies. The majority were quite well paid for their years of experience, often in the $100,000 to $150,000 annual income range. Many were pursuing alternative employment as a result of pending staff cuts and some because they believed they were vulnerable to replacement by younger MBA's entering this job area at annual incomes of $30,000 to $50,000 less than many of them. This is a good example of possibly being too specialized in something where the work in most cases did not require any type of specialized skills.

The author's reaction to the large number of these résumés appearing was that these well-educated, intelligent employees for some reason had not been able to make themselves valuable enough to avoid replacement or reductions in staff. This was possibly true in many of their personal situations. But why did it occur for a large number of them in such a short period of time?

After talking with several of them, the reasons were better understood. Quite a few of them were on the wrong side of mergers or consolidation activities. In these situations, the purchaser or surviving unit usually keeps their valued employers who often survive the inevitable job cuts. Some simply did not understand why, and it was obvious that in some of those situations they were not the most highly valued employees as compared to their peers.

After talking with quite a few of them, the author's assessment was that they became vulnerable owing to lack of things such as job rotation and spending time in other types of sales-and-marketing-related jobs within their companies. In retrospect, if several of these employees had spent time in field sales or field sales management jobs involved with customers and first-hand distribution of their products, many would have enhanced their value as a result of their increased understanding of their business in regard to how it operates and, in many cases, how it could improve.

During this same time period, the author also reviewed the résumés of scores of MBAs who had spent from 3 to 5 years working in management consulting firms. Again most of them started at a comparatively higher level of income than other MBAs and had increased their income level to the level where it was not consistent with most of the available job opportunities for someone with similar education and experience.

The biggest problem, however, was not their income; it was their expertise. Not too many companies were looking for employees who were at the annual income levels of $120,000 and higher and who were primarily working on client project teams unless they had skills relevant to project management opportunities in companies dealing with the highest level of sophisticated technology development and manufacturing.

The problem with most of these individuals was the majority of the content of their résumés showed several years or more of work participating in project teams across the United States and working with customers in different industries. In other words, it was difficult to understand where their skills and expertise existed, even though the majority were educated at some of the best colleges and universities with excellent scholastic achievement.

The problem for most of them in job hunting was that they did not have several years of successful experience with a specifically defined responsibility that is common to other companies outside of the consulting industry.

Even though the young people in both of these examples enjoyed excellent income for several years, strategically they placed themselves in occupations that were too specialized, and, for most of them, their skills were not at the level where it was easy for them to achieve employment outside of their area of specialization.

In difficult economic times when companies need to improve profit and reduce overhead, the higher income specialized jobs are often vulnerable except for those individuals who rank near the top of their profession from a skill and job performance perspective.

It is predictable that the IT profession will go through these same type of cycles or business periods. What has been occurring with programming and software writing will happen with other job disciplines as they become jobs that are quite similar to situations where tens of thousands of employees are doing basically similar work that does not require high levels of specialty skills.

This prediction indicates that IT employees who want to remain relevant and valuable will continually have to be aware of newer opportunities and whenever possible become involved in order to keep their skill inventory somewhat unique and relevant so that their work is always in demand.

The consulting and product marketing examples build a strong case for the IT career value of varied responsibilities. The more applications of technology within separate functional entities that an employee can work with, the more potentially valuable that employee can be. This is particularly true today related to the development of internet applications.

Awareness is based upon study, education, and exposure to new responsibilities or ways of doing things. Increased awareness is the foundation for the motivation to learn new things. Without this motivation today in the IT industry, many more thousands of employees who have held good jobs for years will predictably become vulnerable to further job losses to outsourcing and other technology change if they are unable to keep their skills and relevance updated beyond the level that they become commonplace to tens of thousands.

It is predictable that the IT industry in countries such as India will continue to concentrate their IT education upon the job classifications that have the largest U.S. employee base.

3. Attitude

Attitude, with the exception of potential for educational and skill growth, is possibly the most important aspect of an IT employees career growth and success. Maintaining a "can do" positive attitude even during troubled times requires a significant amount of personal commitment and self-discipline.

Most of us have known and worked with individuals who are primarily focused upon finding fault with most ideas supporting change of any type. The typical person with this type of outlook and attitude is often defeated before he or she starts work on a challenging assignment. There are some exceptions involving employees who use a negative form of expression to motivate themselves, but even this can be disruptive in team and group situations. If this type of attitude is pervasive in team projects, it is often destructive to desired progress within a project. This type of fault finder outlook usually runs hand in hand with the rationalizer who, by their actions, want to avoid any sort of accountability or commitment for solving problems whenever possible. This type of play-it-safe behavior is typical of employees who often welcome participation in teams or groups wherein situations focus is not as great as that upon individual performance.

Individuals who discipline themselves to maintain a positive attitude consistently are more likely to find ways to solve problems when compared to individuals who opt out because of fault finding and rationalization. They are often critical of improvement suggestions from others on work projects, but when questioned, they rarely have solutions of their own, which is a way of avoiding the risk associated with voicing their suggestions. Of course, there are always exceptions to this observation because there are some top achievers within IT who tend to express themselves negatively in many work situations.

It is much easier to be unable to see beyond the barriers and roadblocks associated with a work problem.

If you are committed to achieving significant career accomplishment and success, you cannot be concerned about accepting what some of your colleagues define as risky assignments for fear of failure. Effort applied to worthwhile assignments, sometimes perceived by some as impossible to master, is what takes the mystery out of them and makes them possible to master. Those in the IT profession who are accomplishers will fail at some tasks during their career, but when you study the careers of many successful individuals, occasional failures are synonymous with achieving patterns of consistent career accomplishments of significance.

4. Thinking Ability

Thinking ability is possibly as important as anything else that a person learns during his or her formal education and career. If thinking skills are not developed, it is difficult to look at a problem or situation that is perceived to be impossible to correct and envision what is possible.

Thinking ability is the basis for research and analysis and the organizations of one's thoughts. Proper structure and organization of thoughts is the basis for effective writing of reports, proposals, and other documents with comprehensive content.

If it is to your advantage to improve you thought process structure, consult a science textbook that details the scientific method.

Adopting its structural components mentally is an excellent process for organization and structure of comprehensive variables that are relevant portions of most significant problem solving and development work. This same type of structural framework can be used in the writing of reports and proposals when you are trying to promote any type of change or improvement recommendations that include comprehensive alternatives and relationships for consideration. Today effective writing skills are valued in most IT positions, and many employees can benefit from an improved approach and process.

An effective thinking process is important in detailed report writing and any type of business proposal writing. The ability to organize, structure, and classify a vast of amount of data is important, and the ability to apply principles like those of the scientific method will be valuable in this type of work. If those who are interested do not have access to a science textbook, the structural framework of the scientific method can be located through a search engine.

The reason that the subjects discussed in this chapter have been compiled here is that most IT employees today can benefit from developing new, improved, and better methods of doing things within their professions. These types of accomplishments are not always a function of their IT technical skills, but they are more related to some of the soft skills and personal traits and characteristics discussed during this chapter.

Another important subject that has been the subject of many books for years is the subject of innovation and creativity. The author believes that anyone who does any type of detailed study regarding this subject will, in most cases, find several common denominators that exist in most situations. These are thinking ability coupled with awareness, learning ability and the commitment to a large amount of significant effort over time focused upon the subject matter targeted for improvement.

Based upon awareness, education, and life and occupation experience, thinking ability helps us understand the relationships associated with any complex or comprehensive problem that is beneficial to solve. The author believes that this logic applies to the computer science discipline, and many thousands of employees need to focus on these type of things to enhance their personal career value in addition to doing their jobs to the best of their abilities.

5. Commitment

Commitment is the strongest and possibly most important trait of employees relative to achieving career success. If a person wants to be the best that he or she can be within the chosen profession personal commitment is the most difficult issue with which to deal.

If an individual is serious in his or her commitment to improve, he or she will do whatever has to be done effort-wise to achieve the desired improvement. The problem with many of us is that we do not back the desire up with the necessary sustained level of effort for the desired improvement to be accomplished. We simply are not committed enough to follow through. The problem is that the required self-discipline necessary to accomplish the desired change is difficult, and most of us have other things that we would rather be doing with our time.

During any type of personal reengineering effort, a person should solicit and consider advice and constructive criticism from other people who know them and whom they respect. Of course, it is important that whomever is solicited for this advice is qualified to provide it.

To be very good at something whether it is your occupation, education, sports, music, or another hobby requires thousands of hours of effort over extended periods of time. This is basic to success for any endeavor. If you study the biographies of any individuals who have achieved greatness in their field of endeavor, the two things that you will commonly find existing is a strong personal commitment backed with a significant high level of effort over the years to master whatever the area of concentration.

Two examples of this type of commitment have had a significant influence on the author: One occurred in college, and the other occurred within the past 2 years. One semester in college, the author roomed next to a highly intelligent person who was setting the curve at the University of Iowa in calculus. We had adjoining rooms connected with a dorm-type bedroom. Frequently late at night, while I was trying to sleep, I would hear this individual verbally admonishing himself while working on calculus problems. This personal bashing, which I guess was a way of motivating himself, would frequently go to the extent of calling himself stupid.

Seeing somebody with this level of intelligence acting in this manner made a distinct impression regarding striving for excellence. It was difficult for me then to understand how an individual who had so much talent could be so committed to improving himself. Not only was he an academic leader, but he was also a very good athlete, personable, and well liked and respected by others.

The second event that had a marked impression upon me occurred almost two years ago while I spent several days in a care center recovering from a total hip replacement. After the evening meal every day, usually about 8:00 P.M., I noticed an elderly man walking up and down the hall for the better part of an hour. I was intrigued by this activity, so about the third evening I went out in the hall to talk with him. During our conversation, he told me that he was 80 years old and that, while in the hospital for a hip replacement, he contracted a staph infection that had made it necessary for his hip operation to be redone (the operation in itself is a major one). During our conversation, he told me that he had served in the infantry during the heart of World War II in Europe in the thick of the battle against Germany where he had lost many of his friends. Seeing this type of commitment and effort in this situation really impressed me, and I realized that my personal situation was really nothing.

While in the care center, I saw numerous men and women between the ages of 45 and 55 who were there for therapy. Because most of them were significantly overweight, they were relegated to canes and walkers indefinitely unless they developed significant commitment and effort to improve themselves. I rarely saw any of these individuals putting in extra effort in the halls after their regularly scheduled therapy sessions. It is hard to improve whatever your needs are unless you back it up with a great deal of the right type of effort .

Times have changed within the IT profession, and they will continue to change. Many current IT employees who are not willing to commit themselves to the effort required to keep them viable are being, and will continue to be, left behind.

6. Confidence

Self-confidence is another sometimes elusive trait. Building one's self-confidence is primarily a function of personal interest, motivation, and effort. Confidence building is transferable from one item to another. Most things that people do well are a function of their interests and spending hundreds of hours doing these things. The things that the majority of us master are often more hobby oriented rather than occupational.

Once the author had the opportunity to address a group of some 50 salespeople of whom the majority had excellent personal potential and the skills required for success. However, overall they lacked the motivation and confidence to be a winning organization primarily because they did not make a significant effort and then blamed others and employed personal rationalization.

Most of the group had graduated with good scholastic records from some of our finer colleges and universities. When asked about their daily efforts for class work, term papers, projects, and final exams, most agreed that they had to work hard in college a significant portion of the time. Most also agreed that they were happy that they had successfully obtained a job with what was regarded at the time as one of the most highly regarded Fortune top 100 companies. The question that I posed to the group that puzzled me, was why weren't most willing to work as hard once they had landed a good job with a great company, as they were during college? The majority of the group got the message: Some resigned, some went to work with much more effort, and several became company sales performance leaders. Within 2 years, this company office rose from the bottom of 70 company offices throughout the United States to one of the top few in the company in sales performance.

This type of situation left an indelible impression on the author: Often employees with a high level of capability and potential for success do not achieve career success, are usually their own worst enemies, and frequently put the blame elsewhere when they should be looking at themselves.

Confidence is important in job hunting. In many situations, job hunters lose confidence after they initially experience setbacks. Candidates need to have a good feeling regarding the process and techniques that they have chosen to apply. Repetitive significant effort does wonders for confidence building if you are willing to improve personal effectiveness and try new methods when what you have been doing has not been successful.

All job candidates will make mistakes in the job-hunting process. If a person is conscientious and cares, he or she will learn from mistakes and will not repeat them. If not, that individual needs to question his or her personal commitment to the job-hunting process.

7. Job Competence

Job competence is pretty much self-explanatory. This critical item is a function of many things: attitude, education, skills, effective effort, experience, work methods, ability to get along with others, personal performance standards, health, and so on. Future leaders in IT not only will benefit positively from items such as these but also will be personally challenged to understand how in their responsibilities they can contribute to the future health of their organizations beyond the fulfillment of their basic job responsibilities.

Employees who have concerns like this and are committed to making these types of contributions are the ones who will have strong IT future careers. Most of these individuals do not have the this-is-just-a-job mentality.

8. Interpersonal Skills

As a reader, you may ask yourself at this point what the discussion of the traits and other skills discussed in this section have to do with successful IT job hunting. The answer is a lot. In addition to technical skills, interpersonal skills are important parts of career success. One of the two most successful self-help books ever was written by a now-deceased plastic surgeon who wrote about the personality, self-image, and self-confidence aspects he had observed in patients who had undergone plastic surgery. The other book, which has been purchased by millions of readers, discusses the role of character traits and their relationship to such things as work, family, and mental health. For many IT employees who are frustrated and have not been able to maximize their personal skill and abilities potential successfully, the type of character traits and skills covered in this section of the chapter are potentially as meaningful in any type of career enhancement effort as improved technical skills.

Possibly the most important soft skill in today's everyday work environment is interpersonal skills. This subject was discussed earlier but justifies further mention because of its increasing importance in business and all other type of organizations that have employees. The reason that this subject has gained so much importance is that it focuses upon the basic decency of the individual employee in the work environment relative to the human relations aspects of how individuals relate to each other. It also includes the communications aspects of writing, speaking, listening, and making verbal presentations to others when necessary. The old adage, do unto others as you want done unto you, goes a long way in covering all aspects of this subject.

Several years ago while conducting a technology management search for a Fortune 100 top-ten technology company, the author learned a great deal about the value assigned to the importance of interpersonal skills. The client said that they could evaluate if the technological skills of the job candidate were adequate for the job requirements but that the difficult area was determining the candidate's interpersonal skills. To hear this from what is regarded by many as one of the world's top technology companies made a distinct impression on me.

The client voiced the opinion that having good interpersonal skills had a value of importance as high as 60% of the job that they were filling because working with teams and groups either as leaders or participants is so important. They could not afford to have in a management role someone whose interpersonal skills were not conducive to the necessary chemistry that fostered an environment of cooperation, innovation, and accomplishment within groups or teams.

Today, as mentioned previously, this desirable skill requirement is showing up as much as 50% of time in some IT job specifications within certain occupations.

9. Integrity

This trait is self-explanatory; its importance is understood by the vast majority of employees in all organizations. Traits such as ego and power seem to continue to corrupt some employees and leaders in many corporate entities as well as government organizations. This attribute is closely related to an individual's personal judgment, and occasionally goes astray in the work environment as a result of politics, self-promotion, and greed. Those who practice this type of behavior often show little or no regard for others. They will fail the interpersonal skill test, and sincerity is usually absent in those with this problem. Employees in organizations that continually demonstrate that they are primarily self-absorbed usually will not be trustworthy.

10. Health

Physical and mental health is an important quality to work at throughout one's career. Employees who keep their health in good order tend to show less emotional frustration in problematic situations and also often demonstrate more stamina and resilience.

Maintaining good physical health and stamina is particularly important for IT employees working in the IT and management consulting areas where frequent and extensive travel as well as long work hours are often required.

If, as an IT job candidate, physical health becomes a question mark issue for the potential employer during interviews, you certainly do not want the risk of potentially compromising your opportunity when your situation could be improved by some extra discipline and effort on your part. In many IT jobs, the ability to demonstrate endurance and work effectiveness when projects involve significant additional work beyond normal hours is an important attribute.

SELF-ASSESSMENT EXERCISES

This section contains two alternative self-assessment exercises. Their purpose is to help candidates define their IT-related expertise better than is currently being displayed in the majority of IT résumés. This step is important for candidates who are interested in writing or rewriting their résumés as discussed in Chapter 6.

Candidates should select the exercise that is most appropriate for their needs or complete both. Candidates may choose not to complete this exercise. If they have not gone through a similar process prior to beginning their job-search-related activities, in most cases they are missing an opportunity to better represent their total qualifications.

Assessing Your Skills and Qualifications Questionnaire #1

The first step in résumé-improvement-related efforts recommended for everyone entering into job search or those who have previously been pursuing employment is a skills assessment.

1. What is your expertise? Write a summary paragraph that best characterizes your experience and skills.
2. Summarize your education. List college degrees (BS, Masters, PhD, Associates in major area) and name and location of educational institution. Also list certifications or provide a summary of any advanced courses taken relevant to IT employment.
3. Write a summary description of any industry, vertical market-specific applications experience.
4. Characterize and summarize your development and implementation experience related to any significant applications mentioned in question #3.
5. Profile or summarize any significant experience in these disciplines.

   - Software engineering, programming
   - Web development
   - Networking/communications
   - Database development or administration
   - Systems architecture
   - Operating systems
   - Security systems (network, internet, intranet, extranet, database)
   - Quality assurance
   - Open source
   - Wireless
   - VoIP
   - Project management or participation
   - Team leadership or participation
   - Summary of nontechnical skills

6. For each category, list the vendor-related product or category with which you have experience.
7. Write a summary paragraph that best describes each of the following:

   - Project experience
   - Team or group leadership
   - Exterior client involvement

8. Write a summary of significant contributions of value that improved business processes, increased productivity, improved customer service, or reduced costs. Where possible describe the specific value to your employer of the end result.
9. Explain your experience in end user or client work relative to presentations, important applications modification or implementation, or significant problems solved.

10. Assess your capability in problem solving, analysis, and troubleshooting.
11. Complete a summary statement of up to three IT jobs where you believe that your skills and experience best fit.
12. Write a good summary description of significant projects in which you have participated, and define your role. If you listed several in question #7, only discuss the most significant ones.
13. Summarize your capability with respect to the newer technology developments of the last several years in your area of expertise.

Assessing Your Skills and Qualifications Questionnaire #2

1. Write a paragraph or two that summarizes your computer science expertise and that best describes your career experience, knowledge, and skills.
2. Complete the following.

   • In what areas of computer science do you believe you have skills and experience of significant relevance?
   • Explain why.
   • Do you have good understanding of the primary business practices of any specific industry including the industries' primary applications for IT?

3. Write a good summary statement of your software knowledge and or skills. What languages do you know?
4. Describe your strongest nontechnical skills and what have they helped you accomplish in your work.
5. Summarize your project or team work experience. What skills has this experience helped you develop that has been beneficial to you?
6. Describe some of the most significant contributions or accomplishments that you have achieved. What was the end result value to your employer of each?
7. Describe the type of job where you believe you can contribute the most to your employer.
8. Analyze your answers to each question or category, and write a summary statement of the items that you believe can help you the most to better portray your overall qualifications in your résumé.
9. What are the changes and additions that you believe will strengthen your résumé?

6.   Writing Your Résumé

The Objective of This Chapter

For IT job candidates who want to improve their current résumés, write their initial IT résumés, or test potential employer reaction to alternative résumés, this chapter will provide "how to" help to accomplish these goals.

The chapter concentrates upon maximizing improvement of the traditional IT résumé components and introduces several infrequently used components that can benefit many job hunters when compared to present and past résumé structures that have been used.

RÉSUMÉ IMPROVEMENT OPPORTUNITY ASSESSMENT

During 2004, the author reviewed more than 1,200 current résumés used by IT professionals pursuing new job opportunities. As a result of this analysis, the author believes that more than 90% of these job candidates can benefit from reevaluating their résumés.

It is appropriate to review briefly several of the most significant résumé improvement opportunities that were identified. Things such as common mistakes and items not to be included in IT résumés will be reviewed later in this chapter.

Too Much Content Focused Upon Job Activities Performed

An estimated 95% or greater of IT résumés have too much content focused upon job activities performed. In many situations, it is not that these activities are unimportant but rather that they are not presented in the résumé most efficiently.

Most résumés can be improved to relate more to the purpose of the activities and whenever possible to summarize any significant problems solved or specific value provided to the employer.

Also related to this improvement opportunity is the fact that, in most situations where the professional has been employed in the same responsibility for more than 2 years, very few résumés portray any type of significant accomplishments or achievements. This is not a desirable situation for experienced IT professionals who wish to achieve new employment with annual incomes in the $70,000 to $120,000 range. In many of these situations, it is apparent that not enough thought or time was spent in preparing these résumés.

Résumés That Depict Technical Skills Only

This factor, combined with the previous one mentioned, presents the other most significant opportunity area for improvement; it can benefit more than 95% of the résumés reviewed by the author.

A detailed listing of a candidate's IT-related skills and experience in résumés is an important component. However, when more than 40% of the 70,000 employer IT job specifications that the author reviewed during 2004 list additional items as either required or desired skills, this factor may explain why thousands of IT job candidates are not receiving potential employer interest consistent with their total qualifications. Chapter 5 provides a detailed listing of most of the desired skills and experience that can benefit candidates who have not listed these items in their résumés.

Interpersonal skills is the most significant grouping and is desired today in more than 40% of employer web-posted job specifications. They may be just as important as technical skills in the needs of many employers. This fact is especially relevant in IT consulting firms where much of the IT work is performed at client sites. Today more than 70% of all IT job specifications posted by IT consulting firms require skills related to the interpersonal skills category.

Included in this category are verbal, written, and presentation communication skills; customer relationship and negotiation skills; and the ability to work successfully in teams, groups, or projects while maintaining effective interpersonal relations with co-workers. This includes such things as listening skills, mutual respect, and consideration of the opinions of others.

Industry-Specific Functional Application Expertise

Even though significant industry-specific experience exists today, it is highlighted in less than 30% of IT professionals résumés. Inclusion of some detail regarding this knowledge and experience is important if a candidate is to market his or her total skill, experience, and potential for successful employment.

Any current IT job candidates who have 2 or more years of IT job experience and have not included skills in addition to technical skills in their résumés may be missing an important opportunity. A summation of industry or functional application knowledge and experience, interpersonal skills, and value-related contributions are all important items for presentation in IT job hunting.

Because the quality of your personal résumé is of critical importance in applying for today's IT jobs, the author believes that a candidate's assessment of his or her IT and personal skills as introduced in Chapter 5 and the content of this chapter are critical items for the majority of IT job applicants who want their résumés to receive consideration for interviews.

As stated before, your résumé may be your only chance for potential employers to develop any type of specific interest in you. The author believes that the content in this chapter and in Chapter 5 cover the important aspects of what most IT job candidates should consider regarding the potential of improving their résumés. Also the author believes that the format and component structure of your résumé and the possibility of strengthening it by incorporating one or more opportunity items mentioned at the beginning of this chapter are much more important in successful job hunting than sample résumés. The main value of sample résumés in this book is to show examples of improved résumés in which some of the opportunity items discussed earlier in this chapter have been incorporated.

This chapter's section on résumé component structure will illustrate how the opportunity areas for improvement can be incorporated in IT professionals résumés to strengthen them as well as to show how to incorporate the type of content that will motivate potential employers to consider the revised résumés.

Why Most Résumés Are Not Successful

Of the more than 60,000 résumés that the author has reviewed during his career and most specifically the more than 1,200 IT professional résumés reviewed during 2004, more than 90% contained or indicated that one or more of the following conditions existed.

1. Personal skill assessment has been incomplete in most situations where job candidates desire to be paid $60,000 or more annually.
2. The author's overall impression is that for at least 40% or greater of résumés reviewed, less than 3 hours was spent in résumé preparation.
3. Less than 20% of résumés reviewed did an adequate job of explaining the value of contributions or achievements in jobs that were held for 2 years or more.
4. For résumés that were mailed, a significant number were printed via ink jet printers, which showed a "splattered look" for words. Additionally, A significant number of résumés printed on laser or xerographic devices were received with images not fused or smudged because the equipment was not performing properly or the wrong paper stock was used.
5. Many résumés sent via mail were not sent to the person or organization to whom they were intended because the candidate did not double-check prior to mailing.

If your résumé writing experience is exempt from the aforementioned items, and you have not achieved the desired results in terms of potential employer interest, then you may be able to benefit from such things as a change in format, comprehensiveness, or quality and relevance of the content. The most obvious potential problem from the prospective employer's viewpoint is that approximately 70% of the résumés received for online IT job postings do not meet the employer's job specification requirements. This fact suggests that most candidates could spend more time analyzing job specifications before posting their résumés.

What Most IT Employers Want to Learn from Your Résumé and Cover Letter

If between your résumé and cover letter or web message you can answer the following questions, your skills and experience match well and are tailored as much as possible to the employer's job description. The following questions are good guidelines to follow in résumé preparation.

1. What are your technical skills, additional relevant skills, level of expertise, and experience for key requirements of the posted job?
2. Summarize your responsibilities and accomplishments of significance for your most recent jobs.
3. In addition to your technical skills and experience, what additional skills do you possess that have best served you in your career?
4. Describe your work experience and type of projects where you have successfully participated with teams or groups.
5. What is your understanding of some of the newer IT technology and applications that are recently being applied?
6. In addition to basic accomplishment of the job description, what other strengths do you possess that could contribute beyond the basic requirements of the job?

If, after reviewing Chapter 5 and reading thus far in this chapter, you believe that the suggestions are too comprehensive, it is recommended that you reevaluate your opinion. Because your résumé is the only document that may be seen regarding your personal qualifications, it truly is the "report card of your career," and most candidates are wisely advised to run the risk of overcomprehensiveness rather than lack of detail. What the author is suggesting here is that published advocates of a one- or two-page maximum résumé in many situations, especially for IT employees with 5 or more years of work experience, is bad advice for candidates who want to be paid $60,000 to $70,000 or higher annually.

A two-page résumé should be adequate for most candidates with 3 up to 8 or 10 years of IT job experience. For those with 10 or more years who have had several different responsibilities and have worked on many projects of significance, a three-page résumé may be more appropriate. Of course, it is inferred that when your résumé is expanded, the quality of content should not suffer but should improve. The section regarding component structure and content improvement in this chapter will help to achieve this goal for most job candidates. Before considering any type of significant revision to your résumé, it is important to understand the little things regarding what not to include as well as common mistakes to avoid before making any revisions in order that the small things are not hurting your résumé's potential for serious consideration.

WHAT NOT TO INCLUDE IN YOUR RÉSUMÉ

Most IT job candidates are aware of what not to include in their résumés. Even though it may be somewhat redundant, these items are reviewed here because, after reading several résumé-writing publications, the author found significant discrepancies in recommended and not recommended items. These items are particularly important for first-time résumé writers and those new to the IT job market.

These are the primary ones to omit: age, religion, personal items regarding family, hobbies, organization membership unless it provides examples of leadership, awards, or other recognition related to the IT profession, and high school-related activities except in situations for first-time job seekers that do not have prior relevant IT work experience and have not completed any type of advanced IT-related formal education. Those in this category should only list items of strong academic nature or leadership (i.e., National Honor Society).

Several résumé-writing publications recommend listing "References Available Upon Request." The author suggests that you not include this phrase. If you move beyond the résumé phase in the hiring process, at some point you may be asked for personal references.

The more astute hiring management will ask for references of specific individuals who can validate your personal skills as well as the quality and type of work that you are capable of performing. If at some point during the hiring process you are asked to provide references you should not provide friends or relatives unless you are asked specifically to provide a character reference. In most situations, when references are requested, they should be for individuals who understand your skills and quality of work.

In your résumé or cover letter, you should not list things such as previous job incomes or current salary expectations, which could eliminate you from further consideration from some situations for which you may be a good potential candidate. If you move beyond the résumé submission step and move further through the hiring process, annual income is a negotiable item in some situations. In situations where new employers choose to verify a person's employment with a former employer, it is the policy of most companies not to verify income, only dates of employment and job title.

COMMON MISTAKES TO AVOID IN WRITING YOUR RÉSUMÉ

Misuse and Overuse of Action Words

Some résumé publications list as many as one hundred action words to use to describe a candidate's responsibilities and accomplishments. For many of the résumés the author has reviewed, this recommendation is a significant mistake because job candidates often appear to concentrate more upon the use of action words than on providing the right type of description of their responsibilities and other relevant job related factors.

The general rule for using action words properly is: If the meaning is unclear or is not significantly improved, don't use them. There are approximately no more than 40 action words that are appropriate to use in computer-science-related résumés. The following list of action words will often have the most meaning in IT résumés.

Accomplished	Invented
Achieved	Led
Analyzed	Managed
Completed	Organized
Configured	Planned
Consolidated	Produced
Coordinated	Reconfigured
Created	Researched
Defined	Responsible for
Designed	Saved
Developed	Simplified
Directed	Solved
Documented	Studied
Facilitated	Trained
Implemented	Trouble Shot
Improved	Wrote
Integrated	

The One-Page Résumé

The one-page résumé is only appropriate for college graduates and other candidates who have not had any prior IT-related work experience or who have had only part-time seasonal or intern work while attending college. A one-page résumé for IT professionals who have had 3 or more years of job experience and more than one IT job is, in most situations, inappropriate. Anyone with 10 or more years of IT job experience who presents a one-page résumé is, in most situations, making a mistake. One-page résumés for professionals with this work tenure poses the question whether or not much was accomplished in skill development for those employed years. This is the type of question that candidates do not want posed, especially if one's annual income requirements or objectives are at or above the $70,000 per year level. The exception to this type of assessment might be candidates with superior skills and type of experience that is in short supply within certain markets and the need cannot be filled by contract workers or consultants. Also it may be difficult for some IT professionals who have basically done the same type of routine process-related work for the majority of their career. In any situation such as this, candidates will want to be certain that they concentrate on a comprehensive definition of their technical and other type of skills as discussed in Chapter 5.

It is not uncommon for candidates for technology-related jobs who have 10 or more years of employment experience, advanced degrees in one or more of the physical sciences, and annual incomes in the range of $80,000 to $120,000 to have well-written résumés that are three or four pages long and that also include additional pages of exhibits that include patent filings, awards and recognition, and summary listings of papers written, articles authored, and speeches given.

Résumé Appearance

The use of fancy formats, fonts, graphics, or special stock for mailed résumés may tend to hinder rather than enhance consideration. Times New Roman is a good type style as are other similar fonts. Résumés should normally be completed in 12-point font size. If yours happens to be three pages or longer, 10-point font size is not objectionable. Bold or regular print is acceptable. Résumés that are mailed and printed on a high-resolution laser printer on 20-pound white paper with an optical brightness or 90 or higher usually provides a good appearance.

Double-Checking for Errors

Résumés that contain frequent spelling errors or are directed to specific individuals with names spelled wrong or titles incorrect do not make the type of impression that candidates want to make. Also when the potential employer is known, candidates should never address a communication to the company or a department within the company. Always call to confirm to whom the cover letter or email should be addressed.

It is common to see candidates' résumés with incorrect or overlapping dates for the jobs they have held. This usually occurs because of carelessness and the failure to review the final product several times for corrections or improvement possibilities. If this is noticed along with things like spelling errors and improper or poor choice of wording, candidates will not receive the type of consideration consistent with their capabilities as a result of carelessness, which is an unacceptable reason for not being considered as a viable candidate.

IT-Related Content Mistakes

Listing only one's technical skills, a description of responsibilities, and the type of work done for each job within a multiple-job employment history is a huge mistake today for most IT job candidates with significant prior experience. The exceptions to this situation in some cases may be professionals with high-level skills and experience in significant demand as previously mentioned.

For the majority of other candidates, including things such as industry-specific experience, developmental work on primary functional applications, description of project-related work and experience, and the entire area of relevant skills other than technical skills is important. Today's frequently required need for interpersonal and communication skills, project management, successful team participation, problem solving, training skill, and understanding of the newer emerging technology and its relationship to IT projects are all items of importance. If you have some of these skills and have not marketed them in your job-hunting activities, you may be limiting your potential for consideration in some of the jobs that you pursue.

The next section regarding résumé format and content will provide several examples of how skills in addition to technical skills can be effectively presented in candidates' résumés.

RÉSUMÉ COMPONENT STRUCTURE AND CONTENT IMPROVEMENT

Résumé writing is a popular but often controversial subject today. It gets further confused by the internet, some of the online job-posting services, and the more than 20 books published during the past several years regarding this subject. A recent key word search on Google for résumé writing listed 1,500,000 listings and 458,000 listings for résumé writing under the information technology category.

Proper résumé writing is process oriented. In many how-to guides, far too much emphasis is placed upon cosmetics (i.e., how the résumé looks, rather than the purpose of the content and options for the job candidate to best represent their qualifications of relevance to potential employers).

During 2004, the author reviewed and analyzed résumés of scores of individuals who have consistently achieved significant accomplishment within technology companies. Most have had employment experience in the range of 8 to 20 years and can be classified as above average to superior performers who were frequently provided increased responsibility by their employers.

The analysis of their résumés revealed that the majority of their résumés were very similar in format, content structure, and method of presenting their employment histories and contributions to their employers. The following results from this analysis provide the basis for a discussion of the primary components that candidates need to provide in their résumés whenever possible. In IT résumé writing, the objective is to maximize the quality of its components accurately and, to the best of the candidate's ability, to make improvements. Whenever possible every candidate will want to tailor his or her résumé as much as possible to the individual job requirements for those jobs for which they want to receive consideration. Applying these basics can help separate candidates from the scores of other candidates who are applying for consideration for the same positions.

Types of Résumés

Three types of résumé formats are discussed in most résumé publications: chronological, functional, and combination of chronological and functional. None of the employees résumés analyzed used combination or functional résumés. They all used chronological résumé formats (jobs listed in chronological order with the last or current job listed first and the first job, last).

The reasons for this are several. First and most importantly is that chronological format is what most hiring professionals prefer to receive. When reviewing hundreds of résumés, you see a significant number of functional résumés. The main criticism regarding this format is that they are often inconvenient to read to gain a good overall picture of a candidate's skills, experience, and qualifications. This confusion exists because most of them are not written in a logically consistent sequence. The end result is that many of them do not receive the consideration that they would have gotten if they had been written chronologically. Chapter 13 provides examples of format, variable recommended section headings and content examples for 30 different IT-related job classifications that represent most of the IT jobs that represent the majority of IT jobs that exist today.

The following are the most frequently employed résumé formats for the vast majority of the résumés that the author analyzed.

Résumé Heading

Over 90% of résumés reviewed placed the heading in the middle portion of the top of the first page of the résumé.

James L. Wilson
45 East Ridge Road
Lexington, Kentucky 72245
(606) 487-6922
email: jlw2@hotmail.com

Several individuals placed the name at the left border and the contact information a space below their name and across the page on the same line.

Summary of Qualifications

More than 95% of résumés reviewed listed the qualifications summary section after the heading. The purpose of this section is to provide prospective employers with a summary of your experience and qualifications.

It cannot be overemphasized how important this section is. Often an employer, when reviewing candidate résumés, will decide whether or not to review a résumé further based upon the strength of this section.

Completed properly, this section summarizes a candidates skills, type of experience, and achievements and should be completed using no more than five to a maximum of eight sentences.

Of the alternative headings reviewed, the one used most frequently was Summary, which was used in approximately 40% of résumés reviewed. Professional Experience was used in approximately 20% of these résumés as was Professional Business Experience. Other headings frequently used were Profile, Professional Experience Profile, Summary of Qualifications, and Skills and Experience Summary.

The following example provides the résumé reviewer an overview of the candidates experience and capability.

Skills and Experience Summary

Ten years of database development experience within the financial services industry. Have experience and expertise working with Unix/Linux, Windows NT and 2000, Java, Oracle, WebSphere, C++, database security, cold fusion, and embedded systems. Have strong interpersonal, written, and oral communications skills. Highly effective in client/end user work. An effective team player with significant experience working in project teams as a participant and in leadership roles. Desire to continue working with the latest database technology.

Immediately following the Skills and Experience Summary, Professional Summary and other headings used, all résumés reviewed used Employment History, Employment Summary, or Employment as the next heading. More than 80% reviewed use the Employment History heading.

List the last or current employer first followed by job title and dates of employment. Most of the résumés reviewed listed headings in bold type, while the descriptive data of the position was either in bold or regular type.

Employment History

IBM Corporation, Westchester County, NY   **2003–present**
Programmer/Analyst AIX/Linux Programs

In this format dates employed are placed at the right margin. The employer and job title are placed on the same line, or the job title is placed directly below the employer's name. In situations where the candidate has had several job responsibilities for the same company, the first line of the heading should cover the total employment time and the job title line the dates of employment in that job title.

Next is the content for inclusion under the job title.

IBM Corporation, Westchester County, NY   **2003–present**
Programmer/Analyst AIX/Linux Program

Primary responsibility has been development work on the AIX operating system. During the past two years, have primarily worked on Linux applications for the banking and insurance industry sectors.

- Work has been evaluated at the consistently exceeds standards, superior level.
- Awarded department recognition for contributions for the year of 2003.
- Developed project team progress review simplification procedure that has resulted in time savings of a minimum of fifty hours monthly for my project team.

A word of caution. Many résumés that the author reviewed told too much story regarding the company and type of business and frequently the companies were large, well-known ones. This should not be done. If a candidate's work experience is primarily in a small, not well-known company or organization, it is appropriate to use one but not more than two sentences to summarize the type of business after the job title.

Many of the résumés that the author reviewed used dots for bullet-type emphasis directly under their responsibility descriptions to highlight any type of special recognition or accomplishments achieved. The candidate's responsibilities and job-related activities are best placed as summaries directly under the job title without any type of highlighting.

The majority of the 1,200 IT résumés reviewed did not make significant mention of accomplishments, recognition for contributions, awards, or business-value-improvement-type contributions regarding their work.

As a society, many of us were taught or advised that it is better judgment to not display any type of self-acclaim publicly or in the presence of others. After review of hundreds of current IT résumés, the author believes that this may represent the thinking of many current IT job candidates.

In job hunting, specifically in résumés, it is time to take credit for significant accomplishment or contribution beyond the basic requirements of one's responsibilities. It is a mistake not to place a brief description of any type of such contributions or recognition under the job title where this occurred.

The author has viewed résumés where, for example purposes, senior company financial officials have taken personal credit for significant growth of annual company revenues. Things such as this are marketing and/or sales-related and claims such as this will get candidates disqualified from consideration quicker than anything else.

In reviewing hundreds of professional's résumés, the author observed that the majority of job candidates can certainly improve the way in which they describe the value of their work contributions to their employers.

It was rare to find several résumés of IT professionals with fewer than 5 or 6 years of IT employment whose résumés showed any indication regarding the value provided by their work. This is definitely a problem for many candidates who would like to improve their job-hunting results and is an important subject to many potential employers. It will receive further discussion later.

This type of value definition primarily appeared in résumés of candidates with 15 or more years of IT experience, and in these résumés, it occurred less than 20% of the time. Nevertheless, IT professionals should incorporate significant accomplishments or examples of value provided to employers that made significant contributions or solved important business problems.

What the author is suggesting here is that if most IT professionals better understood the value of their work and the business contributions that they have made or have participated in making, their résumés would be much stronger from a personal marketing standpoint.

At this point in the résumé-writing component and content improvement area, these questions apply to all IT job candidates evaluating their employment history.

- Can you incorporate any additional personal recognition or employee value contribution in your résumé?
- In your résumé have you mentioned industry-specific functional application knowledge or skills other than technical skills such as interpersonal, communication, and project management.

Employment History—Content Example

LL Bean, Freeport, ME	February 2002-Present
Data Warehouse Engineer	

Responsible for maintenance and modification of intelligent customer database for sales and supply chain management systems. Supervise three programmer/analyst, administrators.

Employment History—New Version

LL Bean, Freeport, ME	**February 2002–Present**
Data Warehouse Engineer	

Manage development and modification of sales and customer supply chain database.

- Customer internet sales increased 25% for 2002, 18% for 2003, and 21% for 2004 through database modifications and overall improvement.
- Implemented data mining software that improved the viability of the customer database while increasing its size 17% during 2003.
- Supply chain improvements helped reduce customer order to shipment time by 25%.

A significant number of the well-written résumés that the author reviewed used main headings in bold type. After the initial several sentences, accomplishments were listed under the job title when there are a significant number of items. Dot-type bullets are listed directly under the accomplishment heading.

Another effectively used heading in many of the IT résumés that the author reviewed were inserted at the conclusion of the discussion of the specific job title activities and accomplishments in a section entitled Environment. This is a summary description of the specific jobs skills used such as operating systems, programming languages, protocols, and other technology categories used for that particular job.

Technical Skills, Skills Summary, Skill Sets, Skill Profile

After Employment History, at least 50% of IT résumés that the author reviewed used this category; most used the Technical Skills category. Many candidates placed this category prior to Employment History which is not objectionable, especially if a candidate has skills that are in high demand.

The majority of résumés where one of these headings was used listed skills and their related components under several of these categories within the heading: Operating Systems, Programming Languages, Protocols, Database, Networking, Communications, Additional Software, Security, Quality Assurance, Testing Equipment, and Scripting.

The headings of Skill Summary or Skill Profile are more appropriate when skills other than technical skills are included. The primary problem associated with candidates providing a listing of technical skills only is that there is no way for potential employers to evaluate their proficiency, unless candidates provide a good detailed summary of work or projects, their purpose, and what was accomplished. When using headings such as Skill Summary or Skill Profile, such items as interpersonal skills; writing, verbal, and presentation communications skills; team participation; specific-industry knowledge; functional application knowledge; problem solving; analytical skill; project management; troubleshooting; and training and team building are appropriate to include in addition to technical skills. A trend exists to place more value on these soft-type skills by many employers.

The following is an example of a Skill Summary. It should be placed after the Employment History section but before the Education section.

Skill Summary

Operating Systems: Windows NT/2000, Unix
Programming Languages: Visual Basic, C, C++, Java
Database: SQL Server, MS Access, Oracle
Internet: ASP, VB Script, JavaScript, HTML, XML, Cold Fusion, Dreamweaver, ASP.NET, Java Server, Perl

Excellent team and project participation skills with strong interpersonal, verbal, written and presentation skills, good analytical and problem solving skills, project management experience, and good awareness of latest technology.

Education

In this heading list the degree(s) awarded first, followed by the institution and location.

BS Degree Computer Science, University of California, Berkeley, CA

Dates are optional. If multiple degrees or majors exist, list them. If significant hours of study (usually more than 20) exist in disciplines such as mathematics or any of the physical sciences in addition to computer science study, list them.

List associates degrees or certifications obtained in this section. Also if any significant level of scholastic achievement occurred, list it.

For those who do not have computer science degrees, list any certifications or significant IT-related course work at technical schools such as DeVry Institute or ITT Technical.

Professional Affiliations and Awards

Placed appropriately after education. This section includes things such as IT industry-related professional affiliation or association memberships, any special awards or other recognitions, publications, papers, speeches, and IT industry presentations.

If this section is extensive, consider including a supplemental page entitled Supplement to Résumé of (your name) for listing these items. It is not uncommon for individuals with advanced degrees employed in the physical science disciplines with 10 or more years of employment experience to list several pages of this type of items in a supplement to their résumés.

For candidates who want to limit their résumés to a two-page document but believe that they have additional information that may be of value or interest to employers, a Supplement to Résumé may be appropriate. A good example to consider would be a summary description of project work where significant value was provided. Other items that are appropriate for inclusion would be examples of industry-specific functional application work where a significant portion of a candidates skills were used.

For candidates who have additional relevant content that does not fit well within their résumé, a supplement may be a better choice. Also, there is nothing wrong with having a three-page résumé if a candidates work history, accomplishments, and overall qualifications justify it.

Page Headings

It is a good idea to place your full name including middle initial at the top margin of all résumés more than one page long. This is a good idea because often emailed or mailed résumés get misplaced or are placed in stacks where pages are often intermingled. For résumés mailed, stapling of the pages is not recommended.

ADDITIONAL EXAMPLES OF RÉSUMÉ CONTENT

The remainder of this chapter contains additional discussion regarding the content of the most important portions of candidates' résumés: Employment History, Skill Summary, and Supplement to Résumé. The author believes that the majority can improve their résumés by addressing these three items; consequently, additional thought regarding these items and their potential relevance to each candidate is important.

The first section contains several examples of the suggested format and content for inclusion in the Employment History section of job candidates' résumés. In the author's review of 1,200 current IT résumés, this section for most candidates presented the most important opportunity for significant improvement.

Employment History Examples

Project Manager

Bank of America, Boston, MA   **April 2003–Present**
Project Manager, CRM Implementation Project

Lead project manager for CRM implementation project focused upon improving marketing/sales results in the consumer retailing division. Responsible for coordinating and supervising work of four team members.

- Successfully modified and implemented CRM modules in ten months, two months ahead of schedule.
- After six months of use, new system has increased active customer lead database by 30% with a corresponding increase in internet and other direct contact-related sales results by 24%.
- System has successfully reduced cost of customer contact from an average of ten dollars per customer to seven dollars.

Software Engineer, Applications

Reader's Digest, Pleasantville, NY   September 2002 to October 2004
Software Engineer for Subscription Services

Responsible for leading development team that built and implemented a new web-based application for processing customer-subscription-related transactions.

- Project completed on schedule and 15% under planned cost.
- Enables Subscription Services to process up to 50% more transactions per day than previously possible.
- Processing error rates have been reduced from previous rate of 2% of total transactions to less than 1/10th of 1% resulting from improved processing software.

Environment

J2EE (EJB, JSP, Java Servlets, JMS), Struts, JavaScript, C++, XML, HTML, SQL, CGI, Unix Scripting, Weblogic server

Wireless Engineer, Developer

Xerox Corporation, Rochester, NY   **2001 to Present**
Wireless Engineer, Developer

Participated in design team responsible for development of a new wireless communications system for use by the 10,000 plus employee field technical service organization. System design incorporated latest WIFI and WiMax technology.

- Initial six months of field testing of new system indicates no deterioration in quality of services compared to present system used with potential annual cost savings to be realized in excess of six million dollars annually.
- System incorporated design and controls associated with provision of a real-time customer communications interface capability.
- Early field test results from large customers with networked enterprise document publishing systems indicates new system is a valued customer service improvement.
- Project team was presented with the Company President's Award for innovation and excellence.

Quality Assurance Test Engineer

Texas Instruments, Richardson, TX   **1998 to present**
Test Engineer Microprocessor Testing
  Department   **September 2002 to present**

Participated on a team that developed a new test process and test cases for microprocessor prototype development, using C++, Java, Perl, and Shell Scripts. Included development and implementation of a Unix network used as a repository for test cases processed on SGI-Linux with NT servers.

- Average test cycle time was reduced by approximately 40% as compared to the previous method.
- New process permitted elimination of the majority of previously required duplicate testing.
- Improvement in test cycle time and elimination of the need for most duplicate testing is projected to enable the doubling of the previous amount of testing completed each month with no additional resources required.

Java Architect

Genuine Parts Company, Atlanta, GA   January 2001 to August 2004
Java Architect

Lead developer for a team that converted a Windows-based client server parts information/inventory system that included quote processing, purchase order processing, shipping and other supply-chain-related activities to a intranet web solution. System was written in Java (JSP, Beans, Servlets, JavaScript), HTML, DHTML.

- System reduced average order to shipping fulfillment time by 50%.
- Inventory stocking and turnover improvement resulted in annual cost savings in excess of four million dollars.

Database Administrator

SBC Communications San Antonio, TX   March 1999 to present
Database Administrator assigned to
   Corporate Marketing   May 2003–present

Member of IT team assigned for implementation of WhisperWire CRM software for field sales organization. Primarily involved in maintenance, troubleshooting, and modification work for customer database.

- Since implementation, system has maintained 99% plus uptime.
- System's real-time sales cycle data provision feature is helping reduce average customer sales cycle time required by 30% as a result of quicker access and provision of better customer data.

Environment

Unix, CGI, HTML, Perl Scripting, Cold Fusion, SQL Server

Skill Profile, Skill Summary Improvement Opportunity

Another important area of improvement opportunity for most IT job candidates is the skills area because the majority of IT job candidates' résumés that discuss skills, primarily list only technical skills. The fact is that technical skills alone do not always equate to employment success. The more astute employers today already understand this, which is why 40% or more of employers are requiring skills in addition to technical skills.

A comprehensive Skill Summary or Skill Profile heading appropriately can include this type of additional content. Those candidates who do not believe that items such as these fit well in the résumés may choose to use a Supplement To Résumé document, which is discussed earlier in this chapter and is further reviewed in this section.

Technical Skills: List specific summary items in these or other relevant categories: operating systems, programming languages, database, networking, protocols, communications, testing tools, scripting, additional software, security tools, project management.

Other Skills: Includes interpersonal, communications, verbal, written, presentation, problem solving, analysis, troubleshooting, project management, training, team work, team building, planning, negotiation, creativity, and leadership skills.

Industry/Application Knowledge: Includes specialized industry business practices, listed by name and industry; industry-specific application knowledge unique to industry and functional discipline (i.e., marketing, engineering, or finance), listed by name.

Additional IT Job Category Qualifications: List any other potential job classifications that you are qualified to perform.

If necessary to properly list your total skills and expertise, this section may take up as much as one half to three quarters of one page in your résumé.

In addition, for candidates who have extensive project participation or management experience, it is a good idea to provide an additional supplemental page to your résumé under the heading Project Experience Summary as a Supplement to Résumé.

The reason for considering the use of a supplement is that most IT résumés today are of the one- or two-page variety. If a candidate has more than 7 or 8 years of job experience and during this period has had several different jobs or job titles, it is difficult for most candidates to explain their qualifications properly and for the résumé reviewer in many cases to gain an adequate understanding of a candidate's potential qualifications.

For any candidate who has extensive project experience, a supplement provides an opportunity in a summary paragraph, each with a project name heading, to explain the type of work that he or she has done and are capable of doing. This task is often difficult to explain in a one- or two-page résumé.

A Supplement to Résumé is a better method for handling this task than telling a story under each job in the Employment History section of the résumé.

Before ending this chapter, it is important to discuss another often confusing item that has important relevance in IT job-hunting activities—proper use of cover letters. This section also applies to message windows used in conjunction with candidates emailing résumés directly to companies or to job-posting service sites.

PROPER USE OF COVER LETTERS

Cover letters represent another improvement opportunity for most IT job hunters. Most job candidates do not receive the benefits that they should from cover letters.

Cover letters should always be tailored as much as possible to the job for which candidates are applying. When an employer is mentioned in the job's web posting or ad, candidates should always contact the employer to determine to whom the résumé should be directed. It is a professional mistake to address the cover letter or web site message to a company or to a department within the company when a candidate could obtain the name of the contact who will be responsible for evaluating the résumé when, with some additional effort, they could obtain the contact's name and title.

A cover letter presents an excellent opportunity for candidates to do some additional marketing regarding their qualifications and interest in the subject job. In all situations where the hiring company is known, it is a good idea to do some research on the company and to mention this fact in your cover letter or web site message. Too many cover letters read something like this.

John S. Davis
49 West Avenue
Huntington, NY 10004
(917) 875-6121
email: jsdaviscp@aol.com

October 10, 2004

WR Grace Company
P.O. Box 9712
New York, NY 10007

Att: Human Resources Department

My résumé is enclosed in response to your current job posting on your web site for a systems administrator. I believe that my qualifications and experience are a good match for your job description.

I look forward to the opportunity for the possibility of being considered to interview for this opportunity.

Enclosure (one)

Sincerely,

John S. Davis

Cover letters somewhat similar to this one may seem to be acceptable, but most miss significant marketing opportunity for job candidates to generate further interest in themselves. This is primarily because the cover letter or email window message in many job situations may be the first thing that the employer's reviewer may see, and it is important to make as strong an impression as possible. This and similar letters will often miss this opportunity. The following letter is a sample of the type of cover letter or body of the message for web-posted jobs that has a much better chance of generating the interest of the résumé reviewer.

John S. Davis
49 West Avenue
Huntington, NY 10004
(917) 875-6121
email: jsdaviscp@aol.com

October 10, 2004

Ms. Judith French
Human Resources Manager
WR Grace Company
P.O. Box 9712
New York, NY 10512

Dear Ms. French:

Enclosed is my résumé for consideration for your web-posted systems administrator position. My skills and experience meet the job specifications. I have previous experience in systems administration within the chemical processing industry and have good understanding of and experience working with industry business practices and their related applications.

My technical skills are current relative to the latest IT technology for systems administration work, and I also have strong interpersonal, communications, internal client, and team work skills.

I have researched WR Grace Chemical Division business and believe that I have the type of skills necessary to make the type of business contributions that are necessary for this position. I will plan to follow up with you later this week to discuss the possibility of scheduling an interview for this opportunity.

Enclosure (one)

Sincerely,

John S. Davis

Candidates should consider cover letters as an opportunity for additional marketing of one's qualifications. If writing a quality cover letter or email message or attachment requires some additional research time and effort to prepare, it is wise to make this investment. This is important because in many situations candidates who take the time to write a comprehensive marketing-type cover letter may receive a consideration advantage from the employer when compared to many other candidates who do not take the time to do this.

A more detailed discussion of cover letters is provided in the résumé distribution section of Chapter 10.

In all job-search-related efforts, it is a good idea to locate all situations possible where a candidate's total qualifications may place them in some type of advantage over other candidates.

The potential value to IT job candidates of industry-specific-related business practices and applications knowledge as well as other important skills in addition to technical skills has been stressed throughout this chapter. These factors represent a potential self-marketing improvement opportunity in résumé writing and in the job-finding process for an estimated 90% or greater of IT job seekers today. When these factors are effectively developed, they can help generate increased interest in IT job candidates by employers.

7. IT Employment Strategies

The Objective of This Chapter

Because of change that is ongoing within the IT profession today, this chapter discusses the importance of having an updated career plan and its components. Also contained is a discussion of the different categories of IT employment and some of the unique challenges of each as well as suggested strategies for job finding for those in each primary employment category. The employment categories discussed are the unemployed, college students and recent graduates, those considering career change, those considering industry change, those participating in outplacement, and IT employees with 20 plus years of IT experience.

CAREER PLANNING

In addition to annually reviewing and updating your résumé on a PC, it is a good idea to do the same for your career plan. For those who do not have a career plan, it is a good idea to establish one even for those who are 10 or more years into their careers. A formal career plan can be no more than a one- or two-page document, and it is a good thing to have since most IT employees will spend between 30 and 40 years or more in their profession.

The following sample career plan format shows the types of components that an employee would look at once a year to assess how he or she is doing regarding progress against the plan.

Sample Career Plan Format

What is my employment objective 10 years from now? (Goals such as retiring, achieving a significant level IT management job, pursuing additional education, moving into different IT jobs, and improving certain specific skills are the type of things that would be included.)

What are the most important components that I will have to achieve to accomplish these goals? (Define the specifics of the key parts of skills that you want to improve, any job rotation or exposure to different types of responsibilities such as project management, leading a team, working with end users to define application specifications, verbal and written communication skills, certain vendor certification, and improved level of performance in annual performance appraisals. These types of components belong in this section. Initially, you would select the three or four most relevant components and detail each of their parts that relate to the desired improvement or skill acquisition.)

Where do I stand today against these additional needs? (Summarize the type of IT work that you are capable of doing by category. Basically, these needs should reflect the qualifications data contained in your résumé and other items of importance that relate to the desired change.)

What additional work experience including job exposure or rotation is an important item in achieving my plan?

What is my plan and time goal for achieving this additional experience?

What can I do in my current position with its defined responsibilities to make myself more valuable to my employer? (Review of previous performance appraisals might help clarify this item. If they don't, asking your manager or a colleague who knows your work and skills and whose opinion you respect could help here.)

As of today, what things do I need to think about in terms of the change that the IT profession is undergoing that could result in my skills becoming obsolete or outsourced during the next several years?

Are there any things that require my attention relative to this potential vulnerability during the next couple of years. If so, what are they? If there is nothing apparent today, which things do I need to watch closely during the future?

The following is an example of a one-page summary format that could be used for a career plan profile.

10-Year IT Career Plan for_____

Current Job Title   Current Technical Skills   Additional Skill Needs

Next Job Goal   Targeted Date to Achieve by:

Ultimate IT Career Goal Description

Summary of Additional Job Experience Needs (update present status and progress)

Additional Education Needed to Achieve Career Goals and Continue Relevance (update present status and progress)

Date résumé last updated: Date career plan last updated:

As part of a career plan, it is also a good idea for IT employees who are seriously committed to having a successful IT career to give some thought to the following situation annually.

For items that appear to be evolving as potential problems that could result in employment vulnerability, what can I do to offset or minimize their potential threat? This may at times include consideration of a new employer depending on changing conditions in one's current work situation.

Having the type of a career plan that you can look at and give thought to each year is planning for career success. Lack of any type of similar planning in this day and age is more like planning for increased employment vulnerability where many of us can learn from previous mistakes.

UNEMPLOYED

The U.S. Department of Labor, Bureau of Labor Statistics estimates that there are approximately 253,000 information industry employees who are currently unemployed in the United States. Thousands of computer science professionals have and today are experiencing situations similar to these. "I have twenty years of computer systems experience and was laid off. I was ultimately replaced by a recently graduated computer science MBA at 60% of the annual income that I was earning." "My job was recently oursourced to some type of staffing or contract employment company that is taking over responsibility for several of our functional applications. I do not know whether or not I will have a job opportunity with the outsourcing firm." "My job and several other software applications jobs in our company were recently outsourced outside of the United States."

Individuals who have experienced this situation, are currently unemployed, and have been searching unsuccessfully for a good job, in most cases, need to reengineer their career. The Bureau of Labor Statistics also predicts a U.S. increase of approximately 1.5 million IT jobs between now and the year 2010. Larger corporate outsourcing of jobs such as call and help center work and the simpler application and hosting work will continue to be sent offshore. Many industry consultants and employment industry officials continue to predict no appreciable growth within the IT job sector. The author believes that the projected job growth will occur but that it will primarily come in public and private companies of which there are close to 388,000 today in the United States with total employees in the 50 to 500 employee range. Also a significant portion of this hiring will occur in the government IT job sector.

What does this mean to the currently unemployed and the future unemployed IT professionals who are trying to find employment? It primarily means that you must reassess the job-hunting process that you have been using for adequacy and relevance as well as consider acquiring the additional skills and education that may be necessary.

Whether the issue is one of retooling skills for improved relevance through supplemental formal education, restructuring the résumé, implementing an improved job search process, or initiating more professional marketing of themselves, or in some cases all of the above, major change in approach to job finding is necessary for most job hunters.

The first mistake made by many job hunters is the lack of consistent daily effort. This means putting in an 8-hour day, Monday through Friday, pursuing job-search-related activities. This obviously requires strong personal commitment and self-discipline and in most situations, a different and improved approach and process as compared to what has been used.

Supplemental education is relevant for some. Advice from respected, qualified acquaintances in computer science work can be helpful here. For those who believe they have exhausted their network to no avail and have spent hundreds of hours submitting résumés to corporate and online job-posting job sites, three potentially viable options may be appropriate for them to consider.

1. Improve and upgrade the quality of your résumé. This activity includes tailoring your résumé with multiple alternative options for emphasizing such things as specific industry, functional experience, and other specific applications experience. Start the process with the skill assessment activities outlined in Chapter 5.
2. Improve your research of potential opportunities. This activity suggests that you focus on opportunities of interest more quickly and respond with more comprehensive research of the hiring organization. The material outlined in Chapter 8 regarding the job-hunting process will be helpful in this activity.
3. Consider implementing a self-marketing campaign to learn if this is a more effective method of stimulating interest in your qualifications. The best way to test this concept is outlined in Chapter 9 in the section entitled "Tailoring Your Job Search." This might entail sending out a series of query letters or researching and contacting smaller companies in your geographic areas of preference. Also the possibility of contract or project work, covered in Chapter 9, also could be helpful with this.

You should also continue with your previous job-hunting activities because timing is important to the job search, and there may be jobs out there that fit your qualifications. The problem is that there is not one single source that can identify the potentially relevant opportunities that exist for you at any given time. Additionally, computer science employment opportunities change daily.

After reviewing the components in Chapter 8, you should select the components which you believe are most relevant for you to pursue.

Step # 1. Rewrite your résumé based upon the results of your self-evaluation outlined in Chapter 5. In addition, you should follow the rewriting steps outlined in Chapter 6. Standard items such as the personal information contained at the top of your current résumé will remain the same as will the job chronology with dates, the last job listed first.

Step # 2. If you want to try to test a different approach for specific opportunities such as contract employment, specific industries, and functional applications, or smaller- and medium-sized companies as compared to your previous employment, the following strategically related steps are important for testing new approaches that require tailoring of your résumé for a more focused type of job hunting.

(a) In query letters to small- or medium-sized growth companies, if you have the relevant experience, you might present yourself as being capable of handling multiple responsibilities that normally may be handled by two or more employees.

(b) Willingness to come to work on a trial basis to prove your value is another approach that might be of interest to some companies. If this sounds like a bad idea, remember that some computer science employees who were laid off from dot com companies in Northern California were willing to work without pay for specified periods to gain experience.

(c) Outline a summary of your responsibilities. If you cannot list a minimum of three or four significant accomplishments for any job that you have held for 2 or more years, you need to spend more time thinking about what the potentially meaningful accomplishments were. How did the work that you performed improve or help contribute to significant company business practices?

(d) If you use Job Objective at the beginning of any of your alternative résumés, do not list more than two jobs as your primary priorities. Remember that most computer science résumés normally do not include data regarding important skills other than specific computer-science-related skills that describe the applicant's job experience. These skills can be listed prior to chronological job order as Summary of Qualifications or prior to formal education with a heading such as Additional Skills if you believe either of these formats could benefit you. Again, these alternatives are good items to test to determine if résumés sent out with different formats and components generate more interest in your résumé. The most relevant items for inclusion in an Additional Skills section are the ones listed in the Employer Ranking of Nontechnical Skills in Chapter 5.

(e) Testing of a tailored, specific approach focused upon fast-growing companies or specific industries or functional applications is an approach that is not that frequently used by the majority of applicants who are competing for jobs of interest to you. The primary goal of sending out your résumé today is that it generates enough interest to be put aside for further consideration by hiring management. A tailored, more focused approach can be tested on a small scale and has the potential of providing you with improved results as compared to the previous approaches that you have used. The main thing to keep in mind is that jobs posted via the internet often have as many as several hundred applicants. Your challenge is to distinguish yourself to generate interest on the part of the hiring company.

COLLEGE STUDENTS AND RECENT GRADUATES

As you already know, job finding in this era is much more challenging, and you are and will continue to experience much more competition for the available computer science jobs. The U.S. Department of Labor forecast job growth within the computer science sector is forecast to grow from a current level of 2.8 million jobs to a level of 4 million by the year 2010. For the some approximately 200,000 new IT jobs that will appear each year, college students will have some degree of advantage in pursuing these jobs as long as their computer science education has been in relevant areas such as software programming and engineering, web development, security, networking/communications, and database development and management. There are other areas of importance, but these disciplines are where most of the new jobs will be.

The competition for these jobs will continue to be severe indefinitely. When you consider that there are currently as many as 200,000 or so IT professionals unemployed and as much as 15% of the current IT employment base will consider job change each year coupled with the estimated 200,000 IT students coming into the job market each year after completing some type of IT education, the job hunting in IT will be extremely competitive.

Students graduating with the best scholastic records in IT curriculums that are in demand by company recruiters will have the advantage. Because we all cannot have that distinction, where are the opportunities for the majority? First, new graduates have a distinct advantage over the thousands of unemployed who have 10 or more years of job experience providing that technical skills are similar. The reason is that the entry-level starting salaries provide the new graduates the advantage. If a graduate has done relevant summer and college employment, their comparative advantage increases further.

A strong personal time commitment for most students in their last year of college will be required for most in order to identify available employment opportunities.

This section addresses three distinct classifications of college students relative to résumé writing and the job-finding process.

1. Those still in college
2. Those in their last year of college
3. Those recently graduated and still job hunting

Common to each of these three categories is the need to complete the highest quality résumé possible. The process that will assist you in building your best possible résumé is outlined in Chapter 6. Most college students and recent graduates should focus on optimizing the one-page résumé.

Those Still in College

This category addresses "what to do" for all students not in their last year of formal education.

The items of primary importance are

- Your courses
- Internships
- Your placement office
- Research
- Résumé building

Your Courses

While doing management recruiting for one of the frequently recognized top ten managed corporations in the world, it was learned that in a high-technology work environment an individual's quality of interpersonal skills in team and group work situations was often as important as their level of technical expertise. These type of skills are ranked in the Chapter 5 employer ranking of nontechnical skills 2004 survey results. Communications skills—writing, speaking, and listening—are critical to career success. If you do not believe that they are currently one of your assets, you should research and consider the potential value of enrolling in additional courses related to these subjects.

Interpersonal skills is a rapidly growing subject of importance that relates closely to personal communication skills. In addition, it includes such things as how each of us relates to others in such things as sensitivity, empathy, mutual respect, and consideration. These qualities in employees are important in team and work group situations, and when they truly exist, they tend to block out the type of self-centered behavior that often interferes with group cooperation and work progress.

The old adage from the golden rule, "do unto others as you want done unto you" is a good way to summarize the growing importance of interpersonal skills in the work place.

The future leaders in the computer science discipline not only will make significant technology-based contributions to their organizations but will also be respected and recognized as leaders in the interpersonal skill area.

For those that have double majors in computer science and other disciplines such as math, the physical sciences, and finance, pursuing entry-level consulting jobs will have some advantage. Additionally, looking for employment in specific industries where these disciplines are important may provide candidates some additional potential job opportunities. Even if the double major is not possible, a major in the computer science discipline and a minor in the others mentioned can be helpful.

Today, for example, if your major concentration within IT is software engineering, taking courses in other key areas such as web development, networking, security, and relational databases is also a good idea. Jobs within all of these disciplines are expected to grow significantly between now and 2010. Taking advanced courses within these disciplines would be a good investment.

Internships

Much information regarding companies with internship programs can be obtained through search engine access and directories in most college libraries.

A summer or two during college in an IT department-related internship in addition to your curriculum focus is a desirable asset to be added to your résumé. This experience may provide you with an advantage in applying for entry-level jobs over most candidates who do not have any experience of this type.

The importance of internships is accentuated during periods of a tight job market. Although computer science job growth as forecast between now and 2010 by the U.S. Department of Labor is the leading job growth industry (see Chapter 1), the competition for these jobs will remain fierce. When you consider that there currently are an estimated 17 million students enrolled in some type of formal education programs beyond high school and as many as 2 million of these graduates will enter the work force annually, a forecasted minimum of 100,000 individuals annually will enter the computer science job market from some type of formal education program.

With the previous scenario in mind, you need to be able to distinguish yourself to the highest degree possible in your résumé and job-search-related activities considering the competition that you will face in the job market.

Your Placement Office

Early in the year prior to your graduation, you should become familiar with your placement office and the services that it can provide you. During your final year, you should schedule every on-campus interview possible. It is also a good idea to schedule a meeting with your colleges placement director to gain any advice he or she may have. Many of them have been in their jobs for years and can be helpful.

Campus interviewing may lead to the right job for you. If it does not, the interviewing process will provide you with valuable experience. We all make mistakes in job interviews, but gaining experience is the best way to improve. Review the material in Chapters 10 and 11 for suggestions regarding preparing yourself for interviews and presenting yourself in them.

Job Research

Based upon job cuts and outsourcing of jobs outside of the United States, the best job opportunities for the average college graduate possibly will not be in large corporations but in small- and medium-sized companies with 50 to 500 employees, all areas of government, and, to a lesser degree, IT and management consulting firms. There are approximately 388,000 total U.S. firms in the referenceUSA database in the 50- to 500-employee size category, and the majority included in this database will have very good to excellent credit, which is an important factor in initial employment in firms of this size.

It is logical that these types of firms, in addition to government, are where most of the incremental job growth will occur. Typical firms in this category will have IT departments of employee size usually somewhere in the 5 to 20 range and many will be outsourcing certain functional applications today. As they continue to grow, they have the same needs today as larger organizations regarding newer web applications, web and network security, networks and related communications, relational database use, and the implementation, maintenance, and modification of application software.

The large evolving new areas of software development jobs are in the CRM application software developers. There are currently more than 50 of these companies actively developing customer relationship management software primarily for applications in marketing, sales, finance, customer service, human resources, and supply chain components. This high-growth-opportunity industry is relatively new, and leading IT technology market research firms forecast it to grow to the annual revenue level of $75 billion to as high as $77 billion by year end 2007. They will serve to be a growing source of entry-level jobs for college graduates during the next 10 years. When researching them, you need to be aware that there is currently a rapid rate of merger or purchasing of CRM companies. From a career perspective, several years of experience doing IT work with their applications development and customer exposure will serve well anyone who chooses to pursue employment in this discipline.

In a competitive job market, the need for frequent job research is important. In addition to the numerous job posting sites on the internet, the referenceUSA CD-ROM is an excellent tool for you to use to supplement your job-hunting activities. In the section entitled "Tailoring Your Job Search" in Chapter 9, you can receive a brief overview of the features of this database of companies. If it is not available in your library, check other libraries in the area. It also may be available through the nearest state employment or job network office. In these offices, it is called Employer Database, which is another name for the infoUSA product provided by their government division. This is an excellent product that can be used as the base data for sending employment query letters early during your final year. Using this database to identify numerous companies located in your work area of preference can be useful.

There is nothing wrong with contacting companies early in the school year and advising them that you have researched their company and are interested in the possibility of qualifying for entry-level employment in their computer department. A follow-up phone call to your letter within a week of mailing is a good idea. The purpose of this call is to talk with a manager in the computer department or in human resources to determine if possibly they plan to hire any additional employees in the computer department during the year. Most will tell you during the conversation that they do not know of any plans to add employees, but over the months things always change. It is a good idea at the end of the discussion to ask them if you could check back with them several months prior to your graduation date to see if any possibilities exist.

If there are any possibilities that you learn of, it would be a good idea to arrange a visit during one of your vacation periods to talk with management in the computer department or in human resources.

Hopefully you will have your after-college employment arranged midway through your final year. If you do not, you will need to initiate your own personal marketing campaign in efforts to create potential employment opportunities that you otherwise would not have.

If you are not successful in finding employment and the school year end is not that distant, it then is a good idea to check with the staffing services and contract employment firms in the geographic area where you prefer to work. The firms having the most IT jobs at this time are listed in Chapter 9.

Today it is fact that many college students in their final year are not able to find employment prior to their graduation. It is also true that in many geographic locations jobs have been scarce. The fact is that there are jobs out there, but many are difficult to find. Today and in the future, the typical computer science graduate must be extremely resourceful in job hunting, using different approaches, of which several are suggested in this book. And during your final year of formal education, you should schedule a reasonable amount of time each week for job-hunting-related activities until you secure employment.

Résumé Building

After completion of the self-assessment exercise outlined in Chapter 5, move on to Chapter 6. Particular attention should be paid to the section specified for college students in the formats and components portion. This section specifically focuses upon building the strongest possible one-page résumé. The primary areas of concentration are the presentation of your education, skills, work experience, potentially relevant life experience that indicates leadership, and any significant involvement in group or team activities where you committed significant personal time and effort as well as any significant recognition achieved. Those who have personally financed 50% or more of their own education through work in summer and during the school year while maintaining a good scholastic record should note this significant accomplishment. (This does not include student loans.)

Because of lack of significant computer science work experience, completion of the best possible résumé is a significant challenge for most students and one that requires a significant amount of thought and effort to bring it to the level where it best represents your total capabilities and potential for development and resultant job success.

Those in Their Last Year of College

During your last year in college, your curriculum has been finalized, and you are probably totally into the process of finding and securing employment. Unless you have done internship work in computer science, your network probably has primarily been your professors and your college placement office. In addition to knowledge of some currently available positions that are not posted, ask them what companies they know or can think of that have previously hired students from your college.

By now, you either have scheduled or completed on-campus interviews with prospective employers or are in the process of establishing them. If at this juncture you do not have any promising possibilities, you will want to put significant effort into researching companies that you want to contact and periodically review the online job-posting services. This activity should begin about 6 months prior to your scheduled graduation. Excellent profiles of leading U.S. companies by industry are provided free by the web service WetFeet.com.

Job-posting services do not offer very many opportunities for entry-level jobs, and the ones that you find may not be in locations that you want to consider. However, there is value to this type of research. It can provide a good sense of the type of entry- or low-level jobs that are available throughout the United States. If the results of several periodic sessions reviewing these opportunities are not promising, these sessions will provide you with an indication of the amount and type of effort that you are going to have to spend pursuing alternative sources of jobs as outlined in Chapter 9. Several online job-posting services that cover the college graduate and those new to the IT job market are reviewed later in this chapter.

It is a good idea to start your job-finding research early in your final year or even earlier during periods of problematic economic conditions. Finding availability of the referenceUSA database as discussed in Chapter 9 is possibly the best method available for building your own prospective company list for contact.

When using this system, you are able to identify the senior IT official in many companies. If you plan written contact, it is a good idea to call and confirm the name of your contact and its spelling, you contact's title, and the company's address. Many of these companies have changes that don't get updated for awhile. Query letters sent to companies for the purpose of inquiring about potential future job opportunities should be short and to the point.

The following is an example of the content that is appropriate.

Addressed to Mr. H Steven Gilbert (obtained from the referenceUSA
database)
Corporate Human Resources Executive
Flour Corporation
Aliso Viejo, CA 92653

Dear Mr. Gilbert:

The purpose of this letter is to inquire about the potential of computer science employment at Flour. I have researched Flour thoroughly and believe that it is the type of company where I would like to work and make significant contributions to Flour's business objectives.

I will graduate this June from San Jose State with a BS degree in computer engineering. My major was changed from architectural engineering eighteen months ago. During summer employment I worked with CAD CAM design hardware and software. I have taken courses for FORTRAN software writing within a UNIX operating system environment, which I understand is used at Flour. I will plan to follow up with your office within a week to learn of any potential positions that are consistent with my training as well as to whom I should follow up with and whether it is appropriate to forward my résumé for future consideration.

Thank you.

Sincerely,

Alison Cole

Street address, phone number, and email address

Alison tailored this query letter to a company where her total college education was relevant even though she changed her major. She also had relevant summer job experience and has learned software that is relevant to the company's business.

If Alison wanted to make queries to other companies within a 30-mile radius of where Flour is located and in a similar industry classification but down to an employee size level of 50 employees or more, she would add more than 60 additional potential prospective employers to contact.

The reason for contacting Flour first is because of its size. It is more likely to have more than one position available for which Alison may be qualified for consideration.

During your company research work, if you have difficulty learning about the business affairs of any company on a search engine, there are other good sources in your library business directories. If you want to research companies that have several hundred employees or more, you need to find access to Lexus-Nexus Academic Universe business news portion. Lexus-Nexus is a concentrator of news and other media-related articles for corporations, and their archives go back several years. They may have information of interest for companies that you are not having much luck finding information about after spending hours scanning search engine data. If Academic Universe is not available, another good source of business-related information is the ProQuest ABI/Inform service. These services are both available in electronic form. For those wanting to contact or visit the career data in the web sites of the several thousand largest U.S. companies by industry classification, WetFeet.com is an excellent free source of this data. WetFeet has summary profiles of the leading companies by industry designation, including their contact data.

Those Recently Graduated and Still Job Hunting

At this point, you are probably somewhat frustrated and disappointed, which is understandable. It is suggested that you read the first section in this chapter related to the unemployed because some of the content in this section also applies to your situation. Continue with the type of job-hunting activities that you have been pursuing. A lot of job hunting is timing and significant employer contact effort combined with occasional good fortune.

While continuing your job search activities, review Chapters 5 and 6 to see if your résumé can benefit from any of the content in these chapters. After you have made any appropriate changes to your résumé, move to Chapter 8. You probably have been doing many of the things mentioned in this chapter, but the purpose of reviewing this material is to pick up new ideas or approaches that may prove helpful to you.

You should pay particular attention to the data regarding the infoUSA and referenceUSA data mentioned in Chapter 9 and in the earlier portions of this chapter. Significant effort placed upon companies that you identify in this database followed up with contact and job-query-type letters could help you in developing a better and larger list of companies to pursue. As mentioned earlier, the small- and medium-sized firms included in this database are forecast to have a significant portion of the new jobs in your targeted geographic area. If you contact them through query letters, you may find some that have employment needs that have not posted their jobs in the job-posting services, thus reducing the competition for jobs as compared to those posted on the web.

Also you should not overlook the possibility of contract, project, or other entry-level computer science jobs that you are able to locate through employment staffing and contract staffing companies; their contact data are listed in Chapter 9. The most important thing that is recommended for your consideration is the spending of a significantly larger amount of time each day pursuing relevant activities that can lead to the potential scheduling of job interviews.

You also need to judge whether your previous efforts have been at a sufficiently high level of quality. The effectiveness of your personal technique in how and what you do and say regarding verbal and written contact with potential sources that could lead to employment is a critical item. If you think that this is an item for concern, you need to decide what and how you might improve your personal effectiveness in these areas.

Chapters 10 and 11 talk about marketing yourself to get interviews, preparing yourself for interviews, and taking steps to achieve maximum possible effectiveness during interviews with the prospective hiring company or agent representing them. These subjects are critical aspects of the job-finding process for most job candidates. They encompass items that understandably most new job applicants struggle with in the early job search activities. The only way that you will become effective with these items is by going through several potential hiring situations. There is always some degree of fear of the unknown until job candidates new to scheduling and participating in interviews experience it.

Web Job-Posting Boards and Résumé Posting for College Students

At the time of writing this book, two job-posting sites appeared to have the most comprehensive selection of entry-level jobs for college graduates pursuing entry-level jobs. In addition to reviewing the IT job posting in these sites, they are good places to post your résumé.

MonsterTRAK

monstertrak.monster.com

Site portrayed as the number one web site for job-hunting college students.

CollegeGrad.com

www.collegegrad.com

At the time of writing, this job posting site appeared to have the most jobs in its database for college graduates pursuing entry-level jobs in the IT profession (more than 500). It also contained a significant amount of helpful information for job hunters to consider in the job-hunting-related activities.

StudentJobs.gov

www.studentjobs.gov

During late 2004, although this site listed more than 300 student jobs, there were very few for those with IT educational backgrounds. It is still a good site to review and does not include all federal jobs. It also contains helpful information regarding job search in the federal discipline.

It is also a good idea for college students doing IT job hunting to check for entry-level positions and to post résumés where possible with the IT, management consulting, staffing, contract employment, recruiting, and software companies reviewed in Chapter 9.

CAREER CHANGE

If you have 10 or more years of previous business experience and you are considering a career change to computer science, an important question to consider is, How can you benefit from your previous experience without having to consider taking a significant cut in annual income? This is an important question that many who want to change career functional responsibility have and will find is often an issue of concern.

If you have decided to pursue a career change into the IT discipline and you do not want to consider relocation to another geographic area, the most logical place to consider for the desired change is your current employer. If you have had a successful employment record of two or more years with your current employer, have had good annual performance appraisals, and are satisfied that your employer is a good place to work with a good future outlook for success, then considering the change to IT with your present employer has several advantages.

First, you avoid the effort, time, and costs associated with what may be a lengthy job search. Second, you probably have a good understanding of your company's business practices, functional applications, and culture, and in many cases, you probably have a good working relationship with key functional employees. If most of this is accurate, you may have some parity when competing with outside candidates who have significant IT job experience. Finally, you may be able to keep your annual salary consistent with the level where it currently is, which may be difficult to achieve in an entry-level IT job with another company.

If you have a good standing and are respected in your present company, you should discuss the desired change with your current manager. If they are receptive to supporting you, you need to move the request to the human resource department for involvement with the IT department. If there are possibilities, they may take some time to move forward, but overall you may have equal or better opportunity than you would if you went outside. In some cases, you might be able to achieve a work program permitting you to spend some work time in IT along with your present responsibilities.

The important thing to remember in pursuing new opportunities is that many hiring managers in computer science today are very astute. If a person has 10 to 20 or more years of work experience in another discipline it is logical to expect that their skills developed and accomplishment achieved during their careers should be much more significant than an individual who has 5 years or less of prior work experience. If you are unable to demonstrate skills and accomplishments of significant relevance it is logical that for most employment opportunities you have, you will be expected to consider a significant reduction in annual income to make the career change.

The problem with the majority of résumés completed by candidates who desire a career change and have significant years of employment in other disciplines is that they do not appear to be stronger than candidates with considerably fewer years of work experience. Your goal is not to put yourself in this situation primarily by strengthening your résumé to the maximum degree possible and handling yourself appropriately in the personal interviews you are able to secure.

There are several important steps that a person needs to involve themselves in when contemplating a career change. This is particularly true for those that want to move into computer-science-related occupations.

You need to answer four important questions when considering this change.

1. Do you have adequate computer science education for your targeted area of employment? If not, what are your plans to minimize this potential objection of prospective employers?
2. Considering your previous business experience, in what industries do you have good understanding of business practices, functions, and their related applications?
3. Is your functional application's understanding strong enough to transfer into a different industry or are you better off to remain in the industry where you have the most knowledge?
4. Have you had any type of leadership responsibility that might be of benefit to a fast-growing small- or medium-sized company? Many of them may need this type of experience for the many business situations because of the rapid growth they are beginning to experience.

The reason for giving some detailed thought to these questions is that you need to have the assessment of these potential issues clearly in your mind before taking interviews. Many recruiters may have an industry-type bias and believe that they need employees from the same industry as theirs. To overcome this objection in some situations, you need to be able to defray any potential concerns or doubts by the strength of your résumé and your discussion during interviews. The fact is that most functional applications are similar across industries; only the terminology is different, which is a small thing. The only exception to this would be for businesses that are heavily based in the higher levels of the physical sciences.

The main point here is that in interviews you have to be able to confidently relate excellent knowledge and a strong command of the relevant skills for serious employment consideration in many potential employment situations.

For example, a person may have spent 20 or more years working in sales and marketing-related activities for a well-respected company but for the most recent several years worked in another function. This individual has updated his or her computer software knowledge with several courses but is having difficulty locating potential prospective employers.

This person's previous efforts in company research did not cover one of the fastest growing businesses in the United States, the market for customer relationship management software. This industry is forecast to grow by several of the largest computer industry research firms to the level of some $75 billion to $77 billion annual revenue by the year end 2007. The primary applications within this segment are for sales automation, marketing automation, customer service, supply chain, and financial software. There are currently more than 50 independent companies pursuing this market, and many of them are growing rapidly. Those who have knowledge of these functions and can develop and modify database software could be significant job potential opportunities. Look for these types of emerging opportunities where your previous business functional and applications knowledge may have value.

When you are considering career change, the skill assessment step is critical. What skills of significance do you have that are transferable? Be certain to review the top 10 traits and skills listing and discussion in Chapter 5. These items may represent some areas of additional skill and strength for the rewriting of your résumé.

If you are enrolled in distance learning or part-time or evening classes, have you pursued contract or project employment opportunities with the contract and staffing companies in your geographic area?

After you have completed your skill assessment, redone your résumé, and have had some degree of experience with the components of the job-hunting process as outlined in Chapters 8 and 9, most people who want to consider career change and are committed to accomplishing this will have to develop a new and improved strategy for job hunting, which is discussed at the beginning of the chapter.

It is the author's belief that less than 5% of IT job hunters have a written formal job-hunting strategy that serves as their action plan for their job-hunting-related activities. It is the author's hope that some of the content in this book will provide job candidates with some additional awareness and ideas regarding the job search process that will motivate those who do not have a formal plan to develop one. An action plan is critical, especially for candidates that are having difficulty in their job search.

Other than emerging opportunities such as CRM, most individuals will want to implement a job-hunting strategy and adopt some of the processes outlined in Chapter 9 in the section entitled "Tailoring Your Job Search."

When you have reached the position where you are under serious hiring consideration and you are beginning the employment discussions, do not make the mistake that many individuals with significant work tenure often make. They are rigid in the annual income expectations because of the income level of their prior employment. This fact often causes many to lose their opportunity as quickly as they get it.

In these situations, you opted to go for the career change; it wasn't any concern of the prospective hiring company. In many cases, they may not simply be able to pay you at your previous level. If you are reasonably close, this should not ever be the reason that you do not get a job. Such things as length of vacation offered are other items where you may have to be flexible. Each company has its own policies for new hires.

If you are too far apart on annual income, you may be able to gain commitment for salary adjustment consideration at the 6-month or 1-year mark based upon the value that you have provided the employer.

INDUSTRY CHANGE

If you have computer-science-related skills and experience and want to change industries, you should first complete the skill assessment and résumé rewriting needs following the recommendations in Chapters 5 and 6. The biggest challenge that you will possibly face will be the research effort to identify potential job opportunities that fit your skills and experience.

As mentioned in the previous section, you may also face a certain amount of industry bias by hiring management who spent most of their career within their current industry. They will rarely mention this, but you must address and overcome it if you sense that it is a problem during interviews. This fact is overvalued by many; functional application transfer across most industries is primarily a difference in terminology and company culture except in the scientific disciplines. At the outset of your job search, the level and relevance of your skills will be key factors in determining your job possibilities and the level of interest in you.

If your initial efforts are not promising, you will need to move into every area mentioned in Chapters 8 and 9 regarding the job-hunting process. This will require a large amount of sustained weekly effort. The key thing to remember as you work through these activities, particularly for all jobs listed in corporate web sites and online job-posting services, is the amount of competition that you are facing for the available jobs.

A good thing to remember is that during recent surveys of corporate and online job-posting services, as many as 70% of résumés submitted do not meet the listed specifications for the job. This obviously eliminates these résumés from consideration for most hiring companies, and it is a significant waste of time for those whose qualifications are not close to a match. If your assessment of a job-posting description is that you need more information, where the hiring source is identified or there is email contact information, tell them that you believe that your qualifications may be close, but that you need more information to be sure. Ask them if it is possible to receive a more detailed description for the job. In other words for situations like this, nothing ventured, nothing gained. The 70% mismatch situation occurs because in most situations applicants are simply trying.

OUTPLACEMENT PARTICIPANTS

This section is for those individuals who are provided assistance for their job-hunting activities by their former employer with outplacement companies. There are several priorities upon which you need to focus to gain the best possible utilization of the total days you are provided with these services.

1. Tailor the time allocated to activities that you believe can be the most beneficial to you in your job search. At the outset when you receive orientation, you will learn the possibilities.
2. Some companies use tests that classify your personality type and the type of work situation for which you are best suited. This type of evaluation may be of interest to you, but if you consider taking them, you need to know how they specifically can be helpful to you in pursuing job finding. If the explanation you receive regarding their potential value is not clear to you, don't take them.
3. You will be provided someone to work with you from the outplacement firm. At the outset, you should request someone who has extensive experience working with individuals who have a computer science employment background.
4. When you are using the outplacement office to contact companies regarding potential employment and you are not comfortable telling a potential employer that you are in outplacement, you should have your calls directed to a home office or home number. Potential employers or recruiting companies can figure out that you are in outplacement by the manner in which your messages are handled. If your only alternative for these return calls is the outplacement office and you are not comfortable with this being known, determine if you have the option of the caller connecting with your personal call return message.
5. Once again, the résumé is an area of potential concern. Some outplacement offices advocate widespread use of a one-page résumé with an accompanying cover letter whose body reads something similar to this:

> If you are interested in an Information Technology Manager who:
>
> • Reduced annual operating expenses 15%.
> • Brought three capital expenditure projects in 20% under budget.
> • Developed a sales force automation system that increased sales results 20%.
>
> I would appreciate consideration for the potential of employment with your company.
>
> My résumé is enclosed for your consideration.

The problem with a one-page résumé with a cover letter similar to this is that they are often sent out for candidates with 10 or more years of work experience whose annual incomes are at or above the $80,000 annual level for which a one-page résumé is not adequate in most situations.

The other problem is that this type of letter is often sent out in the same bold type style, making it recognizable as being sent out from an outplacement firm, which some candidates may not desire after they realize this. You want to control the format and content of your résumé and while being open to considering improvement recommendations, you should not alter your résumé unless you can identify significant improvements. This, however, should not include changing to a one-page format. The time spent in outplacement can be helpful, but you need to understand what is possible at the outset in order to select the most potentially beneficial items to focus upon for the time that you are spending in the service.

20 PLUS YEARS OF IT JOB EXPERIENCE

IT employees who have 20 plus years of IT job experience and who are considering job change face many of the same challenges as the unemployed and those who desire career or industry change. It is a good idea for anyone in this category to review each of these other sections in this chapter for ideas to consider.

The problem today in the U.S. IT job market is that many employees are career challenged as early as age 30. What is the significance of this relative to IT job seekers with 20 or more years of IT work experience? The point here is that many of those employed for as little as 8 to 10 years are facing a problem of whether or not their skills and experience are relevant as well as whether or not their income expectations are also realistic. This situation also applies to many with more than 20 years of work experience.

If skills and experience are somewhat outdated and supplemental education to fix any problems of this type is not realistic, then the job-hunting strategy must be much more specific and focused in order for success.

The further reality is that unless your overall business understanding, industry, functional application, and related skills are superior and in demand, in many situations you may be competing with recent MBA-type graduates in computer science with good academic credentials and people skills who are more current in much of the newer software and other data-related technology.

Therefore, in completing your personal employment strategy, you first need to determine in what situations your skills and experience best fit, and then you must decide where you are most likely to find the type of work that best fits your qualifications. Other than those situations where there is still a large need to work with the old legacy software-type applications, some of the better opportunities may be in the application services provider area and some of the smaller IT consulting organizations that either outsource applications or have basic functional applications contract work. Also it is a good idea to review regularly the contract and limited-term job offerings of the staffing, contract employment, and recruiting firms listed in Chapter 9.

The other best source of firms that may fit your employment strategy plan is the company database sources discussed in the section entitled "Tailoring Your Job Search" at the end of Chapter 9.

8.   The IT Job-Hunting Process

The Objective of This Chapter

This chapter will discuss the job research components that cover a high percentage of existing IT employment sources and related data services. To understand each, this chapter provides candidates involved in IT job search the characteristics of and potential benefits of effective use of each. At any given time, this listing of job sourcing alternatives will cover at least 90% of all currently available IT jobs.

NETWORKING

For more information on networking, also refer to the last section of Chapter 1 regarding the best sources of IT jobs today.

In the past, publications have stated that networking was the source of as many as 70% of all jobs found. This may have been true in the past, but it is somewhat doubtful today, especially in times of economic uncertainty. If you have acquaintances who know and respect your capabilities and who are aware of what is currently occurring in computer science employment opportunities in your geographic area of choice, this is still possibly your best option to find employment without going through a comprehensive process.

In any job search, the reality is that the candidates with the highest level of skills that are relevant and in demand today are the ones who will get jobs most quickly through network sources or through online application to the job-posting services listings. If you are not in the highest skill level category or are at the entry level with limited job experience and you are acquainted with some individuals who have top level skills, ask them for suggestions regarding opportunities that they may know of or for contacts in their network whom you could contact.

The highest skilled employees usually know others in that category whom they respect and who may prove to be sources of good information regarding opportunities to check out. Networking is simply a form of prospecting to learn of potential job opportunities or new IT contacts that can lead you to this type of information. Its primary advantage in job search is that if candidates put significant effort into networking, they frequently will learn of jobs opening up before they are posted online or advertised elsewhere. Also if you have former or current colleagues in your work who know you and respect you and your work competency, they also can serve as good references for you if needed.

When you are in the job market, it is always a good idea to attend any IT association meetings or seminars to which you have access either as a member or as a guest of a friend. This is also true of any industry trade shows or seminars. Attending any of these events is an opportunity for prospecting to develop new sources of information regarding jobs.

For those in outplacement, try to learn of others currently in outplacement with IT job backgrounds. They can serve as good sources for comparing experience and learning of opportunities that may fit your skills and experience better than theirs.

It is important to keep in mind that not one single source that covers your preferred geographic area knows where any more than 30% of all the currently available jobs are. At any one time, all sources that have web-posted or advertised IT jobs in addition to search and recruiting firms that have been contracted with to fill jobs in total cover as much as 90% of all total IT jobs available. This is why successful job search often takes a lot more effort than most candidates are prepared to provide when they first begin new job search efforts.

State Employment Network Offices

Many states have in their major cities job assistance offices that have independent listing of jobs that are not web listed or advertised elsewhere. Most state-type employment network offices do not charge employers listing fees, so it is a good idea to go to one of their offices periodically to check the listings. The majority of the IT jobs that will be listed in these networks of most states will be the entry-level positions where lower levels of experience are required.

Also in most of these state run offices, there will be access to America's JobBank IT job postings, which at times will have as many as 40,000 IT jobs from throughout the United States. So if you have not visited one of these offices in your geographic area as a minimum they are a good place to research web-posted IT jobs from various sources.

In many states, job assistance offices will have available the Employer Database from infoUSA, which lists more than 13 million U.S. public and private companies. Use of this valuable tool is discussed in detail in the last section of Chapter 9, "Tailoring Your Job Search." Its use will enable IT job candidates to identify scores of companies to contact regarding potential jobs. The advantage of using this database in job prospecting is that candidates can tailor their selections of companies by city, county, industry, and size of company (revenue and number of employees).

The primary value of using this type of contact is that, by contacting large numbers of companies using this method, candidates will find prospective employers in some cases that have not web posted or advertised jobs and will avoid a significant number of other applicant competition as compared to what they will experience in the web job-posting sites. This is particularly true in the large metropolitan areas.

This method of contact by telephone or query letters takes a lot of time, but for candidates who are having difficulty in job search and are committed to significant additional effort, this method can provide them a contact base of potential prospects that are not normally worked by the large numbers of candidates using the online job-posting services. For anyone seriously committed to a large amount of effort, this is simply another source to use for contact. It is much more extensive than the printed or online-type company directories that are available in college, university, and public libraries.

Latest Networking Sources for IT Professionals

Major City Networking Groups

Local web-based networking groups are beginning to appear in some of the major metropolitan areas. *nycwit.com* is established and has helped IT job candidates find jobs. This New York City-based online networking group is for technology professionals. Expect more of these self-help-type networks to appear in other cities during the next year or two.

Social Networking

Social networking is still a relatively new concept for networking and several companies have established networks for those participants with business and job-finding interests. These networks can also serve as sources to establish contacts for pursuing IT consulting and contract work.

Tribe.net

The most advanced of these web service providers for the IT profession as of this writing is *Tribe.net*. *Tribe.net* has a series of customized forums called tribes. When reviewing the more than 600 tribes related to technology, the computer, and the internet, the author identified 55 specific tribes with significant membership that related to significant responsibilities within the IT profession. Most noteworthy were tribes related to the web, Linux and open source, . NET, Mac OS X, Perl programming, PHP developers, wireless, Java, and HTML. This service is presently free; however, it may eventually carry a small monthly charge. The service offers an excellent privacy control feature.

Linkedin.com

Linkedin targets senior management business users. Currently this service includes over 2,000 senior-level managers including more than 500 CEOs and more than 700 users at the VP level of responsibility. This service does not presently include listings for job opportunities; it only lists contacts.

For chief information officer candidates, this service could provide relevant contacts.

Ryze Ltd.

ryze.com is primarily a network for business people with participants primarily at a lower level of responsibility than *Linkedin.com*. The Ryze basic service is currently free, but it does not include the search capacity. Today Ryze charges $9.95 monthly for its Gold subscription service membership, which includes the search feature.

There are several other social networks in beta testing at the current time, but they do not have a significant current focus on either business or job-finding networking.

A review of these sites may provide IT job search candidates with another potential valuable source of networking that could be beneficial in job search activities. There is no doubt that these type of networking services will increase in popularity and use by IT job hunters during the next several years and should periodically be reviewed by IT job search candidates as another potentially valuable networking source.

ONLINE JOB-POSTING SERVICES

At any given time, online job-posting services will have as many as 500,000 IT-related job listings. In order not to waste a significant amount of job hunters time, this section will list the web job-posting sites that post as much as 90% of total IT jobs available at any given time. At the time of publication of this book, only online posting sites were listed that consistently had 100 or more IT jobs posted.

Job hunters who use these sites need to remember several important points.

1. You need to keep a log or a copy of the job description for every job posted to which you reply. This is necessary because you may find the same job posted more than once in the same service, and you may find a particular job listed in more than one posting service.
2. Remember that it is a good idea to cover every potential job-posting service because no one knows where they will find the jobs that are of interest to them in the listing of the services most active posting IT jobs.
3. The third thing to remember is that posting your résumé in the résumé-posting services alone may not always gain you the amount of interest that you want. Therefore, it is a good idea to review the numerous sources of potential IT jobs listed in Chapter 9.
4. Rarely will one source provide you with the majority of jobs that may be of interest to you. The reason for this is that today not one single source of job postings concentrates all of the IT jobs that are listed in the web job-posting sites. A good example of this is the jobs that

more than 1,000 U.S. search and management recruiting firms are contracted with to source qualified candidates. Their jobs because of confidentiality requirements, in most cases, will not be posted in the larger job-posting sites, and in total these firms place thousands of IT job candidates annually in good jobs.

5. Don't underestimate the effort required to find the number of jobs that meet your personal qualifications. Acknowledging this fact is important for most job hunters because many have posted their résumés to scores of job-posting sites and so experienced a false sense of security only to find that they have not achieved the level of interest that resulted in job interviews. If you are unemployed, job hunting should be a full-time job 8 hours a day when possible until you are successful. If you are currently employed, evening and weekend work will be necessary in most cases to identify an adequate number of potential hiring sources of interest.

Web job-posting services are the choice today of the majority of computer science job seekers. When this book went to press, some of the job-posting sites that consistently posted the largest number of IT jobs were America's JobBank with approximately 40,000 plus computer science jobs in their database; Dice.com with 30,000 plus IT jobs; PurePower.com, a large job-posting concentrator, with more than 20,000 IT jobs; Yahoo HotJobs with 30,000 plus IT jobs; CareerBuilder with 23,000 plus IT jobs; Monster with 5,000 plus jobs; ComputerJobs.com with 8,400 plus jobs; Computerwork.com with 7,000 plus jobs; Career.com with 1,000 plus jobs; ISHunter.com with 3,000 plus jobs; JustTechJobs.com with 6,000 plus jobs; and SoftwareJobLink.com with 5,400 plus IT jobs. Over the past several years, these sites have consistently posted the largest number of IT jobs at any given time.

The most active web job-posting sites for IT jobs are profiled at the end of Chapter 9. They all consistently list a minimum of a few hundred to thousands of IT jobs. Although they may not have as many listings, it is also a good idea to check periodically the national database or the local offices of all the IT and management consulting firms and contract employment and staffing firms profiled in Chapter 9 for jobs listed in your desired geographic area(s).

Effective Use of Web Job-Posting Services

Those IT job candidates most likely to have good results from using these services are the candidates who most closely meet the job specifications for skills and experience. If your skills are accurately portrayed as those of a top performer and your experience is highly valued, using the posting services (other than the web posting of your résumé) is possibly the best option for your job finding other than a high-quality network of contacts.

When you understand the convenience of using online job-posting services to apply for hiring consideration, it is easy to understand how some applicants may become discouraged after applying to as many as 100 job postings over a 30-day period, without receiving any significant interest from potential employers. The competition for good IT jobs that candidates will encounter in large metropolitan areas is often significantly greater than in smaller metropolitan areas.

Unless your skills are highly in demand and your résumé portrays a good match to the jobs skill and experience requirements listed, in most cases the total volume of your online applications needs to increase significantly because of the large number of job candidates that often respond to these postings, although frustrating.

For example, if you devote one weekend, at least 8 hours per day, reviewing the majority of the web job-posting sites that list the largest number of IT jobs and you review as many as 300 listings and identify as many as 30 job listings of interest to you for jobs posted within the past week, you should be able to post your résumé for those 30 job listings during the weekend. If you are having difficulty in your job search, this is the type of activity and effort that you must generate when you are not receiving the desired level of employer interest.

If after doing this for three or four weekends, you still have not received any degree of specific meaningful interest, then you should seriously consider moving to the tailoring-your-job-search methods outlined in the last section of Chapter 9 or undertaking some of the other job search alternatives reviewed in that chapter.

Even though the job-posting sites have some degree of repetitiveness and redundancy, other than periodical ads, corporate web site job listings, and government job-posting services, the larger web services have the largest database of full-time jobs and are much easier to access.

The primary problems that applicants can encounter depending only upon these sources are several. The number of applicants will often exceed 100. In a high percentage of these postings, the hiring company is not revealed, and it is difficult to learn more about many of the opportunities because most of the job specifications do not comprehensively explain the responsibilities and skill requirements. When the hiring organization is identified in the posting, go their web site for the possibility of gaining additional information regarding jobs in which you are interested. If this effort is not successful, call the IT or human resource department of the organization to see if you can obtain a more detailed job description than that which appears in the web posting. A detailed specification can be helpful to you in preparing a more meaningful and impressive response, tailoring your résumé to the individual job posting.

Other than company web sites and government organizations, the online posting services listed at the end of this chapter will list as many as 2,000 or more new IT jobs every day. Always the most potentially valuable listings to pursue are the new ones that have been posted in the past week not ones carried forward from previous postings. This is another reason for keeping and updating a contact log if you plan to use the online services extensively for job hunting. It is recommended that you look for new listings as often as twice weekly and respond quickly to those where you have interest.

Remember in posting that a frequent complaint of the job-posting sources is that as high as 70% of résumés posted do not meet the requirements for experience and skills of the job description posted. If it is not clear to you whether or not you meet the majority of the requirements posted, you are not able to gain additional job description data, and your qualifications are somewhat marginal, in most situations the time you spent will put you in the 70% category of improper responses from the hiring organization's perspective and assessment. This happens because, for most good jobs posted, the posting sources are often deluged with as many of several hundred responses within the first week or two; Consequently, résumés that they consider to be marginal will go to the bottom of the pile.

For situations where you believe that your qualifications are a good match for the posted job description, you may have a competitive advantage compared to the scores of others who apply by tailoring your résumé and cover message to the organization's business whenever you are able to identify the hiring company. Your ability to achieve this information quickly may increase the frequency with which you are contacted by the hiring sources. If you have skills and relevant experience at the top of the scale, this type of thing probably won't be of much value, but for most applicants it can help.

The best source is to call the hiring company's IT department and ask to talk with an employee who understands the requirements of the posted job. If someone will talk with you, they may refer you to their human resource department or employment office, which is not where you want to be.

If this occurs tell the person who answered the phone that you already have basic job information and that you would like to talk with someone who understands the work associated with the job's requirements so that neither the company's time nor yours will be wasted. Then say, "If you could help me or direct me to someone who could help, it will only take a couple of minutes to answer several questions that I have, or possibly you could help me with them."

If you are not successful in this contact effort, quickly go to a source such as Hoover's on-line, the Edgars database of the SEC, or *SEC.gov* for company annual report filing. Also if you have access to the Lexus-Nexus Academic Universe database of business news, this source could help you tailor a more professional response to the job posting. The Nexus database is an excellent source for doing research on companies. Nexus is a concentrator of business articles, and the database contains articles from all sources of media where you can search many months of data. This service is primarily found in the larger libraries in metropolitan areas as well as in college and university libraries.

The important thing to remember is that anything that you can do to better understand the business and needs of the hiring organization can help you prepare a more professional response than the majority of often a hundred or more applicants who will submit their résumés within a week to 10 days after the job is posted. So if you have any interest in a posted job and you believe that your qualifications meet the specifications, your quick response is important. In some situations, this extra preparation can make the difference between your being contacted and your résumé being placed on the bottom of large piles.

Response to online job posting is the most convenient and quickest way to find available computer science jobs today, but it is also possibly the most difficult source for the average person in terms of success unless they have done a superior comparative job in marketing themselves, which means considering different and more professional approaches. If your personal rate of return interest has averaged three or less return responses for one hundred responses to web posted jobs, you need to consider using other methods of contact outlined in Chapter 9.

Waiting to apply for jobs that have been posted for more than 10 days to 2 weeks may be too late in most of the larger metropolitan areas or those areas listed by the Bureau of Labor Statistics as having the largest current IT employee populations. By the end of a 10-day or 2-week period, prospective employers in most cases have narrowed down their selection of applicants for follow-up contact. The only frequent exception to this may be for the candidates whose résumés display high-level skills that are a good match for the posted job specification.

IT JOB-POSTING SITES WITH THE MOST JOBS

At the time of writing, the following sites were those that consistently had the most IT jobs posted the author researched. This changes every month and in any future revisions or updatings, sites will be added or deleted.

Americas Job Bank

www.ajb.com

Consistently lists more than 60,000 jobs in the computer and mathematics category.

CareerBuilder.com

www.careerbuilder.com

Consistently lists 20,000 plus IT jobs.

Career.com

www.career.com

Consistently lists more than 1,000 IT jobs.

CareerSite

www.careersite.com

Occasionally lists 100 or more IT jobs. Consolidates jobs advertised in selected local newspapers.

ComputerJobs.com

www.computerjobs.com

Consistently lists more than 8,000 IT jobs. Web site home page lists number of current jobs listed by industry and by specific job and skill categories.

Computerwork.com

www.computerwork.com

Consistently lists more than 7,000 IT jobs. provides capability to search job database by job classification (i.e., enables applicants to pinpoint such things as network engineer jobs without listing all IT jobs with "engineer" in the title).

ContractJobHunter

www.cjhunter.com

Specializes in technology contract jobs listing more than 200 IT jobs.

Dice, Inc.

www.dice.com

One of the larger job boards specializing in technology. Consistently lists more than 30,000 technology-related jobs.

FlipDog.com

www.flipdog.monster.com

Specializes in job listings from employer web sites. Consistently lists more than 200 IT jobs.

HireAbility.com

www.hireability.com

Lists as many as 700 IT-related jobs.

IEEE

www.ieee.org

More than 150 IT jobs posted.

ISHUNTER.COM

www.ishunter.com

More than 3,000 technology jobs posted.

ITWorld.com

www.itworld.4jobs.com

Over 500 IT jobs posted. Permits search by twenty-nine different IT job classifications.

JobBankUSA

www.jobbankusa.com

500 plus technology jobs listed.

JustTechJobs.com

www.justtechjobs.com

Has created forty-seven technology-specific job sites listing more than 10,000 IT jobs that are tailored to the leading IT job classifications.

Management Recruiters International

www.mrinet.com, job search site is *brilliantpeople.com*

IT job postings consistently at the 200-job level.

Monster

www.monster.com

Consistently in excess of 5,000 IT jobs posted.

The Perl Job Site

www.jobs.perl.org

Specialized job site for world's one million Perl programmers. Consistently lists more than 150 Perl programming jobs.

PurePower Sites

www.purepowersites.com

Contains ten independent IT job category sites consistently listing in excess of 20,000 jobs. At the present time PurePower has individual job sites for IT jobs including *COBOLJobs.com, CPlusPlusJobs.com, DatabaseJobs.com, DelphiJobs.com, ERPJobs.com, LANJobs.com, LotusNotesJobs.com, PowerBuilderJobs.com, VisualBasicJobs.com,* and *WebProgrammingJobs.com.*

SoftwareJobLink

www.softwarejoblink.com

Consistently lists over 5,000 software engineering- and programmings related jobs. Primary job posters are large software development and management consulting companies.

WantedJobs.com

www.wantedjobs.com

WantedJobs is a search consolidator that includes 120 plus jobs posting sites. Ten selected job categories all list in excess of 500 jobs, which indicates more than 50,000 IT jobs are listed in the participating sites.

Yahoo HotJobs

www.hotjobs.yahoo.com

Over 30,000 IT jobs listed in job database.

Advantages of Using Online Job-Posting Services

- Wider exposure to a variety of jobs than other methods
- Access work can be completed evenings and weekends
- Easy to access and convenient to use
- Less time involved when compared to the alternative of company research and a personal contact program
- Best method other than networking and résumé-posting services for IT job candidates who have top-level skills of relevance today

Disadvantages of Using Online Job-Posting Services

- More than 100 candidates often apply for the same job. Can be frustrating when candidates have posted their résumés for consideration to scores of job listings. Often impossible to receive any type of feedback.

- Often no way to identify the hiring company or to obtain more information regarding the job requirements than the posted description.
- Frequently the résumé goes directly to a recruiting or staffing firm.
- Very little, if any control or influence regarding your potential consideration as a candidate.

ONLINE RÉSUMÉ POSTING

This publication will not examine the frequently covered subjects of preparing electronic format résumés or cyberspace résumés, both of which are major subjects of many job-finding-type publications. The author believes that most IT professionals are better qualified regarding these subjects than most who write on them, including this author. These items are simply not representative of the challenges facing most IT professionals involved in job hunting today.

The primary value of online résumé posting as opposed to applying to web-posted job listings only is that posted résumés are valid and can work for you as long as they are posted. This may be of value to you if you are employed and are not in any hurry to find the right new alternative as long as you are satisfied with the confidentiality features of the résumé-posting sites you choose to use.

Most of the résumé-posting sites just like executive search firms will have your résumé in their database indefinitely, which may represent the best alternative for any candidates not in a hurry other than having good quality personal network contacts.

Confidentiality in Posting Your Résumé

If you decide to post your résumé in an online service and you want to maintain confidentiality because you are currently employed, you want to be certain that you can maintain confidentiality. Most online job-posting services have this feature, but you need to check this out for each one if this is important to you.

IT Résumé-Posting and Distribution Sources

At the time of publication, the following are the majority of the larger services that are active.

Guru

www.guru.com

Guru is a large source of freelance and contract employment with more 30,000 businesses that use their service. Professionals bid for employer's projects that are posted.

Recruiters Online Network

www.recruitersonline.com

rapidly growing search site for résumé posting, job posting, and candidate search by headhunters, recruiters, and search professionals.

RésuméBlaster.com

www.résuméblaster.com

Reasonable fee service that will web-deliver your résumé to recruiters in specific geographic areas in selected IT disciplines. IT disciplines covered are programming, networking/system administration, software engineering, and consulting. Each discipline mentioned contains in excess of 1,000 recruiters. Most individual states contain recruiter listings of 100 to 400 recruiters.

RésuméNet

www.résuménet.com

Stresses ability to broadcast your résumé to thousands of hiring managers. Also has listings of hundreds of IT-related jobs.

RésuméZapper.com

www.résumézapper.com

More than 1,500 recruiters use the service, covering over 30 job categories within the IT profession. Résumé distribution targeted by IT category and geography.

Top Echelon

www.topechelon.com

Résumé posting in database providing access to more than 2,000 recruiters. Job search capability based upon the jobs posted by the recruiters who are providing qualified candidates directly to employers. Site also consistently posts approximately 100 IT jobs.

WantedJobs.com

www.wantedjobs.com

At the time of publication, enables candidates to post their résumés in fifteen specific job-posting sites.

WHERE ARE AND WHERE WILL THE IT JOBS BE?

Chapter 1 listed where approximately 50% of the Bureau of Labor Statistics forecasted 2.8 million IT jobs are located today. Looking at these major metropolitan areas is a good indicator of where to look for jobs. Another way to look at potential employment sectors is to look at the primary employment sectors. Gartner Dataquest, a leading technology research firm, forecast that IT spending during 2003 was comparatively low in the healthcare and government sectors as a percent of gross revenue, 3.9% and 6.6%, respectively. Gartner Dataquest forecast that annual growth in worldwide IT spending between 2002 and 2007 is will be among the largest in healthcare, 12.4%; government, 12.2%; and education, 9.3%.

These projected growth figures are further supported by IT employment data of the Bureau of Labor Statistics. Healthcare shows approximately 67,000 IT employees, government (federal, state, and local) shows approximately 203,000 current IT employees, and education (colleges, universities, professional schools, and elementary and secondary schools) lists total IT employment of approximately 135,000. With these sectors in total showing only 14.5% of the BLS projection of 2.8 million IT jobs as of 2002, the Gartner growth estimate for these three sectors may be conservative.

When you consider that the U.S. annual economy is in the vicinity of $11 trillion, government has historically represented approximately one quarter, education one quarter, healthcare one quarter, and business services and manufacturing another quarter. These relationships indicate that the areas of education, government, and healthcare IT staffing are somewhat understaffed compared to the business services and manufacturing sectors, which has almost 86% of total U.S. IT employment.

The average annual projected growth of IT expenditures in these three sectors of approximately 12% equates to annual IT job growth of approximately 50,000 jobs, which is probably realistic when compared to the approximate total IT job growth of 160,000 jobs annually between now and 2010 as projected by the BLS. The web job data banks listed for education, healthcare, and government in the 2002–3 edition of the *Public Library Association Guide to Internet Job Searching* is a good source for jobs posted for these segments as are the most active IT job-posting sites listed in this chapter.

Chapter 1 provides data regarding where the majority of IT jobs are today. When considering annual IT job turnover of somewhere between 10 to 15%, the metropolitan areas identified will continue to be the major sources of IT employment.

Current IT employees may be considering changing jobs as a result of the improved economy. This fact coupled with normal annual job turnover indicates that as many as 600,000 IT professionals are in the job market, which equates to the need for IT job hunters to have a comprehensive, effective job-hunting process and strategy.

The March 2004 issue of *Business 2.0*, a business magazine from Time, Inc., while working with the econometric research firm Global Insight, has ranked the 61 largest U.S. metropolitan areas for forecasted job growth in the 10 most skilled occupational clusters.

The 20 forecasted top skilled occupational growth areas in the United States are the same as 50% of the high job growth areas of the top 10 IT job categories as tracked by the U.S. Department of Labor, Bureau of Statistics. The job growth is forecast from today through 2008.

The author believes that this information coupled with several other indicators represents the type of data that is meaningful to current IT job hunters as well as those currently considering IT careers and other potential change alternatives within their IT employment.

The following data for the 20 top cities identified from the *Business 2.0* listing includes these items:

1. The projected 2004–2008 total employment increases for the three major job categories for each of the 20 metropolitan areas selected by *Business 2.0*.
2. The Bureau of Labor Statistics current employee job population by each IT job category selected by *Business 2.0* for that metropolitan area.
3. The infoUSA database listing of total establishments in the 100- to 999-employee category for each of the 20 cities selected.
4. A listing of the total IT jobs for each IT category highlighted in the *Business 2.0* selections based upon the author's sampling of 70,000 web-posted IT job listings during 2004.

The author believes that a good indicator of the next several years of IT job growth is the comparison of the ratio of the total number of establishments in the metropolitan area to the total number of IT jobs in that metropolitan area as tracked by the Bureau of Labor Statistics.

The author's opinion is that the majority of incremental IT job growth in the United States during the next several years will be in organizations with total employment in the range of 100 to 999 employees of which there are currently approximately 180,000 as tracked by infoUSA. Another significant factor in incremental IT employment growth is the previously mentioned forecast of the IT research organization Gartner Dataquest, which predicts average overall employment growth of IT employment in government, education, and healthcare to be approximately 12% between today and 2007. The growth forecasted by Gartner Dataquest and the author will be offset somewhat by the continuing outsourcing of software writing/coding programming jobs outside of the United States by the larger high-technology organizations, software publishers, and IT consulting firms.

The ratios of establishments in the 100- to 999-employee range compared to total IT job populations as tracked by the Bureau of Labor Statistics in the larger metropolitan areas of the United States show the average number of IT employees in the total establishments ranging from a low of 10 to a high of 50. The author believes that, on average, the significance of this statistic is that the the annual incremental IT hiring rates in the metropolitan areas having an average of 40 to 50 employees per establishment will be significantly lower than those below the 30-employee range. The results of the composite data provided for the 20 metropolitan areas follows.

#1 RALEIGH-DURHAM, NC

2004–2008 IT job growth projections by *Business 2.0*
Computer scientists	156%
Database administrators	128%

Total metropolitan area IT jobs year end 2002 — **34,350***
Computer scientists	5,300*
Database administrators	960*

infoUSA 2004 database of metropolitan area establishments of
100 to 999 employees	884

Author's 2004 sampling of 70,000 U.S. IT job listings
IT jobs available for Raleigh-Durham metro area	441

Projected 2004–2008 total IT job growth based upon *Business 2.0* forecast
Computer scientists	8,268
Database administrators	1,228

Author's comments: Today there are between 400 and 500 IT job's available for all of the BLS primary IT job categories. Incremental growth of approximately 1,990 jobs annually in these two categories is realistic. Employer's in this metropolitan area report computer scientists and applications and systems software engineers all in the same category. Overall IT employee growth may be lower than forecast because of the current employee ratio of 40 : 1 per establishment in the 100- to 999-employee range.

* Estimate of Bureau of Labor Statistics from employer reporting.

---

2 SAN JOSE, CA

2004–2008 IT job growth projections by *Business 2.0*
Network and computer systems administrators	43%
Software engineers, applications	39%

Total metropolitan area IT jobs year end 2002 — **64,440***
Network and computer systems administrators	4,000*
Software engineers, applications	16,080*

infoUSA 2004 database of metropolitan area establishments of
100 to 999 employees   1,281

Author's 2004 sampling of 70,000 U.S. IT job listings
IT jobs available for San Jose metro area   2,844

Projected 2004–2008 total IT job growth based upon *Business 2.0* forecast
Network and computer systems administrators   1,720
Software engineers, applications   6,271

Author's comments: The average annual increment of IT jobs in these categories projected by *Business 2.0* is significant for this metro area. The projected growth in software engineers for applications is significant when considering the large number of jobs outsourced outside of the United States from this metropolitan area by software developers and other high-technology organizations. With a ratio of almost 50 employees per establishment in the 100- to 999-employee range and considering continued outsourcing, significant overall IT employment growth may be significantly slower than projected for this area.

* Estimate of Bureau of Labor Statistics from employer reporting.

---

3 WASHINGTON, DC

2004-2008 IT job growth projections by *Business 2.0*
Software engineers, applications   57%
Database administrators   30%
Computer systems analysts   18%

Total metropolitan area IT jobs year end 2002   **166,160***
Software engineers, applications   19,810*
Database administrators   6,040*
Computer systems analysts   36,150*

infoUSA 2004 database of metropolitan area establishments of
100 to 999 employees   3,914

Author's 2004 sampling of 70,000 U.S. IT job listings
IT jobs available for Washington, DC, metro area   7,945

Projected 2004–2008 total IT job growth based upon *Business 2.0* forecast
Software engineers, applications   11,291
Database administrators   1,812
Computer system analysts   6,498

Author's comments: Incremental annual jobs in these categories averaging 3,920 is realistic when considering the almost 8,000 jobs available in the sampling. The projected annual growth of more than 19,000 jobs in these categories is consistent with Gartner Dataquest's projection of a 12.2% increase in annual government IT spending.

* Estimate of Bureau of Labor Statistics from employer reporting.

4 AUSTIN, TX

2004–2008 IT job growth projections by *Business 2.0*
Software engineers, systems software 55%

Total metropolitan area IT jobs year end 2002 **31,996***
Software engineers, systems software 3,090*

infoUSA 2004 database of metropolitan area establishments of
100 to 999 employees 936

Author's 2004 sampling of 70,000 U.S. IT job listings
IT jobs available for Austin metro area 591

Projected 2004–2008 total IT job growth based upon *Business 2.0* forecast
Software engineers, systems software 1,700

Author' comments: Incremental job growth of software systems engineers averaging 340 per year is realistic. Also comparative BLS data for other high-growth metropolitan areas indicates a significant growth opportunity for database administrators in the Austin metro area. A ratio of almost 34 IT employees per establishment with 100 to 999 employees indicates moderate growth during the next several years. Significant state government hiring could increase overall IT hiring levels providing state's fiscal condition is good.

* Estimate of Bureau of Labor Statistics from employer reporting.

5 ATLANTA, GA

2004–2008 IT job growth projections by *Business 2.0*
Software engineers, applications 95%

Total metropolitan area IT jobs year end 2002 **73,540***
Software engineers, applications 11,580*

infoUSA 2004 database of metropolitan area establishments of
100 to 999 employees 3,215

Author's 2004 sampling of 70,000 U.S. IT job listings
IT jobs available for Atlanta metro area 1,424

Projected 2004–2008 total IT job growth based upon *Business 2.0* forecast
Software engineers, applications 11,000

Author's comments: An average growth of 2,200 software applications engineers does not seem realistic, unless a significant amount of this annual growth is in the government, healthcare, and education areas, which are forecast by Gartner Dataquest to grow at an average rate of 12% annually between 2004 and 2007. These market segments represent a significant percentage of Atlanta metro area employment. Other IT job categories that should show significant annual growth when compared to other metropolitan area employment are database administrators and network systems and data communications analysts. A ratio of almost 25 : 1 for the average number of IT employees compared to total area establishments with 100 to 999 employees indicates continued healthy IT job growth.

* Estimate of Bureau of Labor Statistics from employer reporting.

---

6 WEST PALM BEACH, FL

2004–2008 IT job growth projections by *Business 2.0*
Communications analysts   40%

Total metro area IT job year end 2002 combined with Fort Lauderdale   **22,210***
Communications analysts in the combined metro area   2,670*

infoUSA 2004 database of metropolitan area establishments of
100 to 999 employees   1,086

Author's 2004 sampling of 70,000 U.S. IT job listings
IT jobs available for West Palm Beach metro area   502

Projected 2004–2008 total IT job growth based upon *Business 2.0* forecast
Communications analysts   1,068

Author comment: A projected annual increase of 214 communications analysts for this metropolitan area does not seem realistic when you consider the current employed and the total number of establishments in the 100 to 999-employee range. BLS comparative metropolitan IT job classification data indicates that the largest potential growth area for IT jobs is the database administrator area. A ratio of just over 20 IT employees to every establishment in the 100- to 999-employee range in this geographical area would indicate a moderate increase in IT hiring that could be attributed to the nature of the work force, which is primarily focused upon the services industry owing to a large number of retirement- and vacation-related businesses.

* Estimate of Bureau of Labor Statistics from employer reporting.

7 SAN FRANCISCO-OAKLAND, CA

2004–2008 IT job growth projections by *Business 2.0*
Software engineers, systems software   34%

Total metropolitan area IT jobs year end 2002   **71,600***
Software engineers, systems software   8,420*

infoUSA database of metropolitan area establishments of
100 to 999 employees   4,210

Author's 2004 sampling of 70,000 U.S. IT job listings
IT jobs available for San Francisco-Oakland area   2,819

**Projected 2004–2008 total IT job growth based upon *Business 2.0*
forecast**
Software engineers, systems software   2,862

   Author's comments: An increase of 572 jobs annually between now and 2008 in the software systems engineer category is realistic. This metropolitan area also has significant employee exposure to outsourcing outside of the United States, and some sources would indicate that software engineers for systems are not as vulnerable to potential outsourcing as basic programmer/software writers, which is questionable unless the majority of systems software engineers have advanced, specialized skills that are needed. The current ratio of fewer than 20 IT employees per total establishments in the 100- to 999-employee range would indicate continued growth in IT employment during the next few years.

* Estimate of Bureau of Labor Statistics from employer reporting.

8 MIDDLESEX-SOMERSET, NJ

2004–2008 IT job growth projections by *Business 2.0*
Software engineers, systems software   77%
Network and computer systems administrators   69%

Total metropolitan area IT jobs year end 2002   **30,680***
Software engineers, systems software   3,790*
Network and computer systems administrators   1,610*

infoUSA database of metropolitan area establishments of
100 to 999 employees   846

Author's 2004 sampling of 70,000 U.S. IT job listings
IT jobs available for Middlesex-Somerset, NJ metro area 4,129

**Projected 2004–2008 total IT job growth based upon *Business 2.0*
forecast**
Software engineers, systems software   2,918
Network and computer systems administrators   1,111

Author' comments: The job growth projections for both software engineers and systems and network and computer systems administrators are believed to be realistic. Other job classifications that should show significant employment growth are database administrators and network systems and data communications analysts when compared to other similar metropolitan areas.

* Estimate of Bureau of Labor Statistics from employer reporting.

9 SEATTLE, WA

2004–2008 IT job growth projections by *Business 2.0*
Software engineers, applications   20%

Total metropolitan area IT jobs year end 2002   **65,120***
Software engineers, applications   11,280*

infoUSA database of metropolitan area establishments of
100 to 999 employees   1,694

Author's 2004 sampling of 70,000 U.S. IT job listings
IT jobs available for Seattle metro area   2,062

Projected 2004–2008 total IT job growth based upon *Business 2.0* forecast
Software engineers, applications   2,256

Author's comment: An average job increment of 456 per year for this category is realistic but could be reduced somewhat because of application programming outsourcing by the largest area employers. The growth of database administrator jobs when compared to employment data from other similar metropolitan areas could be significant. An almost 40 : 1 ratio comparing IT jobs to establishments with 100 to 999 employee is possibly somewhat skewed by Boeing and Microsoft, but it also indicates that overall IT hiring gains could lag the average of other large metropolitan areas.

* Estimate of Bureau of Labor Statistics from employer reporting.

10 BOSTON, MA

2004–2008 IT job growth projections by *Business 2.0*
Computer engineers   76%

This job classification refers to electrical, mechanical, and software engineering associated with computer hardware and peripheral equipment development, which is not a major IT job classification category of the Bureau of Labor Statistics.

Total metropolitan area IT jobs year end 2002   79,460*

infoUSA database of metropolitan area establishments of
100 to 999 employees   4,274

Author's 2004 sampling of 70,000 U.S. IT job listings
IT jobs available for Boston metro area   1,980

Author's comment: The largest IT job gains in this metropolitan area during the next several years should come in the government, education, and healthcare sectors in which IT employment is projected by Gartner Dataquest to grow an average of 12% between now and 2007. Other potential IT job growth areas that appear to have significant growth opportunity when compared to other metropolitan area is database administrators and network systems and data communications analysts. The overall ratio of 20 IT employees per establishment with 100 to 999 employees would indicate that overall IT job creation in Boston will be good for the next several years.

* Estimate of Bureau of Labor Statistics from employer reporting.

---

11 SACRAMENTO, CA

2004–2008 IT job growth projections by *Business 2.0*
Software engineers, systems software   58%
Network systems and data communications analysts   45%

Total metropolitan area IT jobs year end 2002   **22,350***
Software engineers, systems software   3,020*
Network systems and data communications analysts   1,070*

infoUSA database of metropolitan area establishments of
100 to 999 employees   906

Author's 2004 sampling of 70,000 U.S. IT job listings
IT jobs available for Sacramento metro area   273

Projected 2004–2008 total IT job growth based upon *Business 2.0* forecast
Software engineers, systems software   1,751
Network systems and data communications analysts   482

Author's comments: An average gain in these two categories of 447 jobs annually appears to be reasonable unless the state budget problem corrective actions restrict IT hiring. Also database administrators looks like another potential IT job growth when compared to other metropolitan areas.

* Estimate of Bureau of Labor Statistics from employer reporting.

12 PHOENIX, AZ

2004–2008 IT job growth projections by *Business 2.0*

Information systems managers	27%

Total metropolitan area IT jobs year end 2002	**35,080***

infoUSA database of metropolitan area establishments of

100 to 999 employees	2,223

Author's 2004 sampling of 70,000 U.S. IT job listings

Jobs available for Phoenix metro area	398

Author's comments: When the ratio of establishments to total existing IT employees in the metropolitan area is compared to other metropolitan areas, the Phoenix ratio of approximately 15 employees per firm is very low. This indicates that overall IT hiring in Phoenix should be better for new jobs over the next several years than in most other metropolitan areas. The only thing that would detract from this is the high retirement population as compared to employment in technology organizations which would indicate that a lot of IT jobs would be in healthcare and financial services-type organizations.

* Estimate of Bureau of Labor Statistics from employer reporting.

13 MINNEAPOLIS, MN

2004–2008 IT job growth projections by *Business 2.0*

Software engineers applications	79%
Information systems managers	43%

Total metropolitan area IT jobs year end 2002	**54,750***
Software engineers, applications	9,030*
Information systems managers (not available)	

infoUSA database of metropolitan area establishments of

100 to 999 employees	2,854

Author's 2004 sampling of 70,000 U.S. IT job listings

Jobs available for Minneapolis metro area	972

Projected 2004–2008 total IT job growth based upon *Business 2.0* forecast

Software engineers, applications	7,134

Authors comments: An average addition of 1,420 incremental software engineers for applications is realistic when you consider the average number of IT jobs per establishments in the 100- to 999-employee range of approximately 20 employees per organization. Based upon these comparative factors, the Minneapolis-St. Paul metropolitan area should show significant growth in all IT job classifications during the next several years.

* Estimate of Bureau of Labor Statistics from employer reporting.

14 DENVER, CO

2004–2008 IT job growth projections by *Business 2.0*

Database administrators	46%
Computer engineers	38%

This job classification refers to electrical, mechanical, and software engineering associated with computer hardware and related periphery equipment development, which is not a major IT job classification category of the Bureau of Labor Statistics.

Total metropolitan area IT jobs year end 2002   **44,360***

Database administrators	1,910*

infoUSA database of metropolitan area establishments of

100 to 999 employees	1,648

Author's 2004 sampling of 70,000 U.S. IT job listings

Jobs available for Denver metro area	775

Projected 2004–2008 total IT job growth based upon *Business 2.0* forecast

Database administrators	878

Authors comments: The average of approximately 28 IT employees per establishment in the 100- to 999-employee range would indicate moderate IT job growth over the next several years. IT job growth is most likely to occur almost equally across all primary IT job classifications.

*Estimate of Bureau of Labor Statistics from employer reporting.

15 NEW HAVEN-STAMFORD, CT

2004–2008 IT job growth projections by *Business 2.0*

Information systems manager	35%

Total metropolitan area IT jobs year end 2002

Not reported.

infoUSA database of metropolitan area establishments of

100 to 999 employees	1,247

Author's 2004 sampling of 70,000 U.S. IT job listings

Jobs available in New Haven-Stamford metro area	172

Projected 2004–2008 total IT job growth based upon *Business 2.0* forecast

Information systems managers	10–15

Author comments: The only thing that qualifies this metropolitan area as a projected top job market during the next several years is the large number of corporate headquarters located within Fairfield County. It is also difficult to predict what the IT job growth trends will be in this section.

* Estimate of Bureau of Labor Statistics from employer reporting.

---

16 BALTIMORE, MD

2004–2008 IT job growth projections by *Business 2.0*

Data communications analysts	57%
Information systems analysts	30%

Total metropolitan area IT jobs year end 2002	**37,390***
Data communications analysts	2,150*
Information systems analysts	7,940*

infoUSA database of metropolitan area establishments of

100 to 999 employees	1,750

Author's 2004 sampling of 70,000 U.S. IT job listings

Jobs available for Baltimore metro area	457

Projected 2004–2008 total IT job growth based upon *Business 2.0* forecast

Data communications analysts	1,226
Information systems analysts	2,382

Author's comments: An average of 725 incremental jobs annually for these two categories is reasonable. When you compare ratio of establishments with 100 to 999 employees to total IT jobs, the average is just under 20, which indicates that the average annual IT job growth for most of the BLS classifications should be higher in the Baltimore metropolitan area than most of the other areas in the country. This is also probable because of the amount of federal government IT hiring that is projected. Even if some federal agencies or departments experience job cuts, IT employment should continue to grow at the projected 12% rate annually.

*Estimate of Bureau of Labor Statistics from employer reporting.

---

17 SAN DIEGO, CA

2004–2008 IT job growth projections by *Business 2.0*

Software engineers, systems software	54%

Total metropolitan area jobs year end 2002	**34,510***
Software engineers, systems software	3,550*

infoUSA database of metropolitan area establishments of

100 to 999 employees	1,861

Author's 2004 sampling of 70,000 U.S. IT job listings

Jobs available in San Diego area   885

Projected 2004–2008 total IT job growth based upon *Business 2.0* forecast

Software engineers, systems software   1,917

Author's comments: An increment of 383 systems software engineers annually is realistic because there is a larger than normal discrepancy between systems software and applications software engineers compared to most other high-growth metropolitan areas. Also the ratio of less than 20 jobs per establishment in the 100- to 999-employee range indicates that overall IT job growth in the San Diego metropolitan area should be significantly higher than in most of the other high-growth metropolitan area. Significant IT job growth should occur in addition to systems software engineers in the database administration and network systems and data communications analysts areas.

* Estimate of Bureau of Labor Statistics from employer reporting.

---

18 DALLAS, TX

2004–2008 IT job growth projections by *Business 2.0*

Software engineers   108%

Total metropolitan area IT jobs year end 2002   **72,520***

Software engineers (systems and applications)   18,080*

infoUSA database of metropolitan area establishments of

100 to 999 employees   3,917

Author's 2004 sampling of 70,000 U.S. IT job listings

Jobs available for Dallas metro area   1,311

Projected 2004–2008 total IT job growth based upon *Business 2.0* forecast

Software engineers (systems and applications)   19,526

Authors comments: Average annual incremental growth of an average of 3,905 software engineer jobs is a questionable forecast. When you look at the ratio of an average approximately 18 IT jobs for total establishments in the 100- to 999-employee range, the Dallas metropolitan area should be one of the largest IT job growth markets in the United States during the next several years. The current employment in the primary BLS job classifications indicates that the highest growth should occur in the software applications engineer and database administrator areas. There also could exist a significant amount of applications engineer work being outsourced, which could interfere with the forecasted growth.

* Estimate of Bureau of Labor Statistics from employer reporting.

19 CHARLOTTE, NC

2004–2008 IT job growth projections by *Business 2.0*
Systems analysts   67%

Total metropolitan area IT jobs year end 2002   **19,380***
Systems analysts   650*

infoUSA datasbase of metropolitan area establishments of
100 to 999 employees   1,222

Author's 2004 sampling of 70,000 U.S. IT job listings
Jobs available for Charlotte metro area   404

Projected 2004–2008 total IT job growth based upon *Business 2.0* forecast
Systems analysts   436

Authors comments: The Charlotte metropolitan area has one of the lowest ratios of average IT jobs per establishment with 100 to 999 employees, 16. This would indicate that if the overall economy in Charlotte remains good during the next several years, significant IT job growth will exist in all BLS primary IT job categories every year.

*Estimate of Bureau of Labor Statistics from employer reporting.

20 PHILADELPHIA, PA

2004–2008 IT job growth projections by *Business 2.0*
Computer scientists   40%

Total metropolitan area IT jobs year end 2002   **58,100***
Computer scientists   990*

infoUSA database of metropolitan area establishments of
100 to 999 employees   3,468

Author's 2004 sampling of 70,000 U.S. IT job listings
Jobs available for Philadelphia metro area   1,735

Projected 2004–2008 job growth based upon *Business 2.0* forecast
Computer scientists   396

Author's comments: Overall IT job growth in the Philadelphia metropolitan area should remain strong during the next several years. The average of just under 17 IT employees per establishment of 100 to 999 employees indicates that this metropolitan area should be one of the better IT job growth areas indefinitely. Two BLS categories specifically that could expect to experience strong growth are software engineers and systems and database administrators.

* Estimate of Bureau of Labor Statistics from employer reporting.

This chapter not only reviewed networking, online IT job-posting sites, and online résumé-posting but also provided a leading business magazine's perspective coupled with that of the 13 million business establishments represented in the database of infoUSA and the U.S. Department of Labor, Bureau of Labor Statistics data regarding IT employment by metropolitan area, which all represent ways to pursue IT job finding.

There is no doubt today that the web job-posting sites and résumé-posting sites are the most frequently used mediums for IT job hunters along with networking, which until recently has been the primary and most successful source for job hunting. This chapter has attempted to narrow the possibilities somewhat for job hunters who prefer these sources.

However, if after using the sources provided in this chapter, candidates are not achieving the desired degree of success from these sources, they should consider using those outlined in Chapter 9. Several of those source possibilities are considered briefly in this chapter, but if candidates want to find different and more creative approaches to job search, they may be better served by some of the approaches presented in Chapter 9.

9. Creating Your Job Prospect Base

The Objective of This Chapter

This chapter provides a review of the majority of the additional IT job hunting possibilities outside of the three most popular methods—networking, online IT job-posting sites, and online résumé-posting sites. In total, these alternatives will help IT job candidates create new alternatives for their job prospect database.

Even though a few of the other alternatives incorporate the online feature, most are unique and, for the most part, do not receive the level of daily traffic from applicants as do the major web-posting sites.

The purpose of this chapter is to cover all additional potential sources that can lead to identification of more than 95% of all the available IT jobs in the United States at any given time. The sources for this data all have been reviewed for relevance. These sources are changing to some degree every month, but the ones identified here can provide every IT job candidate with multiple possibilities for potential job identification regardless of experience or skill level if their sources are worked consistently and effectively.

The process detailed in the last section, entitled "Tailoring Your Job Search," will be new to most IT job applicants and when worked properly can result in identification of job opportunities that will not be posted in the online job-posting services. Using this database will identify for contact potential organizations that, for the most part, will not receive a significant amount of contact from other IT job candidates. The author has used the infoUSA database successfully for more than 6 years to identify job candidates while doing employee search work and believes the database to be an excellent tool for job search.

EMPLOYER WEB SITES

Employer web sites often have very high applicant response because, in most situations, it is difficult to talk with someone who understands the job's responsibilities and skill requirements. In most situations, it is to the candidates advantage to try to obtain a more comprehensive formalized job description than was used for the online posting. Formal job descriptions usually exist in most organizations. When successfully obtained, a detailed description may provide some advantage in tailoring your response to the posting.

In situations where you do not have success in learning what you would like to know, a quick call to the Chief Executive Officer's office may be helpful. First, you will rarely get the CEO on the phone. If you happen to reach the CEO, in most cases, he or she will be glad to tell you to whom you need to talk with or may direct you to someone who will be able to help you. Most frequently, you will get an assistant's voice mail and, after several tries, will reach one of the CEO's assistants.

Tell the assistant that you want to write the Chief Information Officer or Chief Technology Officer a letter. In most cases, he or she will provide you with the information or direct you to someone who can provide the individual's name, spelling, title, and mailing address.

If the assistant happens to ask you what the purpose of the letter is, just say that it is a personal matter, which will suffice in most situations.

In some corporate web sites, the name of the Chief Information Officer or Chief Technology Officer will be listed with corporate management in the investors information portion of the web site. In most companies, this information usually accompanies the listing and profiling of the board of directors. If you have access to the referenceUSA database (an infoUSA product), there usually will be a listing of the senior IT official's name in the company profile summary data. However, in most cases, you will able to receive the name and title from the main operator or by directly contacting the IT department, which is often referred to as data processing.

After obtaining the name, a phone call to that individual's office requesting with whom you should talk regarding the job posting of interest may get you the desired information. If you are not successful, a short cover letter stating your interest and requesting to whom you can talk should be sent. A follow-up phone call to confirm receipt and to determine if a contact for you has been designated is appropriate before your letter gets mixed in with scores of others. Your follow-up call should be made within the first week after your letter has been mailed.

SEARCH FIRMS

How to work effectively with search firms as a potential resource is not properly explained in most job-hunting publications and is not discussed at all in some. Search firms are often improperly referred to as employment or recruiting firms, and often published information regarding them is inaccurate and misleading.

Search firms should not be overlooked by any IT job candidate who wants to begin a comprehensive job search. The reason for this is that search firms today are still responsible for thousands of IT job placements each year in the United States. Although web job posting has made significant in-roads in taking away business that in the past was handled by search firms, they are still a significant factor in employment each year.

If you are seriously committed to job search, you should have your résumé on file or in the database of every search or recruiting firm that pursues placement of candidates in computer science jobs.

A reliable source of this information that has been published for more than 30 years is Kennedy Publications' *Directory of Executive Recruiters*. The 2004 edition lists the following approximate numbers of contingency and retained search firms in the index that pursue IT job candidate placements in these categories:

Information technology	2,000+
Software development	600+
Systems integration	600+
Network administration	200+
Database administration	200+

As you can see, this is another potential source of job finding that has significant possibilities. Most data published on job hunting improperly refers to executive search or search firms as employment services or staffing firms, neither of which is correct.

Reviewing the Kennedy Publications document for search firms that make computer science job placements and that focus upon industries of interest to you in your income range is an additional source of jobs that most applicants do not pursue. In most situations, if your qualifications are a good match for assignments that they are trying to fill, your competition will be significantly less than that for jobs where you posted your résumé for consideration in the online posting services.

The reason for this additional widespread résumé distribution is that not one single source knows where all the computer science jobs are at any given time. As a single entity, America's JobBank with their file of an estimated 40,000 computer-science-related jobs in their database is one of the largest known sources of computer science job listings at this time. Even with this large database, they cover significantly less than 10% of total computer-science-related jobs available at any given time in the United States.

The reason for sending your résumé to a large number of search firms throughout the United States is this. A search firm principal located in Montana may be a friend, relative, former work associate, or college acquaintance of a company human resources or computer science department head located in a geographic area in which you are interested. No one except the creator ever knows when and where a new job will show up. This is why it is important to cover all possibilities. Computer science jobs listings change each month in many companies.

When incorporating the use of search firms in your personal job-hunting strategies, remember that there are two distinct types of search firms. They each use different approaches to help place candidates in jobs, and you need to understand their differences in order to use them as effectively as possible as an additional resource that may be able to help you get job interviews with top organizations. The author will explain how to work properly with the two different type of search firms for IT job hunting.

Two Types of Search Firms

In the Kennedy Directory, there are two sections: One lists contingency search firms, and the other lists retained search firms. There is a significant basic difference between the two types of firms. You should review the listings for both types because, again, only the firm that has the job listing usually knows about the job it is trying to fill. Some search firms in their web site will post summary descriptions of jobs that they are trying to fill. These descriptions, for the most part, are purposely general in nature without revealing any type of information that will identify the company client with whom they are working.

Retained Search Firms

Retained search firms primarily work on assignments for significant level management or specialized IT jobs that require higher level skills where the annual incomes are at a minimum level of $80,000 to as high as several hundred thousand dollars. Some of the larger firms do not work on assignments below the annual income level of $125,000. Retained search firms are paid a fixed, usually guaranteed, fee plus some expenses to locate and screen four or five qualified candidates and to ultimately fill a job for the company with whom they have contracted.

If they are interested in you as a potential candidate for any opening they are trying to fill, they will contact you providing your résumé is in their database. They will also contact several others and conduct initial screening interviews by telephone with every candidate whom they believe may have the proper qualifications. If after the telephone interview with you and the others selected, they can eliminate only one or two from a group of usually four to seven, they will conduct personal interviews with the remaining candidates. After the conclusion of these interviews, they will move forward to schedule personal interviews with client hiring management for normally anywhere from two to four candidates whom they believe all have the potential qualifications to be hired.

Early in the process, the search firm will provide all the candidates of interest with a detailed job description, comprehensively outlining the objectives and responsibilities associated with the position. In almost every retained search, you will compete with several other candidates until a hire decision will be made. The process may take as much as one month after you have completed the client interviews before a job offer is formalized.

Most retained search firms are not a good source of contact for jobs below the annual income level of $80,000. It is a waste of your time to contact them if you are targeting jobs with annual compensation below that level. Many of the IT jobs at the annual income level of $50,000 and below are handled by employment services and staffing companies.

Contingency Search Firms

Most contingency firms do their work for IT jobs at the annual income level range of $50,000 to $80,000. Contingency firms are not guaranteed a fee and only receive a fee for placing a candidate in a job for which the hiring company has agreed to pay them. However, there is no certainty that they will be the successful firm in placing the candidate in the job. From a candidate's perspective, there are two primary differences.

1. The contingency firm rarely has an exclusive for the search, and you may be competing with multiple candidates who are being presented by several contingency firms concurrently.
2. Most contingency firms will send your résumé to multiple companies that have job openings, often without your permission unless you make it clear at the outset that your résumé is not to be sent unless discussed with and approved by you. At times, this requirement is both good and bad. Some ambitious employees may send your résumé to every possibility where they think appropriate openings exist whether or not the opening that exists may be a good fit for your qualifications. Some firms have members who are much more professional in these matters. You need to choose whether or not to participate based upon your own comfort with the firm.

One firm, Management Recruiters International (MRI) based in Cleveland is a successful franchise firm that has approximately 300 offices located throughout the United States. Their web site *BrilliantPeople.com* is another good online source of job postings. Occasionally MRI will secure a large national contract for placement of employees. Their web site is a good place to have your résumé posted.

The internet through corporate job listings and the online job posting services have cut significantly into the annual business of search firms during the past several years. However, if you are serious about new job search, you should contact them because they still place thousands of computer-science-related job candidates annually.

When reviewing the Kennedy Directory or any other search firm directories, pay particular attention to firms that have been in business for 5 years or more and that mention information technology, computers, or computer science. Many of these firms still may have good clients with computer science jobs due to their past success and reputation for quality services. If you are involved in or planning a comprehensive job search initiative, you should seriously consider posting your résumé at all the search firms that do work in IT and handle jobs in your annual compensation range.

The primary advantage of working with a search firm as compared to other options is that if their officials believe you are qualified to be considered for a job opening they are trying to fill, they personally promote you for interview consideration, which can be very helpful in securing interviews with quality organizations.

The majority of IT job candidates will probably fall into the annual income range that is pursued by contingency firms. There are several hundred possibilities for contact in the Kennedy Directory; consequently, those candidates interested in this potential job source may want to test-contact 20 or 30 firms to see the reaction. Consider contacting firms that have the largest number of firm principals listed because, in most situations, those with the largest number listed will have the largest annual fee revenue. Also those candidates who are willing to consider relocation or who reside in the metropolitan areas listed in Chapter 1 may want to focus their initial contacts in these geographic areas, which may be the most active ones in IT hiring today.

Online Résumé-Posting Services Working with Search and Recruiting Firms

The online résumé posting section of Chapter 8 lists the following services that specifically work with search and recruiting companies: Recruiters Online Network, RésuméBlaster.com, RésuméZapper.com, and Top Echelon. These are the major sites known to the author at the time of publishing, and they represent another potential source to provide IT job hunters coverage against the total base of IT jobs.

IT AND MANAGEMENT CONSULTING FIRMS

Large technology and management consulting firms are another excellent source of IT jobs. These companies are primarily for those candidates who have good skills and experience in their specific IT discipline.

Today, candidates who have good skills in disciplines such as open source software, security, database engineering, the web and network engineering, VoIP, and wireless should continue to be in demand. Some of the jobs available through these firms are project- or contract-oriented, and many will require significant travel. Those candidates who have significant successful project management and project participation skills in the disciplines in demand will have an advantage in some cases. In reviewing several hundred IT job profiles listed by the large management consulting and IT consulting firms, the author found that approximately 50% of these companies require good oral and written skills and frequently good verbal presentation skills. Also good interpersonal skills are often desired because of the requirement for work on project teams and often directly with client employees. If candidates have the type of skills discussed they will have a significant advantage in many of these job situations when applying for jobs that require significant prior experience.

Several of these firms also will value more highly qualified candidates who have industry-specific application knowledge and experience. Most identify their industry focus in their corporate web site home pages.

Contact information for the leading U.S. consulting firms that currently provide IT job hunters convenient access to their current job needs at this time are profiled at the end of this chapter. Several of the larger companies that have significant IT consulting and/or computer outsourcing contract business are Accenture, BearingPoint, Booz Allen Hamilton, Computer Science Corporation, Computer Associates (software), Cap Gemini Ernst and Young, EDS, and IBM Global Services (acquired PriceWaterhouseCoopers).

Employment opportunity within each of these firms is annually significant, and because of replacement and contract growth needs, they are recommended web sites to visit weekly to learn of new opportunities. All these companies represent good opportunities for new college graduates who have computer science masters degrees or undergraduate computer science degrees combined with business or finance advanced degrees and excellent scholastic records.

Some of these companies often contract for projects where large system conversion work exists. These types of projects require experience and proficiency in the older programming languages such as COBOL, which can present good opportunities for individuals with system conversion experience. Mentioned earlier was the research study of E5 Systems in conjunction with Bain Capital that indicated possibly as high as 80% of software writing done annually is still primary focused upon legacy systems. Software programmers who are experienced and proficient in the older languages such as COBOL and FORTRAN should not overlook this area of employment.

Booz Allen Hamilton, which in the past had primarily been known as a business-strategy-type consulting firm, during the past several years has moved into the federal government contract area. During the past few years, Booz Allen has secured several large contracts that include computer science skills; this firm's web site should also be contacted regularly to learn of new employment opportunities.

Each year most of the larger firms hire a significant number of entry-level employees with masters degrees in the computer science and good scholastic records from colleges and universities that have good reputations for computer science education.

Also IT employees who have specialized functional and other application development experience within certain industries or functions will want to research the company web sites to understand the firms type of specialization; this information can be to your advantage if you have experience that matches the hiring company's requirements.

Researching employment opportunities within this segment may also provide some candidates who have as a goal becoming more relevant in working with the latest IT technology a limited opportunity to work on projects that can help them become more relevant. In some cases, candidates may have much more success pursuing this type of opportunity than they have had pursuing opportunities on the primary web job-posting services.

IT Applications Services Providers, Value Added Resellers, and Outsourcing Companies

This category of IT services can provide a significant number of IT jobs annually. Many of these jobs will be of project or limited-term contract jobs. Sources of these jobs can be located from several of the large search engines such as Google, Alta Vista, MSN, and Dogpile.

Jobs with these types of companies that do not begin as full-time permanent opportunities often will have the opportunity to become full-time jobs. These companies can also provide the opportunity for job candidates to work on limited-term projects that provide them the opportunity to become more relevant in skills and experience in working with some of the latest IT technology. Job candidates should not overlook this possibility when pursuing these types of companies. Scores of them exist today in the United States that have built annual revenues in the range of $50 million to several hundred million dollars. Job candidates will also find jobs for many companies in this category listed in the job databases of the staffing and recruiting companies reviewed later in this chapter.

Large IT and Management Consulting Firms That Provide Job Hunters Convenient Access to Their Current Job Postings

At the time of writing, the following companies consistently had the most IT jobs posted.

Accenture

www.accenture.com

Currently list more than 80 IT jobs available.

BearingPoint

www.bearingpoint.com

Consistently lists more than 200 IT jobs available.

Booz Allen Hamilton

www.boozallen.com

Currently lists more than 300 IT jobs available. The majority of jobs are located in the Mid Atlantic sector where Booz Allen has significant federal government contracts.

Computer Sciences Corporation

www.csc.com

Currently lists in excess of 300 IT jobs available.

IBM Global Services (acquired PriceWaterhouseCoopers)

ibm.com & *pwcglobal.com*

Consistently lists 150 to 200 IT jobs available.

Other IT Services and Consulting Organizations with Significant Jobs

Affiliated Computer Services

www.acs-inc.com

Currently has more than 100 IT job listings.

AETEA

www.aetea.com

Consistently posts more than 100 IT jobs.

SRA

www.sra.com

Consistently lists 50 or more IT jobs available. Significant number of jobs are in the metro Washington, DC, area as a result of a large amount of government-contract-related work.

SAIC

www.saic.com

Consistently lists availability of 100 IT jobs or more. Known as a technology research and engineering firm. Business built upon providing scientific operations research-type software.

GOVERNMENT EMPLOYMENT

Most states, federal government departments, and larger local metropolitan areas today have their own online job-posting sites. Listings for the major federal web job postings are included in this section.

Many of the larger cities or metropolitan areas post their IT jobs online today; however, the job quantities posted will usually be much smaller than in the state and federal listings. You will also find postings at the consulting firm and applications services provider sites for contract work employment that is being done at government sites where organizations have outsourced projects on a contract basis.

Many IT applicants avoid government IT job postings because they perceive the process as being too complicated. A good reason to consider applying for government jobs is that, in most situations, you will not face as much competition as you might in those sites primarily focused upon the commercial sector.

IT professionals who have security clearances will also often have advantages in consideration as will military veterans who meet the job skill and experience specifications for the jobs to which they applied. The Gartner Dataquest study discussed in Chapter 8 cited government IT jobs growing at an average of 12% over the next several years, thus supplying a significant number of new incremental IT jobs in most areas of government.

Major Government Online Job Boards

For those job candidates interested in employment at the state, county, and city level, contact the web sites of those individual entities in which you have interest. The author is not aware of a large concentrator of IT jobs that spans all government entities within the United States. The *govtjobs.com* job board concentrates job listings state by state, but as of this writing, it did not list a significant number of government IT jobs.

Federal Jobs Digest

www.jobsfed.com

This job board concentrates federal jobs by state. As of this writing, it listed more than 500 IT-related jobs throughout the United States.

USAJOBS

www.usajobs.opm.gov

This is the official job site of the federal government. It consistently lists more than 150 IT jobs. The site also does an excellent job of preparing job applicants for the federal applicant process as well as providing individual federal agency data.

STAFFING, CONTRACT EMPLOYMENT, AND RECRUITING FIRMS

Staffing, contract employment, and recruiting firms are another large source of computer science jobs today. Many of the jobs that they are contracted to fill may be of short-term duration, often for less than one year. Often jobs are associated with one-time projects such as new software implementation or system redesign work. These types of projects should not be overlooked as potential sources of employment because many situations can lead to full-time employment opportunities.

Several of the largest firms in the contract employment and staffing business that fill part-time to full-time IT jobs and contract/project type work are Spherion (formerly Norell/Interim), Robert Half Technology, Manpower Professional, Kelly Services, Hall Kinion, Adecco (Olsten), Kforce, Net-Temps, Allegis Group, and Technisource. Hall Kinion's primary focus is IT jobs. The web sites and other contact information for these firms are listed at the end of this section. Most of these firms have offices in major U.S. cities.

Several of the staffing companies are full-service companies. For example, Spherion provides outsourcing staffing, outplacement services, contract employees, interim management, and temporary staffing. Their outsourcing staffing business handles large-scale projects where they hire, provide, and manage the employees. This type of project often involves contracting to provide functional-type application services for large companies on a full-time basis. The web sites of this type of firm should be visited regularly to review contract employment opportunities that, in some situations, have durations for significantly longer than one year and can sometimes become permanent jobs.

Staffing and Contract Employment Firms with Significant IT Job Posting

Adecco Technical

www.adeccotechnical.com

Consistently lists more than 300 IT jobs.

Allegis Group

www.allegisgroup.ie

This family of companies includes TEKsystems' *www.teksystems.com* and *www.thingamajob.com*, which consistently list several 100 IT jobs.

Robert Half Technology

www.roberthalftechnology.com

Have listed as many as 700 IT jobs during the past several months.

Hall Kinion & Associates

www.hallkinion.com

Technology-specialized staffing in five industries. At time of writing, plans merger with Kforce. Lists more than 300 IT jobs at time of writing.

Kelly Services

www.kellyservices.us

Currently lists in excess of 130 IT jobs.

Kforce

www.kforce.com

Presently lists more than 500 IT jobs. Merger planned with Hall Kinion as of this writing.

Manpower Professional

www.manpowerprofessional.com

IT job postings recently are at the 200 level.

Net-Temps

www.net-temps.com

More than 7,000 IT jobs listed as of this writing.

Spherion

www.spherion.com

More than 400 IT jobs consistently listed.

Technisource

www.technisource.com

300 plus IT jobs posted at this time.

Additional Staffing and Recruiting Firms Consistently Posting Numerous IT Jobs

Greythorn.com

www.greythorn.com

An international staffing company based in London. Consistently posts a significant number of IT jobs in the United States, primarily for their Seattle office.

Hudson Highland Group

www.hhgroup.com

Hudson Global Resources is part of this group, *www.hudson.com*, that consistently posts 50 to 100 IT jobs.

HMS Associates Of Tri-State, Inc.

www.hmstri.com

Posts a significant number of IT jobs primarily in the Northeast.

Wanted Technologies

www.wantedtech.com

This rapidly growing recruiting data firm states that their database includes over 12 million employment opportunities, which should equate to more than 500,000 IT-related jobs.

SOFTWARE DEVELOPMENT COMPANIES

The largest software development companies are another excellent source of IT jobs. Although the majority of their job postings may be related to software engineering and programming-related jobs, many of these companies also have needs for software and systems engineering jobs related to the web, database technology, networks, wireless, open source, security, and VoIP.

Activision, Inc.

www.activision.com

More than 1,000 employees. Rapidly growing to video (small video) game development company.

Adobe

www.adobe.com

Over 3,000 employees. Desktop publishing software industry leader.

Autodesk, Inc.

www.autodesk.com

A leader in computer-aided design software.

BMC Software

www.bmc.com

Software to manage complex and decentralized IT infrastructure of large enterprises.

Cadence Design Systems

www.cadence.com

Leader in the provision of electronic design automation software used in design of semiconductors and complicated electronics.

Computer Associates International

www.ca.com

Software provider to manage the critical aspects of data across enterprise data systems.

Compuware

www.compuware.com

Leading provider of network and application performance management software.

Electronic Arts

www.ea.com

Computer games software developer.

Hyperion Solutions

www.hyperion.com

Developer of business analysis software used by large corporations.

IBM

www.IBM.com

In software development business, possibly only Microsoft is larger. Excellent present opportunities for candidates capable of open source software development.

Intuit

www.intuit.com

Developer of financial management software for individuals and small business.

Microsoft Corporation

www.microsoft.com

World's leading software developer.

Oracle Corporation

www.oracle.com

Industry leader in database software.

PeopleSoft, Inc.

www.peoplesoft.com

A leader in enterprise resource planning and CRM software.

SAP

www.sap.com

An industry leader in enterprise resource planning (ERP), customer relationship management (CRM), and supply chain management (SCM).

Sybase, Inc.

www.sybase.com

Provider of enterprise software solutions, wireless software, and vertical-market-specific software solutions.

Symantec

www.symantec.com

Industry leader in the provision of information security software.

TAILORING YOUR JOB SEARCH

If in your job search initiatives, you want to place effort into job search activities where you are not competing with hundreds of other candidates for available jobs, you need to consider using nonconventional job-hunting approaches. Information in this section will help you do this.

The best process for implementing a tailored job search is to use the private and public company data provided by info/USA of Omaha, NE. infoUSA has an active U.S. database of more than 13 million private and public companies in their files. They have three basic CD-ROMs that contain this database; infoUSA American Business Disc; Employer Database, which is found in many states' employment assistance type agencies; and referenceUSA, which is found in many college and university libraries. Some public libraries also provide this service. The following are the standard components of the infoUSA database that provide job hunters the opportunity to build an employment prospect list that can be tailored specifically to each individual's personal criteria. Tailoring is possible for such items as geographical location, size of company (either by revenue or by number of employees at a location), and standard industrial classification (SIC code). You can obtain the desired SIC code information from the Federal Securities and Exchange Commission web address *sec.gov/info/edgar/siccodes.htm.*

The various infoUSA databases will enable job hunters to identify all companies to contact based upon their selected criteria down to the level of an entire state, one or more counties, one or more cities, or the metropolitan areas of the larger U.S. cities. Also when using the referenceUSA database to identify companies to contact, candidates will also be able to identify the senior IT official in most of these listings. When directly contacting that individual, it is a good idea to call and verify because changes in holders of these jobs occasionally occur. The database identifies the locations of company headquarters as well as branch-type offices. All of the necessary contact information for each company of interest for the mailing of query letters or résumés is included.

The following data outlines the structural content of the standard components of the infoUSA database that enable you to tailor your own personal prospect list for companies to contact. Its primary potential value is that it facilitates your finding some potential opportunities to consider, which the hundreds of applicants who apply to every listing in corporate web sites or the online job-posting services will not necessarily have access to.

Geographical Selection Criteria

State
County
City
Metro Area
Area Code
ZIP Code

Location Size by Number of Employees

1 to 4	50 to 99	1,000 to 4,999
5 to 9	100 to 249	5,000 to 9,999
10 to 19	250 to 499	10,000 +
20 to 49	500 to 999	

Using this process you are able to make cumulative selections. For example, you have the option of tagging only one category or selectively tagging every site in the database in several of the listed categories. At the outset of use in the individual industries you have tagged for search or for all companies in the selected geography you have the option of reviewing the total number of companies that exist in the categories that you have selected. You can also complete the same type of search using annual sales of the organization located at each site you want to review. The annual sales criteria often provide a significantly different picture of a company, especially when compared to number of employees. What you often find is that companies with significantly lower numbers of total employees at a location often have significantly larger annual sales than many companies with much larger employee populations.

Using this process combined with the best possible résumé and well-written cover letters is an excellent alternative for anyone who has not been satisfied with the conventional methods of job search that are available.

Effective use of this process will help you generate more potential alternatives for employment. Remember that it takes only one possibility if it is the right one. Use of a process such as this one can increase your job possibilities in organizations where you will not encounter the same level of competition that you will for online job postings. Effective use of query letters as outlined in Chapters 10 and 12 is another alternative method of contacting the companies identified.

In the business size section of infoUSA, you can tailor your company selection by sales volume.

Sales Volume Categories

less than $500,000	$20 million to $50 million
$500,000 to $1 million	$50 million to $100 million
$1 million to $2.5 million	$100 million to $500 million
$2.5 million to $5 million	$500 million to $1 billion
$5 million to $10 million	over $1 billion
$10 million to $20 million	

To illustrate the potential value of using the infoUSA database to identify companies to contact for prospective employment, the following is an example of the database of companies with 500 or more employees in the Los Angeles/Long Beach metropolitan area during the first half of 2004.

In this area, there are approximately 5,100 organizations listed with 500 or more employees. Firms with $100 million and greater in sales volume total approximately 2,300. Firms that included the name of the senior IT official totaled approximately 1,400.

Having the capability to further break down this data to individual companies in specific industries including their contact information, you can see the potential value of using this database for job search purposes.

This different type of approach for IT job seekers will enable them to make significant contact coverage in their selected geographic area and save themselves significant amounts of time as compared to the research time required by alternative methods. The author believes that this type of approach, aggressively pursued, can be helpful to those unemployed or having difficulty finding the type of potential IT employment opportunities that meet their qualifications.

Use of the infoUSA database is possibly the best method available today for IT job candidates who want to create potential hiring sources where they may have limited competition for jobs.

Most job candidates use networks, post their résumés on the web job-posting sites, and apply for consideration for jobs posted on these sites. These methods may be successful for as many as 70% of today's IT jobs that are filled. Because of the change that the profession is experiencing today, through outsourcing and type of IT jobs available, there is available an abundance of public data that can assist IT job seekers in determining the potential alternatives to pursue.

Used properly, these data sources can help IT job candidates find job alternatives that in many cases will provide them better personal opportunity for career success.

As an additional source of IT-job-related information the best potential indicator of where to look for IT jobs is the U.S. geographical areas where the majority of IT jobs are today. Using this information as base data in conjunction with the web-posting services that list the majority of the IT jobs posted can be helpful in career planning as well as immediate job hunting.

Data provided by the U.S. Labor Department, Bureau of Labor Statistics indicate that today approximately 83% of the nearly 2.8 million U.S. computer science jobs reported by employers, are located within 126 Standard Metropolitan Statistical Areas within the United States.

There is a strong correlation between current IT employment in these metropolitan areas and the approximately 1.2 million computer science jobs that the Bureau of Labor Statistics projected would be created for the period between 2002 and 2010.

10. Marketing Yourself

The Objective of This Chapter

This chapter focuses upon all aspects of the process associated with securing personal job interviews. Chapters 8 and 9 help job candidates identify the primary sources available at this time for IT job search. Based upon personal interests and situational analysis, the chapter will help job candidates tailor their search to avoid significant unproductive effort and to identify the potential sources where they are most likely to achieve the desired results.

Identifying the optimum search process is a function of personal situation analysis regardless of your situation. This analysis is particularly critical for candidates who are unemployed and for those who have expended considerable effort over months without achieving any type of encouraging progress and results.

SITUATION ANALYSIS—ALTERNATIVES

The first step prior to implementing any type of new IT job search strategy or techniques not previously used, is to complete a skills profile, which is discussed in the last section of Chapter 5. The purpose of using this profile is to determine if there is any other important information that you can add to your résumé to help generate more interest in you as a job candidate than what has been achieved using your previous methods of job search.

This section of the chapter will provide you with several alternatives that you could use in your job search activities. Before considering their potential use, you first need to evaluate what you have been doing that has not resulted in the type of results that you desire. If your primary job-hunting activity to this point has been résumé posting to web job sites or applying to jobs posted in the web job services, you must remember three important things. Employers that post their jobs on the various web postings services have indicated in surveys that as much as 70% of the respondent's qualifications do not match the posted job's specifications.

The second thing to remember is that many of the posted jobs may have as many as several hundred applicants during the first several weeks of posting. This means that if your qualifications are not a good match for the posted job and if your skills and experience are viewed as marginal as presented in your résumé, your chances of being considered further are not good.

The last item to remember is that if you do not respond to a job posting of interest within the first week or 10 days of its being posted, often times the employer has already chosen the applicants to be contacted for consideration. Unless your qualifications are very good and a good match for the specification, your chances for being contacted are diminished if you do not post within the first week after the job is listed. These are a few things to consider when evaluating your personal situation regarding productive use of your time in job-hunting activities.

If your skills and experience are of the caliber and type that are in high demand today, you may not have to go beyond résumé posting and applying for jobs posted on the web. In many situations, this type of search will generate significant enough interest in you to move you toward job offers. For those in this situation, your concern should be focused primarily on the process used to research interested employers and your interviewing skills used with these employers.

Situation Analysis # 1—Alternatives First IT Job Candidates

New or Recent College Graduates

1. Review your résumé with an eye toward strengthening it. Review the data in Chapter 5 regarding nontechnical desired skills and the data in Chapter 7 for college students.
2. Concentrate on job- and résumé-posting sites that focus upon college graduates and entry-level jobs identified in the section in Chapter 7 for college students and recent graduates.
3. For those candidates who have strong academic records or dual majors in computer science and other disciplines such as finance, marketing, engineering, mathematics, and the physical sciences, review the web sites of the IT and management consulting firms as well as the CRM software developers discussed in Chapter 9. These types of organizations may also have possibilities for those with a computer science major and minor concentration in the other disciplines mentioned.
4. If, in addition to computer science, you have significant education listed in point 3, the section in Chapter 9 entitled "Tailoring Your Job Search" may provide potential sources justifying contact. Identification of companies in your preferred work area using the referenceUSA database in conjunction with industry SIC codes will help you identify additional possibilities for contact such as engineering, biomedical, and pharmaceutical companies and companies with R&D organizations. As discussed later in this chapter, query letters directed to these types of organizations may have the potential to generate interest in your qualifications.
5. Don't forget to review the government job-posting sites as additional possibilities for consideration that are identified in Chapter 9.

Those Pursuing IT Employment as Career Changes

1. Explore any potential of existing possibilities within your present employer if you are currently employed. If you have a good employment record and believe that your employer has a good potential future, this could be your best alternative. If you are respected and understand the current business practices of the company, in situations where this can provide you good personal opportunities, this arrangement may make good sense to the employer. Your advantage in these types of situations is that, in many cases, employees in this situation are able to provide significantly better value much more quickly than they would be able to with another employer because they understand the company's business. A formal proposal detailing such possibilities in situations desirable to a candidate can represent a better alternative when compared to extensive new employer type job search efforts.

2. Strengthening your résumé by integrating any industry-specific or functional application knowledge experience into it can be to your advantage when you are compared to other candidates. Also review the employer ranking of desired nontechnical skills outlined in Chapter 5 for potential résumé inclusion. If you need to search outside of current employment situations, strong experience and expertise in these types of capabilities can help generate interest in you as a potential candidate as compared to situations where they are not included. The methods discussed in the section entitled "Tailoring Your Job Search" in Chapter 9 can identify industry experience related potential companies for telephone or query letter type of contact, which may represent some of your better potential opportunities.

3. Consider selective application to entry-level-type web-posted jobs. Also, review the job posting of the staffing companies listed in Chapter 9. First-priority-type résumé posting would be for job postings that require one or more of the nontechnical skills for those candidates who have them as discussed in point 2.

4. Concurrent with other search-related activities, initiate query-type phone calls and or letters to relevant industry-related prospects that you identified from the referenceUSA database discussed in the section entitled "Tailoring Your Job Search" in Chapter 9. The small- and medium-sized firms identified in this database may in most situations be more likely to have more entry-level IT jobs than larger organizations.

5. Review the government job-posting services, which again may be a potential source of entry-level-type jobs.

Situation # 2 Analysis—Alternatives
Those Unemployed or Potentially Vulnerable to Job Loss

1. Complete a skill profile assessment as outlined in Chapter 5.
2. Strengthen your résumé by incorporating any industry or application-specialized experience and knowledge. Refer to Chapter 6 when doing this to identify any potential opportunity to strengthen your résumé by the way in which you present your accomplishments or valuable contributions in your previous employment. Employers' most desired nontechnical skills in Chapter 5 should also be reviewed for potential incorporation.
3. After reviewing the potential employment sources listed in Chapters 8 and 9, identify the sources that are most consistent with your skill profile and prior job experience.
4. If interest generated to date in your résumé is minimal, review new web-postings weekly to identify any potential situations where your technical skills are a good match and the employer requires specific-industry or soft skills that you have listed in your revised résumé. This activity represents a good test to determine if you receive any type of improved interest in your résumé. If not, your best opportunity will probably be in contacting potential new sources identified in Chapter 8, that you have not contacted previously as well as a self-marketing campaign involving telephone calls and query letters to companies identified via a database such as referenceUSA.
5. Your use of query letters may be most beneficial when directed to small- and medium-sized high-growth companies with good to excellent credit in those industries where you have prior work experience. Also the *forbes.com* and *fortune.com* web sites may be helpful in identifying some of the fastest growing newer companies in your preferred geographic area. Some of these companies may be good prospects for candidates with prior relevant industry knowledge and experience.

    For those candidates who have IT expertise in more than one relevant IT discipline, presenting this fact in query letters can also contribute to an employer's interest in a candidate in the small and medium-sized high-growth company classifications.
6. Consider the possibility of participating in one of the social networking organizations listed in Chapter 8 that include IT professional networks. These organizations are growing and could prove useful.
7. If you have relevant skills in multiple disciplines such as programming, networks, and databases, the testing of query letters sent to small- and medium-sized companies could prove beneficial. Query letters stressing your multidiscipline-type experience and capability to companies in industries where you have experience may prove beneficial. If you are unemployed, you might propose things like potential capability to handle responsibilities within two separate job classifications concurrently or a test or trial of this type on a limited-term basis.

8. Review listings of staffing companies and application services providers in your geographic area regarding limited-duration contract possibilities.

9. Test sending out query letters to the small- and medium-sized company market proposing the consideration of short-term contract or consulting employment without any type of residual responsibility to the employer if the employer is not satisfied with work quality.

10. Review job postings in government, education, and healthcare, which are all projected as IT job growth markets during the next few years.

Situation # 3—Alternatives
Extensive Résumé Posting on Web Sites—Minimal Results

1. Complete a comprehensive skills profile and résumé-strengthening assessment. Review the skills profile data and employer ranking of nontechnical skills in Chapters 3 and 5 to determine if this information presents résumé improvement opportunity.

2. Review potential alternatives listed in this chapter and the section entitled "Tailoring Your Job Search" in Chapter 9. Select three or four new approaches for testing.

3. Define a different audience of organization type for contact. Review the possibilities listed in Chapter 8. Gain access to the referenceUSA database to select potential prospects.

4. Complete research of targeted organizations through sources such as their web sites, internal company/customer newsletters, local newspaper databases, Lexus-Nexus Academic Explorer business data, and ProQuest ABI/Inform.

5. Generate query letters to organizations that you have thoroughly researched. Test two or three different query letters proposing alternative offers. These two or three paragraph letters would contain key points summarizing things such as have thoroughly researched your company, have detailed industry and functional application understanding of your business, and have capability in several IT disciplines. State that you desire to schedule an appointment to discuss several alternatives that have the potential of helping (company name) achieve its business goals.

6. For all situations where you are able to obtain an appointment, follow the suggestions in this chapter regarding research and in Chapter 11 regarding preparation for the meeting. In these situations, candidates need to go to these meetings prepared to present a proposal of their potential services and be prepared for interview-type questions when interest is generated. Taking along a two- or three-page PowerPoint-type presentation that summarizes relevant skills and experience as well as potential proposed alternatives for evaluating your services is a better method of generating discussion in these situations than using your résumé, which can be left at the conclusion.

As a minimum you need to have something with you to stimulate discussion regarding the potential value of what you are proposing for consideration or the company's representative will wonder why you are there. If a Power-Point-type presentation of relevant skills and experience is not appropriate, a one- or two-page summary of project experience indicating use of multiple skills may be helpful.

The goal of these type meetings which often will not last any longer than 20 to 30 minutes is to quickly generate discussion regarding the potential customer's needs and then, once defined, gain approval to submit a formal proposal outlining alternatives for consideration regarding how you can help. If you achieve this at the conclusion, always try to schedule a firm appointment (time and date) to come back to review what you are proposing for consideration.

Situation # 4—Alternatives
Job Candidates with High-Level Skills and Experience in Demand

1. Your first priority is to be realistic regarding your self-evaluation that your skills, experience, and total qualifications justify this evaluation.
2. Your primary activity should focus upon posting your résumé in web sites, determined to be secure ones if this is important. As a backup, you should also apply to web job listings of potential interest where your overall qualifications appear to be a good match.
3. If you have skills in specialized disciplines such as security, wireless, VoIP, and open source software, you may want to review the job listings of IT consulting firms and applications services providers in your geographic area.
4. If you want to move to newer fast-growing companies, you may want to research CRM software developers and high-growth companies listed in the *Forbes* and *Fortune* annual listings of top growth firms, which can be obtained through their web sites.
5. For job candidates with high-level relevant skills, don't overlook the potential value of distributing your résumé to selected retained search firms discussed in Chapter 9. These organizations often will have exclusive control of some of the best IT jobs available where their clients prefer not to have knowledge of these jobs made available throughout the IT profession and other recruiting sources.

   The primary advantage in working with these firms is that they will do the marketing on your behalf for any situations where they believe that your qualifications meet the needs of their client. Most of these firms' searches will primarily be focused upon IT senior management jobs and specialty-type jobs at the higher end of the pay scale.

Situation # 5—Alternatives
20 Plus Years of IT Job Experience

1. If unemployed or potentially vulnerable to job loss, and most opportunities that you have pursued where your skills and experience are a good match but annual income is not what you need, you may want to consider management consulting opportunities and other potential employment sources listed in Chapter 9 that you have not pursued.

   If in your job experience you meet most of the following criteria, consulting is a potential option to consider:
   - Good experience in multiple IT job disciplines, programming, internet, database, networks, projects or teams, and end user/client work and good interpersonal and communications skills (verbal and writing)
   - Experience in one or more industry classifications including extensive functional and or industry-specific application knowledge

   If your skills are up to date and you can justify many of these personal strengths or assets, you may want to consider exploring possibilities at several of the larger IT and management consulting firms. If you have already contacted some of them but did not include the type of criteria listed here for candidates who have these types of skills and experience, you should contact all possibilities again stressing these capabilities in addition to your job experience.

2. If you have a combination of the items listed in point 1, you could market yourself as a contract consultant on a project or hourly rate proposal basis. All that is required to start in consulting is reliable transportation, a business card listing your name, IT consultant, address and a phone number with answering and message-leaving capability with a line dedicated to your business when possible. Letter heads, when needed for proposal-type items, can be generated on a PC with a high-resolution laser printer (laser printers are very economical considering the excellent output quality). Including your email address on the business card is a personal choice. If you do, think twice about including an email address that someone might question why anyone in business would choose an email address like that. Your business card could include a summary of the services you offer in small print.

   This is possibly one of your better opportunities to pursue especially if your job-specific technical skills are either not at the highest level or not fully up to date with recent developments. This type of skills set will probably find its best fit in the small- and medium-sized companies where the candidates have relevant industry and key-application-type experience.

   In the fast-growth-type segment of these companies, many may have situations where the majority of their IT employees are not that experienced. Hiring someone who has had several years of experience that the inexperienced IT employee needs to have can be a good investment. The key is locating a grouping of this type of organization within your preferred geographic area and gaining an audience with IT management to discuss their individual situations.

Locating the database of referenceUSA will help you identify companies to target and in conjunction with the necessary research will help prepare you to make effective telephone and/or letter queries into the identified organizations.

3. Marketing yourself as a consultant has multiple possibilities. For example, if you have any employee or end user training experience coupled with significant project participation or management experience, this can appeal to a young, high-growth company where most IT employees do not have significant experience working on important projects. If in your queries, you discover any type of need similar to this and you have this experience and skill, presented and proposed effectively, this situation alone could gain you a work contract.

Individuals who are experienced in working with web or network security applications as well as individuals who are qualified to work with Linux open-source-related projects are in demand. Marketing these types of capabilities individually or, even better, in conjunction with other candidates who have relevant industry-specific functional application experience, offers a potential opportunity. If you are not comfortable with your telephone or letter-writing prospecting abilities, and you have some of the capabilities mentioned in this section, look into the smaller IT consulting firms, applications services providers, and staffing companies as a potential source of contract-type work.

If a significant amount of your IT career experience has been associated with routine, process-type repetitive work of the type that has or is being commoditized for outsourcing, the author proposes in this section a more creative type of approach that capitalizes upon your business-process-related and personal-soft-type skills. For companies that outsource these types of needs, the routine, process-type work can present significant risks and efficiency-deteriorating end results if the work plan and its communication and follow-through are not properly managed. If a candidate has good and reasonably up-to-date technical skills with the commitment to further improve them, coupled with good people and other relevant soft skills as well as good understanding of a company's or industry's primary business practices and customers' related priorities, he or she has potential value to organizations. The primary problem is locating the companies that have these types of needs and gaining a personal audience with IT management.

IT professionals with 20 plus years of tenure today will rarely find a significant quantity of the right type of job matches via the web job-posting services unless their skills and experience are very close to the job specifications.

Creative marketing activities similar to what is being suggested throughout this chapter are potentially the best alternative for job hunting for those who have expended significant previous effort without achieving the desired results as well as those candidates who are just beginning their job-hunting efforts.

The type of targeted, specialized approach suggested here must be well researched and focus upon offering creative-type alternatives that are not pursued by the vast majority of IT candidates presently involved in job hunting. Worked effectively, this type of approach has the potential for most candidates to provide significantly better comparative results than other methods; consequently, its end result is much more professional, which in most cases will improve the overall effectiveness of IT employees in the job-hunting process.

4. If you have not, you should also review the listings of the government, healthcare, and education job listings in your area, all projected high job growth areas.

If you find any of the previous suggestions of interest, you will need a step-by-step approach similar to the following one to use.

1. Review the situations that apply to you.
2. Develop a revised skills profile making improvements where possible.
3. Upgrade the content of your résumé to capitalize on the nontechnical and industry-specific, functional application, and multidiscipline IT capabilities.
4. After completing analysis of your best potential sources of employment for contact, research them and initiate contact.
5. After using telephone contact or query letters and gaining appointments, complete significant prior research. This is of critical importance prior to participation in any type of meeting or interview.
6. For each meeting, have either a formal marketing proposal prepared for discussion or a summary of relevant project experience to serve as a discussion item.
7. At the conclusion of each appointment, gain approval to submit a proposal, more discussion, or a formal job interview whichever in your judgment is the best next step that will lead to a formal job offer or some type of work contract.

All of a candidate's efforts expended toward job finding do not have much value if the candidate is unable to schedule a significant number of interviews with potential employers. For those who are having difficulty with this part of job hunting, it is appropriate to assess what you have been doing from a value perspective. The best way to do this is to complete an objective critical assessment of what you have been doing up to this point.

1. If the majority of your effort has been focused upon résumé posting on job-posting-type services and applying for jobs of interest posted on these sites, the following possibilities exist.

- Your skills and experience as presented in your résumé are not consistent with the job descriptions posted for the majority of jobs.
- If most of your applications to posted jobs have been done more than one week after the job was initially posted, the majority of candidates in which the employer is interested, have already been contacted. Unless your skills and experience are at the top level and are a good match for the specification in most situations, it is doubtful that you will be contacted.
- Your résumé is not impressive enough to warrant consideration, and most of its distribution has possibly been to the wrong places or those of questionable value relative to your qualifications.

2. Your strategy for targeting prospective employers requires improvement and you need to consider the fact that web job-posting sites may not be the best sources of potential employers for you.

- You could be better served by better analysis and research regarding your potential sources of contact.
- If, in your assessment of your résumé, you were able to identify significant opportunities for improvement, this in itself infers that you may have been better served directing your efforts to different sources. Review of the potential sources discussed in Chapter 8 may identify some potential more productive use of your time than your previous methods. As a minimum, this is worth testing.

EMPLOYER RESEARCH AND INITIAL CONTACT STRATEGIES

If you have expended considerable effort in job search and have not achieved the type of response desired regarding potential interest, a basic question of importance is, How comprehensive has your research been for any situations of interest where you were able to identify the hiring company? If your job search activity has been primarily focused upon the web, there have probably been very few if any situations where research has been a factor. What this is probably telling you is that you need to seek out more situations where research is important and you have applied significant effort into researching the prospective employer. It is a simple fact that the more you understand about a particular organization or company in which you are trying to generate interest in you, the better prepared you are, the more likely the quality of your contact effort and its effectiveness is going to be.

In most situations where IT job candidates are not accomplishing anything significant, this is primarily a function of the quality of their search activities, not the quantity. If candidates will focus upon as few as ten situations where they have targeted query activity and concentrate on contact-type activities that are focused upon determining the needs of organizations, they will have the key to developing alternative approaches and proposals that lead to meetings, interviews, and employment and/or contracts. This is most likely to occur in small- and medium-sized growth-type companies. In most situations, the more that a candidate can learn about an organization and its needs, the more likely an IT manager is willing to consider talking to that candidate.

In some situations, arranging an appointment when you are able to gain a brief phone conversation with an IT manager is nothing more than asking, "When can I come in to talk with you for a few minutes to discuss your challenges and needs? It will not take that long, and I commit to you that it will not be a waste of your time." Or in some situations a candidate may favor saying something like "I have done a lot of research on your company and I have several ideas that I would like to review with you at your convenience. They may offer some potential benefit to you." If the manager asks something to the effect of what you are thinking about, say that it will only take a few minutes of his or her time and mention that you have prepared some material that you would like to show the manager. Then ask, "When is the best time for you within the next few days that you can give me a few minutes?" This type of discussion infers preparation of some type of presentation for discussion. A two- or three-page PowerPoint-type concept presentation focused upon opportunity needs analysis is a good concept for consideration.

The concept in this situation is that you are an experienced, available resource and whether an employer's internal IT needs are employee training, project management or other work-process-related enhancements, better end user functional customer relationships, or things such as investigating the feasibility of new technology-related interests. Opening up a discussion putting yourself in the role of a potential resource is the type of thing that can lead the employer to offer you a formal work proposal.

If a candidate has good report writing skills, verbal communication, and end user discussion skills, situations like this also present a good opportunity to propose another type of alternative that may represent a better alternative in situations where the employer is not responding favorably or the candidate is not comfortable making this type of proposal.

The author personally has had significant success proposing a limited type of consulting assignment for a duration of somewhere between 2 and 5 days of work depending upon the proposed scope of the assignment. You too can propose to complete a 1- or 2-day work assignment, for example, to complete an IT needs analysis survey that will identify the primary opportunities and needs for improving the overall efficiency of the IT department.

This type of consulting work can be performed for as few as 2 days— one to interview key IT employees and the other for writing the report and review with the manager. If the IT manager is receptive to this type of short-term assignment and it generates interest, they may indicate that they do not believe 2 days is adequate time, to which you respond that it may take 3 or 4 days but doubtfully more than 5 days.

The next question may involve cost. One thousand dollars per day is a reasonable rate. If the potential client says that it is too much, simply say that you are willing to negotiate this, but, more importantly, ask, "What would be the type of things that you would like to have me review?"

At this point, it is a good idea to take notes for further questions if any clarification is needed. After the potential clients review several of these things, the next question you need to ask is, "With whom should I talk in IT to gain the best understanding of important needs?" Then you need to say, "First if we work this out, I would interview you to gain your perspective and then schedule interviews with the employees with whom you want me to talk. Each interview would probably require between 30 and 45 minutes. In advance, you should send out a brief communication to those selected advising them of the purpose and that I will be contacting them to schedule an appointment."

Most of the opportunity identification/needs analysis projects that the author has done were for a 5-day duration. One that focused upon marketing and sales management in a $50 million supplier of data communication network-related products, network installation, and related software lasted for more than a year. The thing that makes this type of thing work is that a 4- or 5-day commitment is not that financially significant. An important aspect is your ability to convince the customer that you are a qualified resource with an outside objective approach and that you have the potential to develop an understanding of some important items that the IT department possibly does not have time to study.

When your work is successful and provides the right type of value, it will usually set up the possibility of definition of future actions that are desirable to consider for implementation. In many cases, this will be the type of thing that can lead to additional project-type work, and it has not cost the client any significant dollar amount to understand your potential value.

These analyses can go wrong if they are presented as an audit of present practices, which is often threatening to employees and interferes with their ability to cooperate. This type of thing is best presented as an opportunity-type analysis to identify additional support or capabilities that can help the IT department become more effective. This type of project does not ever focus upon individuals and their work but instead on important needs that are not being properly met at the time and that represent the best opportunities for improving the department's services to its clients.

In some situations, IT management may want the candidate to meet with other key employees in other departments that IT serves to better understand their perspective regarding support needs or desired improvements. This is another possibility for proposals for candidates who have good verbal, interviewing, and listening skills and good experience with end-user-type applications and other business practices. This type of situation would present significant opportunity where a candidate has a significant number of years of experience in a particular industry and is pursuing the potential of employment or consulting within small- and medium-sized companies in that same industry.

Taking the mystery out of these types of assignments by doing a few will expand the possibilities for employment or income via consulting for experienced IT professionals who are having difficulty finding employment. After successfully completing a couple of these consulting assignments, the experience gained will not only serve to improve the candidate's personal business effectiveness but will also from a creative standpoint serve to identify other potential opportunities related to this type of work to which the candidate had not had any previous relevant exposure.

YOUR PERSONAL SITUATION ASSESSMENT

At this point of your search, depending upon the degree of success you have experienced, the material in the first part of this chapter should have identified several additional possibilities for whatever situation you choose to pursue. This section will review additional possibilities that will assist you in determining what job-hunting strategies and approaches are best for you.

Two basic questions of relevance at this point are

1. Where could your services be potentially most valuable today? It is a good idea to write a summary paragraph describing what you believe to be the best answer to this question.
2. What are the potential hiring sources where you are most likely to find opportunities similar to what you have defined?

Providing some detailed thought to these two questions can be of considerable value to job candidates. This can be especially valuable to all IT job candidates who are having significant difficulty with their search activities and do not believe that they are accomplishing anything of significance.

Depending upon your personal situation, you may choose to pursue multiple new approaches outlined in this chapter directed to some of the potential hiring sources discussed in Chapter 8. Concurrently, you may want to continue posting your résumé to selected job-posting service sites identified in this chapter. This choice may be a good idea specifically for those who have made significant changes to their former résumés and who want to test two or three different versions by applying to web-posted positions.

If you believe that you could potentially receive improved results from telephone or letter queries, you also should consider alternative strategies of contact. There are all types of potential situations that may be appropriate to test. If you were able to gain access to the referanceUSA database, you will be able to focus upon selected industries and organizations with variable revenue and employee size as well as those with credit ratings in the good, very good to excellent range, which is important to job hunters, especially those who are interested in pursuing the possibility of independent consulting work.

Many job candidates think that applying some of the personal strategies associated with telephone and letter queries to preresearched and selected organizations takes too much time. They also believe that it is somewhat more intimidating mentally because it seems quite difficult.

The primary advantage in putting effort into these types of alternatives is that the competition you are facing primarily comes from your own personal attitude. In the vast majority of situations where you are able to make contact, you will rarely face competition from other candidates. Compare these possibilities to posting your résumé and applying to jobs posted in the web services. For some candidates, after résumé improvement and identification of new potential sources to contact, web résumé posting and application may still be the first strategy to try primarily because it takes much less time.

In many cases where IT professionals who have been unemployed for significant periods of time and who have not given up on job hunting consider using some new approaches, one of the most significant problems that they must deal with is their own personal attitude. This is critical because most of those candidates who are in this situation are aware of the many frustrations associated with extensive job-hunting effort and know all too well what can go wrong.

If those in this category are motivated to try some new approaches, they must improve their daily attitudes by improving their self-discipline so that they stick with the new strategy and do not slip back into the old habit of making excuses, which tends to buffer the lack of success that they had achieved. This is human nature for most of us, and in trying new approaches there will be failures, but the proper attitude is to discipline yourself to be more effective in the next opportunity. Marketing yourself in new ways is not easy for anyone because to most it represents threatening types of changes that are usually not familiar and comfortable.

When job hunting, you must keep one critical thing in your mind: what to do and how to do it to win. This chapter provides numerous possibilities for all IT job candidates to consider using, and if used, they will help the majority of IT job candidates achieve improved results when compared to their previous approaches and methods. What is presented in this chapter are numerous proactive personalized approaches that today are not practiced by more than an estimated 10% of all current IT job hunters.

RÉSUMÉ DISTRIBUTION

Other than the posting of your résumé on the web job-posting service sites and applying to specific web-listed jobs, the remainder of résumé distribution should primarily be to prospective employer's who have requested it.

The other exceptions are mailing it to search firms that you have identified. The Kennedy Directory is one of the better sources for identifying these firms because Kennedy has been publishing this directory many years and it is their primary business. Mailing your résumé to selected firms would represent another potential test.

If your annual income has been at the level of $80,000 and below and you choose to make résumé distribution to search firms, your résumé should be directed to contingency search firms. Many will have the capability to post your résumé on their own web sites. If your annual income goals are at the level of $80,000 and above, you should concentrate your résumé posting or distribution to retained search firms. In contacting search firms, be sure to post your résumé with Management Recruiter's International, which has approximately 300 offices throughout the United States and, for the most part, does contingency work. However, in some cases, they have contracts representing multiple job placements to fill for employers.

If you decide to test different résumé formats with some of the additional potential employment sources listed in Chapter 8, this is another situation where you may want to consider résumé distribution, if you have not previously contacted the employer.

Cover Letters

This subject was previously reviewed at the end of Chapter 6 relative to its relationship to résumé writing. It is discussed in more detail in this section because of its importance in relationship to résumé distribution.

Cover letters are a primary subject of some job-hunting publications, but it is a relatively simple item when compared to the most important steps of the job-hunting process. Cover letters are necessary when mailing your résumé, and their content serves as the message that you want to provide when posting your résumé in response to a web-posted job.

A cover letter should never be as long as a full one-page letter. Having over the years reviewed hundreds of cover letters of more that one page in length, the author's reaction to these letters is: If the content is important enough to the applicant to justify a full page or more, then the perceived content of importance that makes the letter so long should be somewhere in the résumé.

The majority of cover letters are wisely never more than two or three short paragraphs. The letter heading should include your name, address, phone number, and the date. Whenever possible, the letter should be directed to a specific individual in the organization. It only takes a minute or two to call and identify to whom the letter should be directed and to confirm the name spelling, job title, and address if this information is not included in the job posting data.

The reason why it is necessary to provide full personal contact data in the heading is that cover letters get separated from an individual's résumé. It is the applicant's personal choice whether or not to include your email address. It is a good question whether or not you should include it if it suggests any type of thing that would concern conservative human resource individuals to question aspects of your personality. The reason that human resources is mentioned is because when you apply to most organizations, your résumé is most likely to be routed to their human resources or employment section.

Your initial opening paragraph should respond to or identify a specific situation that will indicate the purpose for sending the letter or posting your résumé online. Types of possibilities follow:

My résumé is forwarded for consideration as an applicant for the database administration position that you advertised in the June 10th edition of the *Louisville Courier*.

My overall technical and previous job experience appear to meet the majority of the requirements listed in the ad. I have researched your company comprehensively and believe that I can make the type of contributions in the position that is desired.

I appreciate the opportunity to be considered for discussion as a potential candidate to be interviewed and have enclosed my résumé for review. I will plan to follow up with you regarding this opportunity within the next several days.

Sincerely,

Ruth M. Clausen

My résumé is posted in response to your August 25th posting of job code # 120 in Career Builder.

My skills, experience, and overall qualifications appear to be a good match for the job specification. Additionally my interpersonal skills, project participation and end user marketing application work within the financial services industry is a personal strength.

I look forward to the potential opportunity to be considered for contact regarding this opportunity.

Sincerely,

Stanley R. Jones

In situations where the candidate is taking the initiative to contact potential employers when not responding to a specific ad or online job posting, it is directed to the company senior IT manager.

I am taking this opportunity to contact you regarding potential consideration as an IT software writer who has experience working with web and network security and other functional applications within the federal contractor business.

In addition to having a security clearance, my skills are of current relevance, and I am willing to consider the possibility of limited-term contract work. In addition, I have strong project participation and good interpersonal skills. Enclosed is my résumé.

I will plan to follow up with you soon to discuss the possibility of scheduling a meeting with you to discuss alternatives regarding how my services might be utilized beneficially by your organization.

Sincerely,

Robert L. Smith

The main thing to remember in writing relevant cover letters is that cover letters are more effective when you have researched the potential hiring organization and as a candidate you can tie your skills and total qualifications specifically to several of the requirements listed in the job specification.

When you decide to send your résumé in an effort to generate potential interest in yourself, where possible complete prior detailed research. You also need to tie your skills and overall experience to the specialized nature of the IT work that the firm is doing. When you can do this in query letters and cover letters, your chances for achieving an audience with IT management will be enhanced. By obtaining internal publication copies of the organization and reviewing their web site and other media sources, you may be able to identify several items that, when incorporated in your cover letters, will distinguish you as being somewhat unique compared to the majority of others who submit their résumés.

The point made here is that most résumés and cover letters sent without significant prior research do not get considered in the majority of situations when candidates are making mass-type mailings. The question here is, Why go to the time, effort, and expense of sending them if you are not able to make them appear more professional and relevant than most others that they receive?

STRATEGIES FOR GETTING INTERVIEWS

Alternatives to Pursue and Test

This section is a summary of previously discussed concepts that review several alternative approaches for IT job candidates who think that one or more of these approaches may be relevant. For anyone who is having job search difficulty, it is recommended that you consider testing several of these options concurrently to determine which ones seem to have the most potential for your personal situation.

It is doubtful that any of these alternatives can significantly improve job search results unless they are accompanied by revised, improved résumés and significant research of companies to target followed up with detailed research to understand the business of the targeted companies as much as possible. In the last step, effective telephone or letter query contact with the goal of scheduling an appointment for a meeting with the senior IT manager of the organization is also vital.

This all sounds like a lot of effort, but it is not after a candidate goes through several situations and becomes familiar with the steps included. This type of contact takes effort, but it is quality and uniqueness oriented, which in most cases appears to hiring decision makers as a much more professional type effort by job candidates than they normally see. Several possibilities to test follow.

Alternative Candidate Strategies That Can Lead to Initial Meetings with IT Management

This section has potential techniques for all IT job candidates having difficulty obtaining interviews.

The potential merits of proposing things such as being given an assignment to be tested, employment on a trial basis without recourse if not successful, or a short-term project or a limited-term contract basis can open up the consideration for permanent hiring.

In order to arrange this type of meeting, candidates should make either a phone call or letter query stating that they have thoroughly researched the organization, have relevant IT job experience, and would like to schedule an appointment for a few minutes to propose some alternatives that may be relevant to the IT department.

In this type of short meeting, candidates should prepare a brief summary of their skills and experience. They should state their objectives and then ask to spend a few minutes with the IT manager to review the department's priorities and needs for new things that the manager may want to pursue or existing things that he or she would like to improve.

You could then say, "Based upon this discussion and if you are interested in any employee input or from end user internal clients, with your approval I could spend a few minutes with several individuals you designate and then come to you with a proposal for possible alternatives for you to consider resulting from these discussions. What do I have to do to convince you to give this a try?"

Researching Companies for Contact

After locating a source for the referenceUSA database, which can be found in most college and university libraries and state employment assistance offices, identify all companies within reasonable travel range from your home base and apply your choice of following criteria: industry designation, annual revenue, number of employees, and employers having credit ratings from good to excellent. Many of the companies in this database will list the senior IT executives title and other data such as addresses and phone numbers.

For example, if you identified 125 companies within a 50-mile radius of your home base in two industries where you have significant industry practices and application experience, why not consider contacting them with a postage prepaid return survey card. You would send them all a short cover letter introducing yourself as a potential resource with x years of application development work related to the x industry and explaining that you are interested in learning of any potential needs that they would like to explore.

For example, by this time you may have a network of associates and with one or two of them and your own job experience you may cover most of the important IT disciplines that are popular today. Beyond applications software engineering for the particular industry, you may also have experience with things like network and internet security, voice over internet protocol, and open source work with Linux and MySQL.

Other potential things to survey would be improvement of things such as primary applications for sales, marketing, finance, customer service, and other industry-specific applications of importance. Simply ask the respondent to check items of potential interest and to write at the bottom of the return card any additional items of interest as well as their names, company names, and phone numbers. You should also prenumber the front of the reply cards with the respondent's address in case you are unable to determine the name of the company replying.

If you try something like this, professionally done, it is not unusual to receive a return response as high as 20% of those individuals contacted. The key to achieving this return is that everything must be done professionally. You need to confirm correct name and title spelling and address in advance. Form letters are unprofessional and usually get treated as such. A personal letter with a brief explanation including a simple return reply card with relevant subjects will get results.

Having once used the method described to survey the 5,000 customer base of a technology company for which the author was responsible, the organization received an initial return of 92% of all reply cards. A second follow-up letter with another survey card and a cover letter requesting that the recipient's opinion regarding five basic area of services provided these customers moved the return rate up to 97% of all customers. Each time the cover letters were completed and personalized to the customer employee in charge of services, and the author personally signed each letter.

Officials in companies rarely get personal letters regarding subjects of this nature. They usually receive form letters, which are immediately discarded a high percentage of the time, and, in most cases, they never see them. This is just another type of marketing approach that, when professionally completed and followed up, can lead to contract or consulting work.

In any situations where individuals have good networks of capable IT talent available and where response to the survey was good, the originator might serve as a project manager in order that more than one project may be handled concurrently.

If your search efforts to date have not yielded anything of significance, this type of thing, properly worked, could lead to the establishment of a small consulting organization made up of IT professionals contracting with the originator. There is no doubt that there is more than enough IT talent available today in most metropolitan areas to start several small organizations of this type.

Proposing an Opportunity/Needs Analysis

Proposals of this type can have potential as projects where IT management wants to make significant department improvements and does not have the time or resources to get into an opportunity/needs analysis. In busy companies today, most managers have a full-time job accomplishing their basic responsibilities, and many do not have the employee resources that they need.

In a telephone or letter query to an IT manager in situations where you have as thoroughly as possible researched the company, relate that you have significant industry practices and IT applications and other key IT discipline experience within your industry. You need to explain that you are a resource that may be able to assist the IT manager with some of his or her priority needs and that you would like to schedule a meeting for a few minutes at a convenient time to discuss any potential possibilities. If, in an initial phone conversation or a follow up to a query letter, the IT official says that he or she doesn't believe that they have a need for your services, respond by explaining that it will only cost the manager a few minutes to compare notes because you probably have a significant amount of common experience. The key in situations such as this is to move forward to a meeting. Once that is granted, it is up to you to be properly prepared at this meeting to get the manager to open up to discussion of possibilities for which the candidate can complete some type of work proposal.

Again situations like this may seem threatening to many candidates, but for those for which the employment outlook is not that promising, these are the types of things that you need to try that can lead to sources of income and eventual jobs.

Potential Job Sources Not Previously Contacted

When you have reassessed your skills, completed a skills profile, reviewed your résumé for improvement, and incorporated improvements, does this work present the possibility of new sources of potential jobs for contact? It should in the majority of situations. While testing the potential value of new résumé alternatives coupled with better selection of web-posted jobs, you should also review the alternative potential job sources listed in Chapter 9 for contact.

If you have strong soft skills that serve you well in project team and end user client work as well as good skills in industry-specific IT work and functional disciplines such as sales, marketing, finance, engineering, customer service, other physical sciences, or the supply chain, including these type of things in your résumé can enhance your potential for jobs in IT and management consulting firms, application services providers, and CRM software development companies.

If you have a combination of the mentioned experience in conjunction with good technical skills, analysis of the type of work that these organizations specialize in can result in additional potential sources of jobs for you to pursue.

Higher Growth IT Job Employers

As previously mentioned, IT employment in the government, education, and healthcare professions is projected to be the fastest job growth in the IT professions between now and 2007 with an average composite annual growth of approximately 12%. If you have not considered any of these sources as potential prospects, you should include them in your prospecting.

The advantage that many IT professionals with significant years of experience have compared to many of the IT employees already in these organizational designations is that they have significant experience with the same type of IT work in which these organizations are currently involved. Many of the organizations in these categories are currently behind in the application of the latest IT technology and now need to catch up, which is one of the primary reasons for the significant IT job increases.

IT Research Work

In your potential employer contact work, don't overlook the possibility of doing IT research work for a company. Many organizations want to consider the possibility of acquiring new technology and applications software that they or other functional managers within their company think may have the potential to add significant value to their organization. In companies that are busy and where many are behind schedule, they don't have the time or resources to do thorough research on the possibilities of interest.

Opening up the possibility that you can serve as a potential resource to do research work of this type in meetings or query letters is another possible alternative to consider. This type of work can serve as a source of income while you are pursuing other alternatives. In some cases, where your work is highly regarded and you fit in well with their organization, you could have the opportunity to join the organization initially serving as project manager to implement the new technology and applications that you researched.

In all organizational situations where organizations are supplying products or services to end users, their clients, or customers, these organizations can learn more than 90% of what they need to know by surveying some of their most knowledgeable customers as well as their top-performing sales and service employees who are working with these customers every day.

This type of situation also exists within companies' IT organizations. By conducting interviews with their internal clients who have the responsibility for working with their end user customers for their products and services, they can learn of the majority of needs that can improve internal efficiencies, which often can also improve the services that are provided their end user customers. Where situations like this exist and things such as cost savings and internal productivity related to key business processes can be achieved, these are the types of things, when addressed, that can lead to consulting or project-type work for job candidates.

These types of things represent the creative-type application of IT professionals work skills and overall qualifications. Experience with this type of work can provide IT professionals with valuable experience where they gain a comprehensive understanding of some of the better applications of IT technology where many organizations today have similar needs.

Using Query Letters

Query letters are best used in conjunction with a database such as the infoUSA product reviewed in the last section of Chapter 9. The advantage of using the query letter approach is that, for any employer interest generated, candidates will not experience any degree of significant competition from other applicants as compared to résumé posting on the web job sites.

The subject of query letters received significant mention earlier in this chapter. In many situations, it is more effective than sending your résumé. When an organization reviews your résumé, it is much easier for them to say that your skills and experience are not a good match for their job. This is especially predictable in situations where the potential employer is known and applicants have not done a thorough job of researching the company prior to sending their résumés.

In many of these situations, a résumé and accompanying cover letter could have represented a much better presentation of an applicant's potential had the applicant done the research and taken the time to tailor the résumé and cover letter making them as relevant as possible to the hiring organization.

Sending query letters to organizations that the candidate has properly researched can have significant advantages compared to the mailing of résumés. The résumé, in the vast majority of situations, gets discarded or filed because most of the time preliminary judgments are made that the candidate's skills and overall qualifications do not fit their needs. In most situations, this occurs because the résumé and cover letter were not tailored to the organization's business and often were not well written.

A well-written query will show some understanding of an organization's business and suggests that the writer may have significant relevant experience and skill and be a potential resource to help the subject IT organization achieve its priorities and future plans. Oftentimes queries of this type will pose some degree of curiosity on the part of the IT manager.

The previous paragraph is a fairly simple statement of the content of a query letter and what it needs to accomplish. Written professionally with the correct name, spelling, and title of the recipient, prepared on a PC, duplicated on a high-quality/resolution laser printer on quality, business proposal-type 24 lb bond paper with the candidates personal information professionally PC prepared at the top of the letter is a simple and not that expensive method of generating and mailing between 50 and 100 of these queries. If professionally prepared with an impressive message, followed by phone follow-up within the first week of mailing, it is reasonable to expect to be able to schedule meetings for as much as 10% of these queries.

If you are not confident about your ability to effectively do this, try sending 10 query letters. In most situations, you will get the experience you need to develop the necessary effectiveness for a larger scale mailing. It should be possible to schedule meetings in a minimum of 10% of situations. Consider that web résumé postings on the online job service sites are estimated to average not more than 2% positive responses.

In this situation, of course, your personal effectiveness and getting the follow-up phone conversation is important. In many situations, you may be talking with the IT manager's assistant or leaving voice mail messages. All that you are asking for initially is a good time to call to have a short discussion regarding the letter you sent.

In situations where you achieve the discussion, you must try immediately to schedule a brief meeting to review some concepts relating to IT challenges today. In situations where you have relevant industry knowledge and experience, mention this. Stress that the meeting will not take that long, emphasize that you will not waste the IT manager's time and will come early, late, or any other time of day, whichever is most convenient. Then ask when would be the most convenient time and date to meet.

When you are successful in scheduling these meetings, take along several presentation-style one-page sheets with bold print and a larger font. Each separate page should cover a different subject with the subject heading and five to eight subpoints of relevance on the same page. The type of subjects could be a newer technology research project, an internal IT employee and internal end user needs survey, a 2- or 3-day opportunity/ needs analysis, a summary schedule of IT work for which you are qualified to contract, studies of subjects such as feasibility of moving into open source software, a feasibility study of implementing voice over internet protocol phone services, and a project plan for a priority business practices-related project. These are a few examples, and you might have six or seven alternatives with you that you are most comfortable discussing as related to your experience and skills.

Early on in the discussion, you might begin by reviewing a sheet listing newer and evolving technologies such as security, wireless, open source software, VoIP, and CRM software. This could serve to lead to areas that are a priority need of each individual manager with whom you talk. Be prepared with several presentation or discussion sheets. You would use those sheets most consistent with the individual's needs, which could lead into the possibility of discussion then or at a later time regarding the potential of an assignment.

If you achieve this, ask whether there any specific items that you could prepare to discuss at your next meeting? In this type of meeting, you are participating in the consultative selling process, which is simply establishing and understanding client needs and recommending the specific change-related alternative solutions that have the potential to best serve the needs.

At the end of these meetings, you may be asked for a copy of your résumé as well as a business card.

Other Potential Query Letter Themes

For software engineers who have an understanding of Linux and Unix and who could do work in the open source area, this is the subject of a powerful query today, especially in manufacturing, engineering, and other technology-type organizations. Most larger organizations are probably addressing the subject, but many of the medium-sized ones can be identified via the referenceUSA database will have interest but will not have moved forward. This is logically an area of potential opportunity where you have same industry-type previous experience in the relevant disciplines. Unix for many years has also had a significant presence in large financial organizations where large volumes of numerical analysis and processing are completed daily in brokerage, banking, and insurance actuarial applications.

Send a query letter similar to this:

If you have need for a software engineer who has x years of experience working within the x industry who has the skills and necessary understanding to do open source software work, I would appreciate the opportunity to talk with you.

I will plan to follow up with you regarding this subject next week.

In follow-up discussions with those who do not have current interest, ask if they know of any IT managers within their network who are interested in this subject.

Test a simple query such as the following.

I am currently searching for employment as a programmer/analyst and have up-to-date skills and experience working with most of the popular languages. I am willing to consider initial work as a consultant or for project work on a contract basis cancelable at any time that you are not satisfied with the quality of my work. I will plan to follow up with you soon.

Some candidates who are having difficulty finding work, may be comfortable with a simple query such as this. If you have researched the company and have application experience within the same industry, this is an added point and may stimulate management interest in talking with you further.

A short simple query with an attached one-page summary of technical, project, applications, and industry-specific experience listing soft skills of this type could generate interest.

If you are currently experiencing challenges getting where you want to be within your organization, I would like to be considered as a potential resource to help with this. Attached is a summary of my background and qualifications. I will plan to follow up with you soon to learn of any potential possibilities.

This next type of approach is different than most.

I have comprehensively researched your company and have gained as much understanding as possible regarding the job description for your quality assurance position. I believe that I have the experience and skills required for this position. Who would I have to convince or what would I need to do in order to qualify for a personal interview? I am willing to complete some type of assignment if necessary to achieve this.

This is a type of open-ended, direct query and in situations where a candidate is able to identify the employer and then quickly research them and learn as much as possible about the job, go for the interview. If a candidate has posted a significant number of résumés and applied for job interview consideration without much success, this type of direct approach may provide comparatively better results.

Scores of different concepts and approaches have been discussed in this chapter. The main point is that one or several of them may help you achieve better results gaining personal interviews than what you have previously been doing. You may benefit from trying out several of the concepts that you think may be appropriate for you and with which you are most comfortable. As a minimum, the experience that you will gain in trying several of these approaches will help you become more effective in your job hunting and will help you identify additional new ideas and approaches.

11. Success in Interviewing

The Objective of This Chapter

During periods of tight job markets where there is significant competition for the available jobs, the author believes that the reasons that jobs are not won at least 50% of the time can be traced to inadequate or improper preparation for interviews. He believes that in the IT profession today the competition for available jobs will remain intense indefinitely.

This chapter's purpose is to address every aspect of the process associated with successful interviewing so that candidates will be properly prepared for the interview as well as for the majority of the possibilities that can occur doing interviews so that they will be prepared to win. The author further believes that proper preparation for interviews is necessary if candidates are to perform effectively during interviews and to put themselves in a position to be seriously considered for a job.

PRIOR PREPARATION

Throughout this chapter many components that are related to all aspects of interviews will be covered. The author believes that every important aspect of interviewing is related to the Three Ps.

The Three Ps: Planning, Preparation, and Performance

Planning is the candidate's checklist for winning. It is a simple handwritten or PC-prepared worksheet to ensure coverage and awareness of almost every situation or aspect related to interviews that can occur. The author is confident that every candidate who is properly prepared going into an interview will be more self-assured and will perform more effectively than if he or she were not prepared. He further believes that losing in interviews is usually a culmination of things primarily the result of inadequate or improper preparation. This is really unfortunate when an extra day of effort in most situations may have been all that was needed to move further toward a job offer. In most of these situations, the candidate hears things like "We are going to look further" or "We don't think your qualifications are the right fit for this job." In many cases, however, the candidate does not receive feedback.

When a candidate loses out because of inadequate or improper preparation, this is really a shame. When considering all of the prior personal effort associated with job hunting, the candidate who has secured an interview has achieved the most difficult thing to achieve, next to winning the job. The key components associated with planning will be covered in detail later in the chapter.

The primary value of planning is that it is the overall strategy for winning the job based upon all the important aspects of preparation prior to the interview. If a job candidate has not made the necessary effective effort to be prepared on a minimum of the most important aspects related to the interview, a plan is not that meaningful. The culmination of candidate errors, primarily lack of awareness, is why most candidates do not win jobs once they have achieved interviews. Employers sometimes make mistakes, but most of the time it is correct to assume that once a potential employer has scheduled a candidate for a personal interview, either as a function of reviewing a résumé, a query letter, or a phone conversation, that the candidate is qualified to be considered for employment. This assumption is even more accurate in situations where the candidate has generated the interest through a query letter or telephone conversation. The candidate has already done a significant amount of effective selling of him- or herself in order to achieve the interview.

Proper preparation is primarily a function of prior research and personal items for awareness. The actual interview itself is based upon technique and personal effectiveness in handling questions and responding in a winning way to any important situations that may occur. This chapter will help provide awareness of and potential situational responses to these types of challenges.

Personal performance during the interview is primarily a function of your personal effectiveness in response to any concerns or potential issues that occur.

The Employer's Primary Reasons for Scheduling Job Interviews

Whenever possible it is important to understand the employer's situation and the job for which you are interviewing. This is not an easy task, but by asking appropriate questions while the interview is being scheduled or during other research, it is possible to gain some degree of insight into the situation. This understanding is important because the more you know in advance, the better you can prepare and have a more relevant strategy to apply during the interview. This approach is far better than not understanding anything about the reasons for the interview.

The primary reasons for the interview from the employer's perspective will be related to one or more of these situations.

- They have an immediate need to replace an employee who is leaving.
- They are significantly behind schedule on important projects.

- They realize that they need some different skill sets than what they presently have.
- They have been thinking about adding an IT employee as a result of growth or need.
- They want to talk with you, even though they were not presently looking, because either your résumé, phone call, or query letter generated interest.
- They are screening potential candidates for a job opening.
- They want to compare outside talent to internal talent for a certain position.

The best situation of all of these is where your personal phone call or query letter has generated the interest in talking with you. In these situations, you may win a job without ever having any potential competition, which is any candidate's best opportunity in situations where the job is a good match for an applicant's skills and experience.

At the outset, you need to understand as much as possible about the actual situation relative to how you handle yourself for maximum effectiveness during the interview. It is also important that you not develop any expectations that are not realistic.

For example, if you are competing with other candidates in a screening situation, which may be in person or in some situations initially a phone conversation, the background of the interviewer usually will determine the content of the interview. An IT employee will primarily be interested in what kind of skills, and experience you have and whether or not they believe you are qualified for further consideration, while a human resources employee without significant IT experience will in most cases concentrate on what type of a person they believe you are and how they think you may fit in with the chemistry and culture of the organization. The interview with the human resources employee will be much more subjective and will require a totally different strategy, which is discussed later in this chapter. What type of interview can you expect? This is somewhat dependent on the job responsibility of the people who interview you.

Interviewer's Backgrounds

The Screening Interview

The screening interview may happen over the phone or in person. In this situation, the candidate needs to make a strong positive impression. The purpose of the screening interview is to eliminate job candidates from a group. Those doing the screening from IT will usually want to discuss a candidate's skills and experience to determine if there is a potential fit relative to their needs. They may choose to discuss the type of work a candidate has done and at the same time try to determine the candidate's level of understanding and skills. In this situation, it is important that the candidate, whenever possible, be well prepared by obtaining a job description or being able to discuss in detail the type of work that they have done. If the candidate is able to gain a copy in advance of some type of job specification or description, he or she can tailor responses with some degree of relevance. Any advance understanding of the company's business that can be gained through the various media sources will also help establish that the candidate spent some time in research, and it may help open up the discussion to potentially valuable information that would not be normally discussed in a screening interview.

If the screening interviewer is a member of the human resources staff, a candidate can expect a more general interview with more open-ended questions. The interviewer during the interview will be trying to determine what type of person a candidate is and how he or she will fit into the organization's culture and chemistry. These assessments will be more value judgements so that if a candidate is primarily prepared for an IT skills and experience interview, this type of general, open-ended interview can prove troublesome. Again in this situation everything that a candidate can learn about the company or organization prior to the interview is important. The ability to work in project teams and groups as a contributor and positive influence will often be of interest to human resource personnel. A candidate should also mention any end user or IT employee training experience. A human resource employee will also probably be more judgment oriented than IT personnel on such items as the manner in which you conduct yourself and your appearance.

Interview with an IT Manager

If a candidate is able to determine prior to the interview that he or she will report to the IT manager, this is valuable to know in advance. The IT manager will be concerned about several things. First and foremost, the IT manager will want to know whether the candidate has the type of skills and experience that are needed to help accomplish the business goals of their organization. Second, he or she will want to know how this individual will fit in with the employees who are currently in the group. If the particular job requires interface and work with functional end users, will the candidate be able to do this effectively. These three items most frequently will be the concerns and priorities of the majority of IT managers to whom candidates will directly report.

A candidate's primary objective in this situation is to first convince the interviewer that he or she is qualified with respect to all the previously mentioned things that are covered during the interview, but it is also to a candidate's advantage as a function of prior research regarding the company or organization to try to get the interviewer to open up regarding their needs and problems. In situations where a candidate is successful in achieving this type of thing, he or she has a much better chance of advancing further within the hiring process as long as they are able to contribute some relevant input from their experience and skill that relates to similar needs, problems, and challenges of the organization. Any time that a candidate has the opportunity to do this effectively, that candidate's chances in competing with other candidates for a job will improve.

Interview with an IT Employee Other than a Manager

In most situations, the purpose of interviewing with an IT employee other than a manager is to assess the candidate's skills, experience, and overall qualifications to determine whether he or she has the ability to do what needs to be done and how the candidate will fit into their IT organization. In some situations, candidates will be interviewed by an IT employee because the senior IT manager's skills of the past may not be relevant today or in some cases he or she may have come to IT from another function within the company such as finance or administration.

This is a critical interview because if the candidate does not pass this test, he or she will rarely go further within the process. At an appropriate time during the interview, a candidate might say something like, "I have done thorough research on your company, and I would appreciate knowing your opinion where you think the IT department could do a better job of serving needs." This type of question or something similar may open up the interviewer to talk about things that would not normally come up during the interview. Showing interest in the interviewer's opinion, if the interview has gone reasonably well, can help to get a candidate on to the next step in the hiring process in some situations. This type of question cannot hurt, especially in situations where a candidate is competing with several others.

A Group Interview

A candidate may be directed to a conference or meeting room where two or more interviewers are present. This situation, if unexpected, can unnerve a lot of candidates. After the candidate has been introduced to each interviewer and it is not clear what each of their responsibilities are, it is a good idea to mention that it would be helpful for each to take a minute to describe their responsibilities. The candidate should take notes while this is happening because they may be useful during the interview.

The interviewers have a distinct advantage: While one of them is talking with you, the others are provided time to think about what they want to ask you or to review something that has surfaced earlier during the interview. Knowledge of the type of responsibility assumed by each interviewer will help the candidate better tailor his or her responses to each individual.

Multiple Interviews Same Day

If a candidate has multiple interviews on the same day and this was not expected, this is a good sign that the first interviewer was favorably impressed. In most cases, this is a positive sign. If a candidate is passed on only to one other person, in some cases the first interviewer, if an IT manager, wants a second opinion. If the second interview is with another functional manager, the IT manager may want an opinion regarding the IT manager's favorable opinion if that function is an important internal customer. If the IT manager wants a candidate to talk briefly with three or more other employees, this is usually a good sign. If, at the end of the session, a candidate has the opportunity to talk again with the IT manager, this is a good time to confirm strong interest in the company and job if it exists and to ask, "What is the next step for me related to this job opportunity?"

Interview with Another Functional Manager

In any situation where the candidate's first interview is with another functional manager, it will usually mean that the work the IT department provides this department is currently a major priority of the IT organization and that a significant amount of the new employee's work will be in support of that function working with department managers to be certain that the completed work is relevant to their needs.

In this situation the manager will be interested in a candidate's end user work experience in other projects and will primarily be making some type of judgment as to whether the candidate will fit in well with the department's employees. In addition to satisfying the manager's concerns and questions regarding successful end user work experience and human relations skills, the strategy for the candidate in this situation is to draw out the functional manager in terms of the type of support that is needed from IT, what type of improvements are needed, and the department's priorities related to the IT support needs. If the candidate can acquire this information, he or she should take notes during this discussion and respond to any key points where their experience and skills can help. At the end of this type of interview, if a candidate has successfully been able to get the manager to open up to a specific discussion of needs, priorities, problems, and concerns, the candidate should thank the manger for the candid discussion at the conclusion, and if interested in the job, affirm this, by saying something like, "I hope to have the opportunity to work with you and your organization. I believe that I can do a good job for you." At the beginning of company and job research for an interview, an important question to consider is, What can you do for the employer that they need?

Company and Job Research

As an example, if five candidates from all applicants for a specific IT job, are selected for in-person interviews at the company's location, it is most probable that all candidates selected have similar skills and experience levels. If, for purposes of this discussion, after the initial interviews have been completed, two have been selected to move further in the process, why were the two selected and the others dropped from contention?

In nine out of ten cases, the candidates who performed most effectively in relating to the interviewer moved on. Why were they able to perform more effectively. In the majority of these situations, they were simply better prepared. They spent more time doing higher quality research regarding the job and company or organization, which made them appear more confident and enabled them to provide higher quality answers to the interviewer's questions than the other candidates. In some situations, they were more effective in communicating with the interviewer because they were able to learn some of the things that were important from the interviewer's perspective. Once learned, they were able to build upon these things during the interview. In addition, they may have appeared more professional in their manner and appearance and in some situations if everything else is basically equal, these types of things can also play a part in providing them with an advantage when they are competing with others for employment consideration.

Job Descriptions or Specifications

If an interview results from an IT job that is posted online, the employer's online job listing in many cases is not comprehensive enough to provide candidates with a good understanding of the skills and experience requirements. This occurs because sometimes these postings are not prepared by the individuals who have the best and most detailed understanding of the responsibilities.

In such situations, it is a good idea for the candidate to be interviewed to go to the hiring organization's IT department to see if a detailed job description or specification exists. If it does not, it is a good idea to make a query to determine whether there is anyone within the IT department who understands the job and its related work and responsibilities and with whom the candidate could have a phone discussion. This should be done in every situation possible because it enables job candidates to better prepare themselves for the interview in that they are better able to draw out discussion of the responsibilities and priorities relative to how their experience and skills can potentially benefit the hiring organization. This set of activities is possibly the most important preparation that an IT job candidate can complete prior to a scheduled interview.

If a job candidate has been able to gain some type of detailed understanding of the job requirements from various sources, the next most important item is to complete research on the company or organization itself to better understand what their business is about and whom they serve as customers. This is particularly valuable when the candidate can learn of any industry-specific applications or customer-type intelligence that will help the candidate better relate the potential relevance of his or her personal skills in the interview.

If the interview is scheduled within a few days after the candidate is contacted about it, the candidate must move quickly on the research. The quickest and sometimes best source is to visit the company. If practical, visit their employment office, main reception or public relations office, or investor relations office to obtain a copy of their latest annual report. If they do not publish an annual report, obtain copies of any internal employee or customer newsletters or product or services brochures that describe the organization's purpose. Prior to the visit, try to gain anything of potential value from the organization's web site such as internal news releases or excerpts of other articles where the organization is favorably discussed within the news.

If you have time and want to try to gain more information that could prove helpful for the interview, contact a college or university library or any large public library within your metropolitan area to determine if the have the business database of either Lexus-Nexus Academic Universe or the ProQuest Corporation's database ABI/Inform. Both of these companies are concentrators of business-related information from periodicals, industry journals, and other printed and electronic media sources that go back several years. If either or both of these databases are available, they can prove helpful in your interview-related research activities.

At the appropriate time and opportunity during your interview, try to relate your skills and experience to the needs of the company in a manner that shows understanding of their business and the customer aspects of their products and services. This not only is impressive but will separate you from other candidates who do not do this. It can also provide you with opportunities to relate effectively how your skills and experience fit their internal and customer-related needs. Doing this will often put you in a more likely position to move forward as compared to the other candidates competing with you. In some cases, when your job and company research has been extensive and proves to be meaningful, it may be possible that you will win over candidates who are better qualified than you in skills and experience. They neglected to spend adequate time in job and organization research.

In some situations, if you have time and have been able to gain extensive information about the organization and its business, you may want to consider taking along a three- or four-page Power Point or equivalent presentation with appropriate graphics relating how your skills and experience can potentially benefit the employer's business needs. This again is professional; the interviewers will not see it from most candidates, and it is worth trying in any situations where you are able to obtain comprehensive information regarding the prospective employer. This can provide you with a significant competitive advantage.

Applicant Personal Preparation for Interviews

This portion of the chapter is about the logistics and checklist for the small things that, when not properly considered prior to a personal interview, can add up to create problems that job candidates do not need. It suffices to say that these types of things in conjunction with inadequate research regarding the potential employer coupled with little or no understanding of the job for which a candidate is interviewing are the types of things that individually do not seem like much. However, these are the types of things that, in total, tend to disqualify candidates from consideration, sometimes when they are better qualified skills- and experience-wise to move forward than candidates who do make that effect.

Logistics, Material, and Other Personal Preparation for the Interview

When the interview is initially scheduled, it is a good idea to confirm at that time with whom you will be speaking and his or her responsibility. You will often talk with the senior IT manager's assistant, and it is also a good idea to ask if whomever you will be meeting with has any type of biographical summary that you could obtain. It is also a good idea to ask where you should go upon arrival and whom you should ask for the day of the interview. It is also a good idea to arrive early to accommodate security and other check-in requirements. Some campuses of larger organizations are themselves quite large, and you want to be certain that you are going to the right place. You do not want the interviewer to wait for you because of your inadequate prior preparation. If, however, you have to wait for the interviewer, which frequently occurs, you can often turn this into a personal advantage because most decent, considerate people are sincerely apologetic about your having to wait.

It is also wise to confirm the interview the day prior because employer's often have unforeseen emergencies that they cannot always predict. Your understanding if this situation should occur may work to your advantage. Decent people regret inconveniencing others, which may help psychologically to strengthen your potential candidacy.

A map and directions are always important to obtain in advance. If your interview happens to be first thing in the morning and you are not familiar with the route in large metro areas and don't understand the delays associated with prime-time traffic, you need to gain understanding of this prior to your interview in order to plan accordingly.

Appearance in most cases should be conservative. Business type dress is preferable. Men should wear a suit and tie, or a minimum of a sport coat and tie; women should wear a business suit or conservative dress or pant suit. Do not wear too much cologne. Candidates should show evidence of good personal hygiene, with clean fingernails even for men mechanically inclined. Both men and women should wear leather shoes, shined not scuffed. Clothes should be neatly pressed, not wrinkled. Men should have a fairly recent haircut and neatly trimmed facial hair. To many applicants, these types of things appear to be somewhat superficial and raise the basic question, What do these types of things have to do with my skills, experience, and overall qualifications, relative to what I can provide in terms of value to this potential employer? This is possibly true in many situations, but image is important to many hiring organizations, and it is not wise to disqualify yourself from consideration. If it is your personal choice and judgment in these types of situations to ignore an employer's conservative expectations regarding your appearance, then don't complain about lack of job opportunities when you are not willing to conform to personal items of this type.

As another consideration, everyday work dress is a different story in many organizations. However, in anything as important as having the opportunity to be considered for a new job, which is important to most IT job applicants, why wouldn't candidates want to represent themselves in the most professional and positive manner possible? When you consider that most experienced IT job applicants that interview will be trying to qualify for jobs in the annual income range starting at $70,000 to in excess of $100,000, this is a good question for those who have difficulty with the relative importance of things such as personal appearance.

Even if your personal résumé had been forwarded previously, you should not assume that the person(s) with whom you will interview will have a copy with them at the interview. It is a good idea to take several additional copies with you just in case. Copies of your résumé should always be made on a high-resolution, quality laser printer when possible. It is adequate that the résumé paper is a bright white 20-pound laser printer bond. Résumés do not need to be printed on special bond paper or heavier paper, it is not necessary and the font used for your resume should be a basic business document style font, which is easier for most people to read than specialized more decorative fonts.

If you also have material that illustrates your work end product and is impressive, take a couple of copies with you if it is appropriate for use in the interview. As previously mentioned, when your research effort has been significant and you are able to relate your qualifications to the employer's business and customer base in a Power Point or similar graphics-type presentation, this may be beneficial. Also, if you have extensive project-type work experience that is not covered in a two- or three-page personal résumé, a supplemental attachment detailing this experience could prove beneficial. Before going on the scheduled interview, you should answer the question, What can you do for the employer that they need?

Applicant's Personal Attitude and Manner

An applicant's attitude and manner upon arrival and going into an interview are things that can help or injure a candidate's chances to move forward in the hiring process. After an interview, if there is suspicion regarding attitude or any indication of a candidate being aloof, arrogant, or impersonal, an astute hiring manager will sometimes check with the receptionist and anyone else who interacted with the candidate to get their opinions.

If friendliness is not perceived as being natural and candidates display any type of attitude that shows indifference or disinterest in others, candidates often ruin their chances for employment consideration. This is particularly true when end user contact is important. At times we all can be noticeably preoccupied with what is on our personal minds and appear to be indifferent to others. A job interview is the wrong place to have this occur. Most people in the work place prefer to be around other employees who are considerate of others, generally somewhat friendly, and pleasant to be around. Arrogant, unsociable-type behavior will not work today in most work places where team and work groups are prevalent.

In summary, an optimist with a positive outlook finds ways to make something better or to make it work. The pessimist usually spends energy focusing on why something will not work. In competitive economic times, the majority of times the employer will favor the candidate who reflects a positive outlook even in many situations where skills may not be as good as the candidate who is perceived to be detached and unsociable.

OPENING OF THE INTERVIEW

The interview normally will begin with an introduction by the employee conducting the interview. The candidate should always participate in a firm handshake with a friendly exchange of greetings while maintaining direct eye contact with the interviewer. Avoiding direct eye contact when talking to or listening to the interviewer is a bad sign to many interviewers. It can be perceived as a lack of confidence, not being sincere, or a misrepresentation of some facts. After the introductions, if you have been unable to obtain any prior meaningful information regarding the company, you should ask, "Before we get started, it would be helpful to me if you could take a minute or two to tell me what your concept is of this position and what the most important needs are regarding it. This would help me address the answers to your questions in a more meaningful way."

During the interview your body language and your manner are both important. You want to maintain good posture, be alert but not overanxious, too intent, or nervous. When answering questions as well as when listening to the interviewer, it is important to maintain eye contact. There is nothing wrong with taking notes. It demonstrates that you have interest in what the interviewer is saying, and the notes may be helpful to you at other times during the interview for reference purposes.

During interviews, candidates need to discipline themselves not to exhibit any type of frequent preoccupation with what they want to say. If this happens, they may injure their chances of moving forward in the hiring process. When this becomes noticeable to interviewers, it can create unnecessary doubt about the candidate. At all times during the interview, the candidate should concentrate and focus on listening to the interviewer in order to respond as effectively as possible when appropriate to the interviewer's questions or conversation.

At the outset, the candidate in some situations immediately following a warm greeting and introduction, may experience some difficult questions. For example, the interviewer may ask, "Why should we consider hiring you?" If the candidate has obtained detailed information on the job and completed comprehensive research on the company or organization, he or she is in a much better position to answer this, by stating, "I have reviewed the job description and have done significant research on your company and believe that I have the right skills and experience necessary to make the type of contributions that the position requires. I also believe that your company is the type of company in which I would like to work." The interviewer may ask why. This presents another good opportunity at the outset to show the interviewer that you understand the company and its business and are impressed with the potential opportunity that is offered.

If you did not obtain detailed job information and were not able to gain any type of significant information regarding the company or organization, your responses cannot be impressive. Your best response in this situation is to state that you were not able to obtain any significant information and that it would be helpful if the interviewer could provide you with information regarding the job and its importance to the company. In some situations, you may get by with this; in most, you are already operating at a significant disadvantage, and the interview has just begun. If the interviewer begins with something like, "What do you know about our company?" Again, if you have not completed significant research, you are again at a potential disadvantage. Two questions like this early in an interview where candidates are unable to reply with answers showing time spent in research may in many situations totally rule them out of contention for the job unless their skills and experience are a good fit and the interviewer keeps an open mind and permits them to explain these attributes in detail. If the interview lasts for less than 30 to 45 minutes, there are lulls in the conversation, and the interviewer shows signs of being uncomfortable with the discussion, the candidate can conclude that he or she did not do well and that chances for consideration are poor. This is unfortunate in situations where candidates have the necessary qualifications and could successfully do the job but will not have the opportunity because they did not put enough effort into prior research of the job and the company or organization. In many interviewer's minds, the thought occurs, if they were really interested, they would have invested the time to understand these things. This may seem ridiculous in situations where candidates have the right qualifications, but things like this frequently occur.

It is not wise to put yourself at any type of disadvantage as a result of things that you could have controlled. To do well in the total interview will be challenging enough in most situations, and to put yourself at significant disadvantage at the outset should be avoided whenever possible. Many interviewers tend to make judgments on candidates based upon their perception early in interviews and you want to start as effectively as possible.

Understanding the Interviewer's Perspective

When you go into an interview, it is important to understand the perspective of most interviewers. At the conclusion, they are going to decide whether or not to consider a candidate further. During the interview, most interviewers are trying to determine the following things:

- Your IT technical skills and experience
- How well you may fit into the IT organization
- Whether you have the desired communication skills, manner, and personality to work with end user clients when this is important

- Whether your thinking ability is good as evidenced in the interview
- Whether, in the final analysis, you could do the requirements of the job and be an asset to the company or organization

THE INTERVIEW

Potential Problem Areas for Job Candidates in Interviews

This topic is important. If any or several of the following problem areas exist in your personal situation, you need to give significant prior thought to how you will best answer questions about them in an interview. If they are brought up and appear to be a problem, you need to determine how you are going to overcome any potential damage where they may restrict your ability to compete for a job?

Time Gaps in Your Résumé

It is acceptable in your résumé to include the year you started with an employer and the year that your work ended as an alternative to month and year started to month and year your work ended at the employer. If a person has had multiple jobs over the years it is difficult to remember accurately the month started in most unless you kept records, which most people do not do. The problem with using year to year, is that for any situations where you started and left in the same year, you will probably be asked, at least in some interviews, to explain the situation.

In any job situations where interviewers want to go into detail regarding the circumstances of your employment, you do not want to show any indication of irritability in any sensitive situations, which in some interviews is a quick way to end your potential candidacy. If a candidate shows irritability or any indication of displeasure in discussing individual employment situations, the candidate raises the potential question of emotional stability and control, which candidates do not want to raise.

In those situations that appear to raise concern from interviewers, candidates want to be up front and honest, which is the quickest way to dispose of them and to discourage further questioning by the interviewer. It is rare that anyone who has had several different employers and multiple bosses in some jobs has not had at least one situation where a relationship with the boss has been strained even though the employee's job performance was adequate. Most employees who have worked for 10 or more years have had at least one bad boss along the way. If this situation occurred and was related to job tenure, which is in question, the important thing is the content of your response. If you have had bosses who were arrogant, inconsiderate, unreasonable, or frequently emotionally out of control or whose behavior frequently included one or more of these things or other things of a similar nature that resulted in their acting in manners not in the best interests of the company, explain the situation in this manner. It is also not unreasonable that an employee would have a personality conflict once or twice with bosses during a career. It would be a major concern to potential employers, if it appeared to be a frequently occurring situation during employment history. If this situation has occurred several times in the past and it appears to be a key concern of the interviewer, it is best to be honest and admit that in several of these situations you may have contributed to the situation as a result of a significant disagreement with your manager, which was not related to quality of work. You need to explain that you have not had a problem with this in recent employment and that you can provide references to verify this if desired. In situations such as this you need to try to resolve them as rapidly as possible and to get back to other questions regarding you skills and experience and how they may benefit the employer.

Frequent Unemployment or Unemployment for a Significant Period of Time

Unemployment is easiest to explain in situations where you did contract employment, consulting work, or limited-term project participation, which should all be noted in your résumé. Another easy explanation is where an employer has had financial problems or has made significant employment cuts because of business problems. In this situation where your employment was terminated, and others with similar qualifications were retained, an interviewer may want to know why you were not retained, which requires a good answer if the reason was not related to significantly less tenure.

The best type of answers to questions regarding extensive or significant frequency of unemployment are things like your research and selection of employers could have been better owing to stability, your skills and IT education became outdated in some respects and you have since taken action to correct this (be prepared to explain). If some of the unemployment was the result of relocation for family or personal reasons, mention that without going into anything personal that is not appropriate for discussion. Again in this situation, quickly address and dispose of any obvious concerns and as rapidly as possible try to get the interview back to *areas related* to your qualifications of today and how you believe you can help the employer fulfill their needs.

For any candidate who has experienced significant unemployment in either length of time, frequency, or both, the amount of company and job research that you do prior to the interview is critical. If you have been job hunting for any significant period of time, your situation is more difficult to overcome than that for most other candidates with similar qualifications. Also in your résumé preparation, you need to emphasize any specialized industry or functional application experience where your prior research has indicated that similar needs may exist in the employer. If, in the interview, you can establish that you have significant experience and expertise in areas that have relevance to the specific employer, you can establish potential value that can offset any negatives or stigma attached to the unemployment situation. In reality, you will often need to prove in interviews that you are a better potential risk in hiring than other candidates who have similar qualifications and do not have the unemployment situation to overcome. In other words, in order to win and move to job finalization and an offer, you need to perform better and more impressively in almost every aspect related to the interview and the employer when compared to other candidates. This may even extend to alternative-type proposals for employment consideration in order to facilitate closing out a formal employment offer. Being better sometimes means being much more creative and resourceful than your competition.

Jobs of Short Duration

Unless they were contract, consulting, or limited-term jobs, jobs with tenure of less than one year are most certain to draw attention in interviews. If your situation is not one of those previously mentioned, when questioned, your objective should be to dispose of related discussion as rapidly as possible. If an interviewer keeps asking questions regarding your departure you need to try to end these questions as rapidly as possible, and in some cases the only thing that will accomplish this is the truth. In situations where your employment was terminated, say so, and if it happened to be the wrong job for your skills and qualifications, say so. It is a rare employee today who goes through a work career without having his or her employment terminated once or twice during a career. After the discussion gets to the termination part, the important part is explaining why it occurred. If it was not skill- or job-performance-related and you took the initiative to resign due to a personal situation such as conflict with a supervisor, say so, but again be prepared to discuss the conflict.

No or Low Level of Previous IT Job Experience

This is a frequent situation for those who are making a career change or are new or recently graduated college students. Candidates in these situations find it difficult to effectively convince interviewers that they are not taking a significant risk in hiring candidates in these categories. They must effectively present a history of patterns of success and excellent results in previous occupations or in life's experience in areas where they have achieved anything that has distinguished them within a group or team situation or excellence within other endeavors where they have expended a significant personal commitment of time and effort.

In the final stages during an interview, a candidate might be well advised to say this to the interviewer, "Someone had to take a risk on you when they hired you for your first job, which is true of every official or key employee within your company." If everything else in the interview has progressed reasonably well, this is a difficult statement for an interviewer to dismiss because of its validity.

Candidate Has Had Several Jobs with Employment of Less Than Two Years

Interviewers with concern regarding this situation have two questions: Is this candidate a job hopper? Is this candidate simply unable to hold jobs for any length of time? If the candidate has had a significant number of jobs where his or her tenure was less than two years and he or she left for better pay, say so. Then the concern will move to, What is going to be different here? If this occurs, the candidate needs to have a meaningful explanation as to why this situation would be different. Possibly one of the better explanations is: "Having reviewed the job descriptions and further research into the job requirements, I am confident that my skills, experience, and overall qualifications are a good match for what is needed by your company. In the past, I have had good jobs and have gained a lot of valuable experience related to the specific customer needs within your industry which I believe will help qualify me to provide your company significant value in this job as well as having the potential to provide progressive contributions beyond the basic requirements of the job. In my research I also am impressed with your company and believe it to have a good future."

Another Potential Way of Addressing Employer's Concern Regarding Tenure

"If it would be of any potential value in satisfying your concerns regarding tenure, I am willing to sign an employment contract that commits me to a minimum of two years of employment and that can be terminated at any time by your company if you are not satisfied with the quality of my work and contributions."

Candidates Who Do Not Have College Degrees

Candidates who show on their résumés that they have attended one or more colleges for two to three years but did not graduate are often asked in an interview why they didn't graduate. It is a proven fact that candidates who receive formal degrees in IT during their careers on the average receive higher comparative annual salaries than those employees who did not complete their college work. The interviewer will probably ask, "Why wasn't it important enough for you to find a way to achieve this?"

In this situation, if they thought that the skills, experience, and qualifications in your résumé were good enough to bring you in for an interview, you have some advantage. However, if their recent history is to hire only IT job candidates with degrees in the computer science discipline, you may have a difficult time convincing them to consider making an exception. You do this by researching the job's requirements and the company's key information and understanding the customer base. If during the interview you can relate impressive understanding of these items describing how your skills and experience have the potential to contribute to both the customer-related support and internal functional priorities associated with IT services, your potential for being hired will be enhanced. To do this you need to gain prior insight into the type of IT work that is a priority at the time of the interview and do the best job possible of tying these needs to your background. In these situations, developing this relationship will not only help you gain consideration for hiring but also serve to provide you with a significant advantage over other job candidates who are being considered, unless one has a significant skill advantage for items of relevance.

During Career Applicant Has Job Tenure of Less Than Two Years Per Job

Interviewers will see this as a pattern of concern and want to know why it has occurred. If you can primarily attribute it to job hopping for better annual income, say so. Then be prepared to answer why it won't happen again if they should hire you. This situation also poses the question in some interviewers' minds as to whether the situation is related to the candidate's inability to hold a job for any longer period of time. If an applicant has less than 8 years of total IT job experience after graduation from college and during this time period has held five or more jobs, the applicant will be hard pressed to explain this difficult situation. A potential valid explanation is "At the age I left most of these positions, I was immature and I did not exercise good judgement in several cases. I left several of these jobs due to this immaturity and to lack of awareness, several for the wrong reasons. I am mature enough now and realize my mistakes, and I am confident that the pattern will not continue." This is a difficult situation and an explanation of this type may work in some situations, but it is not likely to work in most of those where concerns exist.

Common Mistakes of Job Candidates During Interviews

Asking Too Many Questions

During interviews candidates need to exercise good discipline to control the number of questions that they ask and to be certain that the questions they ask have relevance to the more important content of the résumé.

Often when candidates become preoccupied with questions that they want to ask, they fail to listen properly to the interviewer when he or she is talking. It is important to maintain eye contact with the interviewer most of the time when he or she is talking. If a candidate is often focused upon what to say next over the course of the interview, the interviewer will see this inattention as a lack of interest or sincerity, both of which are not good. Also if it is apparent that the candidate is not listening, in job situations where they require frequent dialogue with internal functional end users, this is not a good sign.

The types of questions that are appropriate for the candidate during the interview are those that ask for clarification and those that help to provide the candidate with the opportunity to move the discussion toward job-related skills or experience that are a strength of the candidate and that have relevance in the job being pursued.

In situations where candidates continually ask questions, interviewers often are of the opinion that the candidates are trying to avoid discussing certain things in which the interviewer is interested or that they are trying to hide something. Continual question asking by candidates can also be irritating to the interviewer and sometimes takes the outward appearance of nervousness, which again can arouse undesired type of suspicions about such things as lack of confidence.

Candidates' Answers to Questions of the Interviewer

Another area where candidates frequently do not perform well in interviews is in the length and quality of their answers to interviewer's questions. Two dangers exist in this subject: saying too little or too much.

Saying "yes" or "no" in answer to certain types of questions or when making minimal answers or answers that are short in duration often precludes candidates from making the types of answers to questions that can help them win the right to move forward in the hiring process. For certain questions that appear to have more importance, it is not a bad idea to think about the questions for a few seconds before making a response to be certain that you are making the best possible response. In this situation, if the intent of the question is not clear to you and could have multiple relationships, you want to be certain that you are addressing the one desired by the interviewer. In situations such as this, it is a good idea to ask the interviewer for clarification to be certain you are responding to the right meaning.

Most responses to interviewer's questions should take no more than 20 seconds. Exceptions to this would be those questions that have multiple parts or components of significance, which should be addressed individually in some situations and not lumped together. Candidates need to use their judgment for items such as this.

Where most candidates get themselves in trouble is answering questions where their response runs over a minute and often as long as 2 minutes, which often runs the risk of covering ground that is not relevant to the interviewer's question. The longer the answer extends beyond 20 seconds, the more likely the candidate is to have the answer result in diminished effectiveness. In interviews where this type of thing occurs frequently and the answers cover too much material (and the material covered frequently does not touch on what the interviewer intended), the candidates chances of moving forward in the process are greatly diminished. If you believe that you have something important to say or want to make what you believe is an important point in response to an interviewer's question, remember that the longer you talk, the more likely you are to diminish the quality of the answer you make.

Questions That Are Better Held Until the End of the Hiring Process

During first interviews, you are wise to not ever ask questions of a personal nature. If you are sincerely interested in qualifying as a serious candidate and moving forward in the process toward a job offer, personal questions of interest are not appropriate to raise in an initial interview. Questions such as What does the job pay? What is your vacation policy? What are normal work hours? What benefits are included? and What items are employee-paid and how much? are off limits. In a first interview, they are the wrong focus and are better held for later in the process. If you raise them in the initial interview, your chances of moving forward may be diminished because the interviewer may rightfully conclude that a candidate focused upon these things rather than the job at the outset has a potential judgment problem.

Warning Signs for Concern During Interviews

There are several situations that occur during the course of personal interviews that, if not addressed quickly and effectively when a candidate senses that they are or have occurred, will usually result in the candidate not moving forward in the employer's hiring process.

Length of the Interview

Any interview that lasts for less than 30 minutes is usually a certain sign that the interviewer does not consider the candidate being interviewed as a potential one for hiring. The clues to this is the interviewer appearing disinterested or having difficulty moving the discussion, which is dragging. The interviewer's manner is also often a good clue. This situation is very tough to address, and there is some risk in facing it. If you sense it is occurring, the thing to do is to face it, asking something like, "I sense that I am failing to convince you that I am qualified for consideration for this job." The interviewer may say that you are correct and tell you why, which if something you are unable to deal with and change their mind, as a minimum, is good to know in order not to waste time and have false hope regarding the situation. In a few of these situations, the interviewers may apologize and take the blame personally, and you may have an opportunity to get the interview back on the right track and extend it to where you may be able to reestablish yourself, which previously, the way things were going, would not have been possible.

Candidate Overselling of Capabilities

Another particularly difficult situation occurs when a candidate senses that the interviewer may be concerned about the candidate's qualifications. The clues to this occur when an interviewer stays on a particular subject or keeps coming back to it over the course of the interview. It is obvious that there is a suspected problem if an interviewer in sequence asks three or four questions regarding a particular subject. They will ask things like How did you approach this problem? or How did you do this? If something is suspect, the interviewer will test your understanding of the process used in many situations.

Situations of this type are serious because when an interviewer is suspicious that a candidate may be taking credit for something that he or she really did not do, credibility becomes an issue. If a candidate senses that this type of thing has occurred, the only possible damage control he or she can take is to accept the blame by saying, "I believe that I failed to communicate the situation in question properly to you because there appears to be some misunderstanding or concern regarding my explanation." This may not work in all situations. Left alone it will definitely ruin a candidate's potential to move forward in the hiring process. If situations such as this should occur, ask for an opportunity to prove yourself in an assignment for any situations where you believe that you were misunderstood. Sometimes interviewers are wrong in their perceptions, and in these situations the fact that you faced the problem may be enough for the interviewer to be willing to provide you further consideration.

Skill Tests

If an interviewer has some reservations regarding the level of an individual's technical skills relative to their adequacy for the job in question, during the course of the interview, the interviewer will ask in-depth questions regarding the level of these skills to determine the candidate's level of understanding. In these situations, there will be a lot of how do you do this and how do you do that questions. The interviewer may also say, "Take some time to discuss the type of work that you have been doing during the past year and what type of projects you have worked on and what your responsibilities have been. I am interested in understanding the level of the skills that you have developed."

Another more specific example of this type of question occurs when the interviewer says, "Your resume indicates that you have done a significant amount of work with Java, please take a few minutes to tell me your understanding of Java's advantages as compared to other methods relative to integration with the internet." In situations such as this, the interviewer may have concerns relative to résumé-related skills and will often pose open-ended questions to determine how well candidates can communicate their understanding of any IT subjects of interest.

For an IT job candidate, this type of a situation is possibly the most challenging one that they can encounter during an interview. Their skills are being challenged for relevance, and if they are unable to convince the interviewer that their skills are adequate for the job, the end result in most of these situations is they will be advised that the interviewer does not believe that their skills are adequate for the job.

In these situations, if the candidate did not do significant prior research regarding the job and company, he or she has damaged his or her chances for consideration. If the candidate had completed extensive prior job and company research, he or she would have been able to more effectively present skills and experience relative to the employer's business and customer needs. This type of thing can often provide an entirely different perspective regarding the potential value of a candidate's qualifications.

Preparing for Potential Interview Questions

This section includes a selection of potential questions that are somewhat typical of questions that will be asked during interviews. Some of them include explanations of why the interviewer may be asking the question. There are many ways to answer the questions included. For most, the author has included an example of an answer that in many situations would satisfy the interviewer but might not fit the individual job candidate's situation. However, in reviewing most of these situations and thinking as a candidate who was asked the question or a similar one, consider how you would reply. Prior to a scheduled interview it is a good idea to review these questions because they will cover the majority of situations. IT technical skills questions are the most difficult for the interviewer to cover properly in a personal interview. If they receive the majority of the emphasis, a qualified interviewer can determine a level of understanding but not actual skill performance in the work place. An IT senior manager is more likely to pursue questions similar to those listed in this section, while an IT employee who has a detailed understanding of the job in question will tend to concentrate more on technical skills and the type of work experience of the candidate. When in an interview situation where technical skill levels are at issue, if there is concern noted the only way to settle that issue if in doubt, is to recommend some type of relevant work-related test. The sample questions follow.

What type of employee are you?

Applicants should think about this open-ended question before they answer. This type of question could cover almost anything. Because of this, it would not be a bad idea to ask, "In what respect are you referring?" If the interviewer comes back and specifies in the work environment, some of the better answers would be "I take my assignments seriously relative to the quality of my work," "I work well in a team environment and get along well with others," "I am capable of handling multiple assignments concurrently," or "I am process oriented and have good problem solving skills."

Tell me about your planning skills.

"As previously mentioned, I am process oriented, and on a project of greater complexity I first want be certain that I have a project plan in place that serves as a road map for all of the important components and their most important relationships. If this includes the development of the proper specification for the work, if one does not exist, I will develop one that will be the basis for my work plan."

Why are you interested in our organization?

"I did a significant amount of prior research on your company and learned as much as I could regarding the job specification. I am impressed with the potential that I see in this company and believe that I can make the type of contributions that are needed from the job."

What has been your most significant contribution to a former employer?

This type of question requires some thought prior to responding. This could be a project or assignment where you were a team participant that helped improve efficiency significantly for a priority business practice or one that reduced operating costs significantly compared to the prior method. Or it could be an assignment where you had to overcome significant obstacles or problems in project development and or implementation. Sometimes things that were more of a struggle can be more beneficial in the final analysis because of the existing problems that were corrected.

In your last job, what did you contribute beyond completing your basic responsibilities?

When this type of question is asked, interviewers are looking for indications that an applicant may have the potential for handling more responsibility or making contributions of value beyond their basic job responsibilities. The answer for questions like this in many situations may be: "Basically I was totally challenged with the basic work load of my job for which I received good performance evaluations." In this situation, there is nothing wrong with an answer that does not go beyond the sample answer.

Let's talk about your job skills. At this point, your résumé indicates that you have almost 12 years of job experience. What is a good summary of your capability and potential value to a small, growing company like ours?

"I believe that my primary value to a growth company like yours is both a function of my skills and experience. I have knowledge and experience with the latest software writing languages. Possibly the most valuable thing that I offer your company is that during my career I have worked in high-growth organizations, which means in IT that I have successful experience and understanding with a lot of the challenges in IT that you are and will face as a result of your growth."

What have you done to keep your skills relevant?

"During the past couple of years, I have taken two online courses to broaden my knowledge of the latest technology, one regarding network engineering and the other regarding network security, which are both important subjects and will be for most organizations far into the future."

It looks like there is a time gap in your résumé after the job before your current one.

"Yes, I was out of work for several months until I was able to find the type of job that I wanted."

What caused you to leave the employer before your last one?

"The IT manager was under a great deal of personal pressure to complete several projects that were behind schedule and he wanted me to rush my work to get the project I was assigned completed. I was not willing to compromise the quality of my work in this situation, the project was important and I knew that if I compromised the quality that major modifications would be required after implementation to correct problems that would exist. I simply was not willing to do what my manager asked."

What interests you the most about this job?

"The primary thing of interest to me is that I have spent the majority of my IT career to this point working in much larger organizations. The work in those types of companies is pretty much routine. I am looking for the type of opportunity where I can have more impact on the priorities of the business which will develop my skills to a higher level. I believe that your company is the type of company where I can achieve this."

If I contacted the manager that you had the conflict with, what would that individual say about you?

"I really can't say for certain. Possibly that I did good work, but that I was a little strong headed and rigid at times."

Have you failed at any assigned responsibility or job task during your career?

"Yes, early in my career I was assigned to a project related to a functional application where I failed to comprehensively enough define several specification-related aspects related to internal end user needs. This in the end caused me some significant extra modification work, which taught me to do it right the first time and be certain that you have done a comprehensive job of mapping out relevant relationships in the initial work specification."

Describe your influence on others within the IT organizations in which you have worked.

"For the most part I believe that it has been positive except for one or two difficult personalities. I get along well with others and am a positive contributor in team work-group-type situations. I am considerate and respectful of others until they violate this trust through their actions. If someone is continually somewhat detrimental in a work group by interfering with progress, I will confront them about this. I believe that for the most part I am a positive influence on others and that other people that work with me, respect me."

What area of your skills would benefit you and your employer the most to improve at this time?

"That is a good question that I have not thought that much about. Possibly becoming more familiar with and learning more about Linux open source software. I believe that this capability has the opportunity to offer most companies significant cost savings over the next several years when compared to present methods. Also the internet and its applications are here to stay. However network and web security is also going to be a problem that will remain with us indefinitely. The online course I took on network security design was good, but I believe that I can provide significant benefit to my employer going further into the web security aspect."

Take a minute or two to characterize for me how you work under stressful circumstances where you are behind and are in danger of missing important deadlines, which I believe we covered to some degree regarding your employer before your last one.

"Normally I work well under pressure in most situations when my management is reasonable. The only time I have had personal problems with stress concurrent with a heavy workload and deadlines is when I am working on something that was beyond my skill level. Whenever this has occurred, which is not often, I have learned that rather than struggle and lose valuable time, I should seek out a colleague or acquaintance who has a better understanding of the subject than I, which has usually worked well."

You mentioned that you have worked with Java and that you understand the older procedural programs such as BASIC and COBOL. Compare their efficiencies for me when integration with the internet is required.

"Java as you know has become one of the most popular object-oriented languages and is superior to the older procedural programs comparing portability, sharing ability, and security aspects. The older procedural languages are also much less efficient in the integration of such things as networks, databases, and three-dimensional graphics."

Why should we consider hiring you?

"As a function of my skills, experience, and overall qualifications, the primary reason is the potential contributions that I can make to your company. In my previous job experience, I have worked on a large amount of business process and practices-related applications, which has helped me understand the type of contributions that IT work can make to the overall health of the business. This, in my opinion, is beyond the scope of what the majority of software writers with whom I have had experience are able to do. I have always been motivated to learn more than the basic work of code writing."

Which of your nontechnical skills do you believe have benefited you the most during your career?

"Probably my ability to communicate effectively and work well with people who have varied skills levels and come from many different backgrounds."

Why do you believe you are able to do this?

"I believe that I have good skill at understanding things from their perspective, by putting myself in their situation. In other words, I consider how would I react in certain situations if I were them."

What has been the most difficult problem that you have had to overcome in working with others?

"I worked on a project with one individual who continually wanted to make changes and shortcuts on a project, which was not consistent with the project plan that had been established prior to the outset. This type of situation was interfering with the progress that we needed to be making. I finally had to sit down with this individual and force him to discuss the end result and consequences of what he was recommending for several components. At first, he was reluctant to do this and after one or two discussions, I told him that his insistence in making changes was interfering with the progress that we should be making on the project and if he was not willing to cooperate and work the plan as originally established, that I would have to take the entire situation to our manager for resolution. I further communicated that I respected his opinion and was willing to consider changes he recommended if they could be proven to improve the quality of our work or reduce costs significantly without the quality of the end product deteriorating. But at this juncture I did not believe that any of his suggested changes would have any potential improvement benefits. Then I said, 'In the future when you feel strongly about an improvement suggestion, let's talk about it and not go off in different directions.' After this discussion he agreed to stay with the original work plan and specifications for the project."

How could you verify that the quality of your work is adequate for our needs?

"The best way would be to test me. Give me an assignment for a few days that will include the use of the skills that you need. This would probably be the best way. If this is not feasible and you are interested in considering hiring me, I am willing to come to work on a contract basis that states that if I have not proven my value to your company regarding the quality of relevant work and value contributed that you can terminate my employment without any possible recourse from me. If this is not feasible I can provide you two references of people with whom I worked closely for significant periods of time. They know my skills and the quality of work of which I am capable as well as the characteristics of my personality in the work place."

In your résumé, you appear to take a significant amount of personal credit for the results achieved through the use of some sales and marketing application software on which you worked? This type of thing is always difficult for me to understand. Weren't you part of a project-type team that had other participants from IT as well as the end user community? And wasn't what you provided just a software tool for the sales and marketing people to implement and the end results in improved sales and revenues were primarily a function of their efforts and effectiveness? I always have difficulty with things such as this in résumés when IT is primarily a support function.

"Possibly you are correct and I did not state the situation properly in my résumé. The application work was not a packaged software product. It was created by our IT team. The end result of its use after implementation by marketing and sales was successful as stated in my résumé, and you are correct that it could be inferred that my work was responsible for the improvements when in fact it was the total work of the IT team, the marketing people who implemented the program with the sales organization, and their application of the program in the field."

What do you know about our company?

This is a particularly difficult question if you have not done any type of significant research or were not able to secure a job description or talk in advance of the interview to an employee within the IT department who understands the job.

At this point any answer that you could make is not going to impress the interviewer. If this question occurs early in the interview, tell the interviewer that you were not able to obtain any significant information. About the only thing you can do is try to get the interviewer off this subject quickly by saying something like, "Under the circumstances if you could take a minute or two to provide me your perspective on what this job needs to contribute to the IT department and to your company, then I can respond by relating how I believe my experience and qualifications can help you achieve the results that you need to receive from this job. I don't want to waste any of your time, and I am suggesting that this may be the best solution since I did not obtain much prior information."

CLOSING THE INTERVIEW

It is nearing time for the interview to close, hopefully you have made a strong positive impression on the interviewer, and if you have, the interviewer will in most cases advise you what the next step is. They may want you to talk with another person or two. In cases where you have not met with the hiring IT manager, that will have to be scheduled. If you initially interviewed with the hiring manager and were then passed on to several others for short-duration discussions, this is another good sign that you will move forward.

If at this point you have not received any of the abovementioned responses, your situation is probably somewhat in doubt. Exceptions to this would be, explanations that we have scheduled interviews with several other candidates or we intend to schedule interviews with several other candidates.

At this point, it is a good idea to try to get a reading on where you stand. You should ask, "Do you think that I warrant further consideration for being hired for the position?" If the answer is noncommittal, you should try to draw the interviewer into further discussion. Stating something similar to "I am interested in doing what I have to do to be considered for hiring. Is there anything that I can do to strengthen my consideration for hiring?"

In those situations where it is apparent to you that you have not done well in the interview but have not been told that you will not be considered further, you need to take action to try to open up the possibility for your further consideration. A statement to the effect that, "I don't believe that I did very well in the interview, and at this point I think that it is doubtful that you will consider me further as a candidate for the job. I am confident that I have the skills to do what you need done. What could I do to prove this to you?" In most situations such as this, you will probably not receive an immediate response or you may get something like, "I had not thought about anything like that." If the interviewer should happen to say, "What were you thinking about?" You can say, "I obviously have strong interest in this job and your company. I am interested in doing what I have to do for you to seriously consider hiring me. Maybe the best type of test to prove myself is for you to give me some type of work-related assignment, where I could actually perform some representative work for you or prepare a proposal relative to some type of work-related project in which you have interest. I would even consider coming to work on a contract basis for two or three months to prove my value with no further obligation on the part of your company if I failed to prove myself. These are just a few possibilities." After proposing this, ask when should you follow up with the interviewer regarding these possibilities.

The biggest problem with résumés and job interviews is that, in most job candidates' situations, neither are usually a true indication of a person's skills and total qualifications. There is too much subjective evaluation associated with both, often by employer personnel who do not have significant expertise in proper evaluation of either of these primary components of the job-finding process. This is why it is not too difficult to understand why many thousands of IT job seekers are totally frustrated with job hunting. Job candidates can do everything in their power to improve every component of the job-hunting process.

However, the author is of the opinion that Chapter 10 is critical as it relates to a candidate's ability to schedule a significant number of different interviews and then gain some type of commitment in the interview from the employer to warrant further consideration as a serious candidate for the job. Therefore, the most important effort is activity related to gaining interviews. If the conventional methods have not worked for you, you need to try and test new methods, many of which are mentioned within this publication. This is also a function of where you look for jobs and what kind and type of effort you place into contacting potential employers.

In interviews, especially if you have participated in several and have not moved forward toward a job offer, the author recommends promoting a type of trial or test at or near the end of most interviews, done in a low key, friendly type manner. By stating that résumés are very subjective, an interviewer really cannot know whether or not your skills and qualifications will fit their needs until you are tested. The author believes that more of this type of commitment—try me, test me—will get many candidates in the door, which is 98% of the battle. After getting the opportunity, it is then up to the candidate to do whatever it takes effort- and results-wise to win permanent employment.

INTERVIEW FOLLOW-UP

Immediately after the interview, follow up in all situations where the employer has confirmed further interest, you don't know where you stand but you have not been told no, or you have proposed some type of trial or test. You immediately want to send a thank you letter to those who interviewed you. Be sure to call their assistant to verify correct name spelling, job title, and address if you do not already have that data. The purpose of the letter is to confirm your interest in qualifying for the job, to thank them for the interview and further consideration of your candidacy for the job, and to indicate that you are enthused about the opportunity, are confident that you can do what is needed and are anxious to learn what you can do to be considered for hiring.

The following could serve as a type of content framework for this type of thank you letter.

Thank you for the enjoyable interview. I want to take this opportunity to reconfirm my interest in the possibility of being hired by (company name). Based upon our discussion, I am confident that I can provide the type of results in the job that your department needs to provide support of corporate business goals.

I look forward to scheduling further discussion with you regarding several of the possibilities mentioned at the conclusion of our interview. I welcome the opportunity for consideration of any type of assignment or trial that you believe may be appropriate. Thank you again for your interest in me, and I will plan to follow up with you early next week as suggested.

12. The IT Job Outsourcing Challenge

> ## The Objective of This Chapter
>
> This chapter is focused upon IT employees who have lost their jobs to outsourcing outside of the United States as well as those who are vulnerable to job loss in the future. It discusses why and in what type of IT job classifications outsourcing will continue to occur. The primary focus of the chapter will be to suggest some alternative employment strategies that can be used for job hunting as well as to suggest other actions that may be helpful to those already affected and to those who may be affected by outsourcing at a later date. Those who believe that the data contained in this chapter may be helpful should also review the material in Chapter 10, which contains similar but also some different suggestions.

OUTSOURCING IN IT TODAY

During the course of writing this book, the author has become aware of the large number of software writing/programming jobs that continue to be outsourced outside of the United States, the majority going to India. Estimates on this subject regarding total IT jobs outsourced range from as low as 200,000 to a total as high as 500,000 total jobs during the next several years. Several of the leading U.S. IT research firms predict that outsourcing of white-collar jobs will average as much as 200,000 jobs per year over the next 15 years. This includes other skills in addition to software writing/programming such as call center, help desk, other technical support, and certain engineering and other mathematical/operations research-type work. The software code writing occupation alone could lose as many as 100,000 jobs annually for an indefinite period of time.

The important thing for those who are affected and who will be affected is that they understand their vulnerability and most importantly put together a personal employment strategy that can strengthen their employment options. For those who have lost their jobs, a strategy including alternatives that can help them find employment with less vulnerability is an important thing to prepare.

Outsourcing today is primarily occurring in large technology companies and those involved in sophisticated industrial manufacturing, large software developers, large IT and management consulting firms with large IT contracts, IT contractors that have contracts with large corporations, and other large financial services and retailing companies that have large amounts of routine, processing-type work that is not that complicated.

The primary incentive for all these organizations is to reduce costs, and thus improve annual profits, by eliminating head count or the need to hire additional IT employees. A related political issue with some of this outsourcing is that some organizations are outsourcing work that have federal and state government contracts. This issue will continue to surface relative to the use of taxpayer funds and things like unemployment benefits paid to workers who were employed by organizations that have federal and state government contracts but who lost they jobs to outsourcing. This sensitive issue could also extend to any organizations that are specially chartered to do work in the United States by the federal or state governments such as banks and insurance companies as examples.

OUTSOURCING TO INDIA

The majority of the present IT outsourcing work will continue to go to India for several basic reasons. India has one of the largest English-speaking populations outside of the United States. A high percentage of college graduates in India for the past 20 years or so are fluent in English. It is also forecast that within the next 10 years, India will have as many college graduates in the physical, mathematical, and computer science disciplines as exist in the United States. The other important reasons are that the IT occupation is supported by the Indian government, and the companies based in India pursuing IT outsourcing contracts do high-quality work paying software writing incomes ranging from one sixth to one tenth annual wages of U.S. entry level and experienced programmers.

With a good annual wage in India for software writers ranging from as low as $6,000 for basic entry-level work to as high as $12,000 for the more experienced highly skilled worker, it is not hard to understand how U.S. software workers displaced by outsourcing believe that workers from India currently possess an unfair competitive advantage. This is particularly relevant in any situations where government taxpayer funds are financing contracts for any organizations that may be participating in outsourcing of computer work outside of the United States.

Not only has the competitive situation in India hurt U.S. software code writers, but the changes in simplification of the process have as well, making it easier than in the past to be able to write usable software code. This development has tended to have a commoditizing effect on the profession relegating much of it to routine process-type work. To a certain degree, the profession over the years has also done some injury to itself. Several years ago, when programmers were in high demand, job hopping for income increases was prevalent; it was not uncommon for some programmers to have as many as several jobs during a 3- to 4-year period. It is doubtful that this type of activity did much to strengthen the overall health of the profession.

Today it is also important for IT programmers to understand the perspective of the typical IT code writer in India. First, they are well educated, speak good English, and are capable of producing quality work on a consistent basis. Many are relatively recent college graduates, and many are educated not only in computer science but also in mathematics, engineering, and the other physical sciences.

The average programmer has pride in doing good work, wants to learn, and enjoys the newly developed opportunity to earn as much as double what they would have earned in other occupations related to their educational training. It is not hard to understand why the majority of them are enthusiastic about this new opportunity that affords many of them the opportunity annually to double to triple what their educated parents may earn or have earned during their work careers. Sounds somewhat similar to the United States, doesn't it?

After completing their formal education and starting their first job, most of India's new employees are as enthusiastic as many of those in the United States. However, for many in India, it is still a relatively new industry, and there is extra pressure on them to succeed and to work very hard at succeeding.

Most of their work being routine, task-oriented process-type work will not help them develop higher level programming and software engineering skills. India's companies that control the outsourcing work, for the most part, are quite secretive about the type of work they do as well as the range of wages they pay, of which a significant amount may be considerably lower than what is published, which further complicates this situation that will not go away. The outsourcing work is organized and implemented by project managers, many of whom received their education and software experience in the United States.

From a competitive perspective, it is unknown whether India's highly educated PhDs in mathematics, the physical sciences, and certain engineering disciplines can successfully perform the more sophisticated type of software and systems engineering work that technological companies require. If this transition can be successfully made, India will eventually threaten much of the software engineering work requiring higher skills and experience. Most will not have the right type of work or length of experience required to accomplish this; however, with the existing cost advantage, the outsourcing companies can expend a lot of additional employees toward developing the required skill. When you can put four or five employees on a task as compared to one in the United States, at less cost, these companies may be able to master much of the more sophisticated work.

Given the accuracy of the previous content of this chapter and what is forecast, what can U.S. software writers do to remove themselves from these challenging types of situations?

SIX STRATEGIES FOR IT EMPLOYEES LOSING JOBS AS A RESULT OF OUTSOURCING

1. Opt Out of IT, Sign Up for a Lower Paying Unrelated Job

This may be the best solution for many, especially for those who believe that their skills are marginally relevant and that they are not able to afford the time and cost required to build the necessary skills. For those who want to continue working with IT, consider looking into opportunities within education for teaching possibilities.

2. Pursue Contract or Part-Time Employment Based Upon Your Technical Skills, While Pursuing Permanent Employment

Networking organizations can provide a good forum for these opportunities as can the staffing companies discussed in Chapter 9. These companies often represent clients who have short-term project needs. The other possibility is to contact all IT applications services providers in your geographic area to understand their projects and needs, which are always changing.

3. Consider Self-Employment Doing Consulting Work

If you have specialized software writing skills and specialized applications or industry related experience, initiating a marketing campaign by sending out query letters to all of the industry specific possibilities within your geographic area would be a good trial and error type test. The problem with consulting work as an individual is that you always need to be developing prospects for your work which often conflicts with the projects that you are currently handling. The main value is that after doing this type of work for a year or two your relevant experience is significantly increased and due to exposure in working with several organizations you may have good opportunities to consider for permanent employment.

4. While Doing Contract or Self-Employment Work, Take IT Educational Courses That Can Help Expand Your Expertise Beyond Software Writing

Many programmers whose jobs have been outsourced may have some degree of knowledge and experience in other primary IT disciplines. Taking some advanced courses in these disciplines may be a good career investment for many. Self-employment work that you are doing concurrently may also provide the opportunity to put some of the new education to work in conjunction with your software work.

5. Consider Marketing Yourself to Smaller-/Medium-Sized Companies That May Take You Out of the Potentially Vulnerable Position of Doing Routine Coding and Software Writing in Large Organizations

Many programmers would be better off today working in the small- and medium-sized organization sector ranging from 100 to 999 employees. At the smaller end of this range, you might be asked to handle multiple tasks that provide you the opportunity to work and gain important experience with functional applications and their implementation with end users. This is not referring to help desk or technical assistance-type activities, but there also would be some of this because, in the smaller companies, you tend to be called on to do everything for everybody once you have established your credibility and provided evidence that you understand the things that they need to understand.

The main value of this type of position in smaller firms is that you will often have the opportunity to be a part of supporting their most important business processes and can also be responsible for implementing applications and work that involves other key IT disciplines outside of software writing.

This type of work is totally in contrast with basic code writing doing similar work as others in large organizations for long periods of time. The advantage from a perspective of career enhancement value is that you gain experience with the primary business process and practices of successful growing companies, which you would rarely be able to do in large organizations.

For those that have good people skills and can successfully work in and lead groups, the opportunity to grow into IT management positions will exist in these organizations for those that aspire to this.

The referenceUSA database discussed in the last section of Chapter 9 can provide you with the opportunity to identify scores of small- to medium-sized companies to contact within a large metropolitan statistical area or within a 10- to 50-mile radius or so from your personal geographic home base. If you have significant industry experience within one or two industries by SIC code, this database includes the majority of these possibilities for both public and private companies. You can also identify the companies that have very good to excellent credit, which is also an important part of identifying prospective companies to contact.

You may have noticed earlier that the author specified targeting companies for contact in the 100- to 999-employee range, which the referenceUSA database enables you to do. In the author's opinion, the majority of the incremental IT job growth will occur during the next several years in these small- to medium-sized companies, and the majority of these jobs will not be vulnerable to IT job outsourcing. When you consider software writing, the web, databases, security, networks, open source software, and so on, these smaller companies have the same needs as the larger ones, but many are simply slower about getting around to addressing these needs. This is why these type of organizations can provide significant opportunity for experienced programmers. Programming is still the one skill that has a close relationship with the various other IT disciplines mentioned previously. In summary, the potential value of this type of experience to any programmer is that he or she is exposed to business practices, process, and end user work and applications that most would never have the opportunity to work with in large corporations with large software-writing staffs.

6. Consider Other Potential Opportunities to Broaden the Application of Your Skills and Experience

What is being advocated here is pursuing opportunities to broaden the application of code writing and other basic software engineering-related skills. This is the area that needs a lot of leadership by example at this time. In order not to be vulnerable to outsourcing, programmers need to learn to go where the code writers in other countries are not qualified to go and in so doing adding significant value to U.S. companies. In other words, employ some creativity to changing the playing field and reshaping the profession.

This sounds good, but how do you achieve this? It will happen if software writers take on different types of responsibilities in companies compared to those to which they were usually relegated. This is happening today throughout the financial services business in the marketing area through the application of CRM software. Scores of financial services organizations are learning by providing their customer base with more convenient access over the web so that they can use CRM software for data-mining-type analytical work. This activity followed by customer contact regarding their alternative array of services is a comparatively more cost-effective method of growing their revenue than most present methods. Software companies currently developing CRM application software now number over 30, and this number is growing . Some of the more progressive companies are using the utility-type concept of not selling the software but charging for use. CRM software is projected to grow to the annual revenue level of $75 billion to $77 billion by leading IT research firms, Gartner Dataquest and Forrester Research. This growth will also provide significant job-related opportunities in all types of companies that decide to implement various CRM application packages. Currently the majority of this software is focused upon finance, marketing, sales, customer service, human resources, and supply chain applications.

Individuals who are qualified to work with things such as network and web security applications, the application of open source software, and wireless and voice over internet applications should consider approaching CRM from a contract work or consulting perspective. From a self-marketing perspective, these are the types of things where significant effort should be placed in prospecting activities through query letters. Most of them are not the type of things that software job candidates are going to find listed in web job-posting sites for full-time positions where their qualifications are the right match.

The social networking networks discussed in Chapter 8 are the types of places where contacts can lead to identification of potential employment or contract employment opportunities that do not fit into the standard IT job classifications, which is where most individuals do not want to be because better alternatives may exist for them. Identifying these types of opportunities will take a significant amount of effort weekly for those who are committed to finding new employment possibilities.

For large U.S. companies with earnings challenges, reverting to outsourcing may only be a temporary fix. Many are going to discover that their long-term interests can be better served by investing in improvement of their internal efficiency focusing upon things like applications that have an impact on productivity and efficiency within their most critical functions. Outsourcing for many may be like a temporary program patch that will require more attention later.

These types of companies should not be overlooked as potential opportunities for contract work. The thing to remember is that most of them wanted not only to reduce the cost of software writing work but also to reduce the cost of benefits for their permanent employment.

The previous six items are not the only things to pursue when reestablishing potential employment. There are many others, but these are the things that can start new development of applications of software writing skills that can be communicated across the self-help networks that are being established by individuals who have lost employment as a result of outsourcing. The author is confident that these and similar types of things several years from now will redefine and reestablish the application of software writing and programming and its relationship to the business practices of organizations to a level of value provided where it will be much more difficult to commoditize and outsource it. This will occur as the result of the new ground that thousands of programmers will break and prove by applying their skills. This is probably well underway at this time in scores of situations that can serve as models; however, most are simply not documented at this time.

For those IT professionals who have lost and will lose their jobs to outsourcing, the most important thing to have, if you decide to stay in IT, is a set of alternative strategies to be used in marketing yourself for new employment. As a result of the previous data in this chapter and your networking you probably already have implemented several strategies. Most may have difficulty locating opportunities in their preferred geographic area through web résumé-posting sites and the online job-posting sites. If you are willing to consider relocating to other metropolitan areas, your opportunities may increase.

However, for most the job-hunting process is going to be the equivalent of a full-time job until you are successful. You need to be prepared to make this type of time commitment, which can be completed during evenings and weekends if preferred. If you have experienced difficulty or believe that you will, you need to have several alternative job-finding strategies that you implement on a trial-and-error type basis to determine which ones are the best for you based upon your skills and experience. High-telephone activity and the mailing and follow-up of a large number of query letters prior to sending out your résumé is the best way to do this.

At the outset of this type of R&D-type testing, you need to determine where your total skills and experience best fit. It is important to remember that in most cases your strategy should be a new one and with a revised résumé sent after you have generated interest through phone calls and query letters. If you have developed a new and different résumé, you should repost it and apply to a few selected job postings where your background appears to fit.

DEVELOPING AND IMPLEMENTING NEW EMPLOYMENT STRATEGIES

The first step in implementing new strategies for job finding is to develop a profile of skills and experience that in most cases will be in addition to the technical skills and job experience listed in your current résumé. If this exercise is successful for you in making significant improvement to your résumé, it should open up scores of new prospects for you to contact. The use of the query letter as discussed in Chapter 10 will be the best way in many of these situations to generate potential interest. The objective of these contacts is to offer your potential services in numerous forms that will generate enough interest to gain you a significant number of personal interviews. In many of these situations, you will be promoting skills, experience, and capabilities that you were not or are not able to use in previous and present jobs. The total objective in this type of approach is to generate a high quantity of potential interest in yourself, significantly higher than the job-hunting sources used by most other IT job candidates. The first step in this process is your personal assessment of your total skills and experience to determine if an opportunity exists to strengthen your résumé significantly and the expertise offered to be promoted in query letters. The best way to complete a skill profile is to complete a series of questions that will help you build a stronger personal skill profile than presently exists.

- Write a summary statement of the skills and experience that you could offer a small growth type company in the size range of 100 to 500 employees.
- If you have significant industry experience and application development or modification experience, what are the industries and applications?
- Do you have adequate understanding of any of the following disciplines where you would be comfortable doing related software writing or mod-

ification type work: the web, networks, relational databases, CRM or ERP application packages, open source software, voice over internet protocol or wireless?

- Do you have any significant experience working on project teams? Define any significant experience or leadership roles, as well as details of any high-profile projects that related to important business practices.
- Write a summary description of your people skills. Concentrate on team and group participation, and characterize your performance in team or group situations.
- Assess your interpersonal skills focusing upon writing, speaking, presentations, listening, and consideration of others as well as what type of influence you are on others. How would you characterize your skills in a one paragraph summary of these subjects?

Use these questions to stimulate ideas that you may have. These questions should be used to build an approach for job hunting.

This is an example of a potential situation to market that might appeal to high-growth medium-sized companies. It is for candidates who have strong functional applications knowledge and related software writing experience. The candidate could present him- or herself as a potential marketing systems analyst who could be involved in web application development. In this responsibility, the analyst would coordinate projects with the IT department to ensure that the necessary software development is consistent with the needs of the primary functional end users who will benefit from the software. Optimum use of these tools, which is a function of proper development, will make significant contributions to continued growth as well as comparative competitive advantage for years to come. Having a competent marketing analyst or project-type manager who is assigned to marketing and who will work closely with IT to gain the best possible results could prove to be a wise investment.

This type of uncommon position would require good people and end user communication skills as well as the ability to communicate progress and problems effectively to senior management. Experience with this type of responsibility within selected industries might only last for a year or two in smaller- to medium-sized organizations, but the experience gained could be useful in marketing this type of experience and expertise to larger companies. Many organizations over the next several years will want to improve efficiencies within several critical functions or business practices in order to remain competitive and continue their profitable growth.

The overall value of aggressively trying to create interest in positions such as these is that they get the candidate out of the uncertainty associated with commoditized, routine, process code writing and significantly broaden his or her business experience. If worked properly, this strategy can lead to excellent project manager and other IT management or more senior-type positions with higher pay, avoiding outsourcing or job cuts, as long as the employee provides significant value to the organization helping it to remain financially stable and successful.

In order to put new strategies for job hunting to work after completing your revised résumé (consult Chapter 6), and your profile of skills and experience, consider where and how to apply this information to get the desired result of a significant amount of discussions and personal interviews with prospective employers. Keep in mind that, based upon your experience profile, relative to application, functional, and industry understanding, you may be addressing your contacts to senior functional management other than IT. In fact, you may contact both in the same company, and in some situations you may receive more promising results.

The best way to identify industry-specific companies of a certain employee or revenue size within your targeted geographical areas is to locate referenceUSA, which lists the more than 13 million public and private companies. This excellent CD-ROM database, from parent company infoUSA of Omaha, can be found in many large college, university, and public libraries and in many state employment assistance offices. This excellent tool will help you build a tailored prospect list in various industries and will also identify those that have very good to excellent credit which is important. In the "Tailoring Your Job Search" in Chapter 9, this tool is discussed in more detail. Spending several hours with this product enables you to cover hundreds of possibilities efficiently. Printed company directories often contain no more than 3,000 companies, and you cannot define criteria selection in most of them.

After you have developed your prospect list of several hundred potential organizations to contact, the next important step is to research them thoroughly. Most large metropolitan area newspapers maintain a web-based database of company business articles for several years. Try this as one good potential source. If some of the selected companies have web sites, many will include articles regarding them that appear in periodicals or news of any significant developments that have occurred within the organization. If it is convenient, it is also a good idea to stop by each company's reception area or job application area to obtain any internal publications that may be helpful to you in tailoring your query letters or phone calls. referenceUSA company profiles also contain a list of senior company management by function.

When using referenceUSA, you want to call to confirm before making letter or phone contact because across a large number of prospective companies for contact, management changes will have occurred since the last updating.

The most helpful source that the author has used for years to obtain company information that has appeared during the past several years in newspapers, trade journals, and other periodicals is the business information database of Lexus-Nexus, which is often found in college and university libraries as well as larger public libraries. Lexus-Nexus is a large concentrator of these articles and will sometimes contain data that is not available from other sources which is also much more beneficial than expending an extensive search across other sources. In other words, any research is time-consuming, and you want to get to the desired results in prospective company identification and research as rapidly as possible.

You do not want to convince yourself that time in research is really getting you anywhere until you have made the contacts and secured interviews. The best example of this is IT job candidates who have posted their résumés over the months to hundreds of web job postings and have not received any amount of success from these efforts. Don't get into the trap of a false sense of security like many have in posting for these jobs.

If you are unable to locate Lexus-Nexus Academic Universe, another good source is the ABI/Inform product of ProQuest Corporation, also found in many college, university, and large public libraries. This product contains abstracts from business periodicals that go back to 1992, which is another potential source.

The main thing in this process, which is being recommended for use, is that it is more exclusive. Most of the companies selected are not being contacted by a significant number of IT job candidates as compared to web-posted jobs, some companies may be considering adding IT staff but have not advertised or posted, and if you are able to achieve significant current, meaningful information through your research, you should be able to make more professional phone or query letter contact.

The important and most critical thing to remember in job hunting is that, in any type of contact, you need to gain a commitment to talk, whether over the phone or in person. The second most critical thing to remember is that when you get the opportunity to talk, you need to be prepared to converse effectively, in order to ask for a commitment for further discussion or, if this is not possible at the time, to gain permission for a tentative date for follow up to schedule a time. Again, all the effort has gained nothing until you gain commitments for personal meetings or interviews, which in many organizations will be a several-step process.

If your personal strength is phone contact after you have completed your prospect identification and research, use it. If not, use the query letter approach and follow up. The objective of each approach is to gain an appointment to talk in person, or as a minimum to talk further on the phone. In phone conversations whether they are with the senior IT official, or any other senior organization manager, try to avoid getting moved to the human resource department because the majority of time you will end up getting the response, "Send us your resume or come in and fill out an application," neither of which you want to do.

When this occurs and your research has indicated that the subject company you are contacting is the type of business and industry that you believe would represent a good opportunity for you, try to get a personal audience with the manager. A good simple way to approach this is to call the manager and say, "I have researched your company thoroughly, and I would like a few minutes of your time to discuss a new concept in IT related to my skills and experience that could have significant potential benefits for (company name)." Then quickly say, "I will only need 15 minutes of your time and will come in any day you say early in the morning or late in the day or even on a Saturday if this would be better for your schedule. I will not waste your time." If the manager should say, "Let's discuss it now," you need to say "I don't believe the concepts can be properly discussed over the phone." In some cases, you may want to present a brief summary presentation of the concept, which would be a good idea to prepare.

This type of presentation in Power Point or similar could list the summary points of the concepts you want to discuss. An interesting format could be excerpted from several of the summary points made earlier in this chapter discussion. Things such as the relationships of critical functional applications to primary business practices and functional end users can be the basis for a good discussion where that manager sees their internal needs. Include some discussion of the IT mediums that are viewed as most important for development.

If after a meeting of this type, the manager shows some interest and you have taken some notes on what appear to be some key points of interest, it is a good idea for you to ask permission to write a brief proposal on the concept. In addition, ask the manager if he or she believes that it would be a good idea to talk with any employee who could provide input to make the proposal more meaningful. This approach used over and over will generate interest and can lead to job opportunities.

This type of approach represents the most basic marketing and selling of yourself. After gaining some experience with it, applying it in situations that you have researched and that fit your background, and using it in personal phone calls or in-person meetings where you have identified areas of potential interest, you will be ahead of thousands of other IT job hunters. Most of them have become somewhat discouraged due to amount of interest received from many hours of job search type activities that were for the most part too convenient and not risk threatening enough. It is human nature for all of us, when we have worked hard on something as important as job search but have not received the desired results, to become frustrated. Also when something as threatening as making phone calls into organizations where we are not known or were not requested to contact, the fear of rejection always exists, which is the reason that most IT job applicants are not comfortable with using direct contact approaches. After being embarrassed by doing it a few times, most of us tend to become more effective. And when you need a job, the wrong response is not to try it anymore just to avoid the potential unpleasantness.

For anyone interested in trying to use this type of approach, the reason that most who try it are not successful is not that they performed horribly during the phone contact. It is usually more of a function of not being properly prepared relative to research, which often results in a less than professional phone discussion where the manager is not impressed enough to talk further or even as a minimum to direct you to someone else in the firm. In most situations, when you are properly prepared, a brief conversation covering key points of what you are proposing and a suggested next step is adequate. If you sense that it is appropriate, ask for a meeting or request to talk with someone else when necessary in order to gain better understanding of their needs.

All of this can be done in no more than a minute when you are properly prepared for the conversation and relate your interests to their business needs professionally.

After being a few years out of college, the author sold business services to all sizes of business and government organizations for several years. Whenever it was possible to get in front of people, the majority of times without a prior appointment, I asked, "If I can demonstrate to you that our services will help your organization better achieve your organization's business objectives better than what you are currently using, will you consider the possibility of using our services?" By using this quick simple question, the author received a positive response in 90% of several hundred situations during approximately 3 years of sales work. As a minimum in most situations, an assignment was obtained, either to write a brief proposal letter or talk with another manager.

In summary, don't ever make any type of query without attempting to gain some type of further reaction that can lead to a proposal, a meeting, another phone conversation, or a meeting with another official. Lack of effective use of this type of a process is the reason why many IT job candidates are somewhat frustrated and discouraged when they have expended large amounts of job-finding effort and have not been successful. The primary reasons for most failures are wrong sources of contact, wrong approaches, inadequate preparation, or fear of rejection.

For application software and other code writers, the corollary to the author's example is this: "If I can prove to you or the appropriate functional manager that my skills and experience can make significant contributions to your business priorities, would you consider giving my employment a test?" It is predictable that, in some situations, you will receive a response similar to what do you mean, or what are you proposing? When this occurs, you should propose something similar to "If you could either authorize or arrange for me to spend a half day at your company talking with key employees who understand your most important computer-related needs, I could then quickly prepare a proposal detailing how my experience and skill could help contribute to your projects."

After making suggestions such as this, you need to be prepared to determine with whom you should talk to understand the priorities. If it is nor clear to the manager with whom you are talking, then ask if you could arrange to talk with someone who would understand the details of the major challenges for a few minutes while you are there. If the manager with whom you are talking is interested in pursuing this concept, he or she may agree for you to talk with several individuals for a few minutes while you are there, which is even better.

In essence, what you are trying to achieve in situations such as this is quick access so that you can learn of an organization's current IT challenges, which as a minimum may lead to a test-type assignment or in some cases a consulting assignment or in others directly to completing a proposal for employment consideration. The important thing to remember is that in smaller high-growth companies there is a significant opportunity to learn and gain valuable job experience that most would not have gained in their previous jobs.

The problem in the smaller organizations is that once your skills are understood you at times will be requested to be all things to everyone who wants to better understand how applications and other software works. If this represents too much of a contrast that you do not welcome compared to your former code writing and programming-type responsibilities, these types of jobs are probably not for you.

However, if you welcome this type of opportunity to do whatever you can do to provide value and to make meaningful contributions, the experience that you can gain will prove beneficial to your future career success. You will have many opportunities to do the type of things that can broaden and expand your personal skills and qualifications that you would rarely if ever have the opportunity to do in large organizations where many others are doing the same type of work.

The results of effective efforts of the type described in this chapter applied by thousands of programmers, code writers, and other software writing professionals during the next few years will help accomplish several significant things within the profession. Many success stories networked over the web for self-help-type purposes will assist thousands of others strengthen their personal value, making many of them less potentially vulnerable to outsourcing.

Possibly the most important end result is that the hundreds of resultant jobs obtained by using this type of approach will tend over time to redefine the value and status of basic programming work, taking much of it out of the commodity-type, easily outsourced category. A worthwhile objective is the contributions of many entrepreneurs who will break some new ground. They collectively will open up new types of employment possibilities for thousands within the profession. This type of result also has the potential of removing many thousands of code-writing programming-type jobs that would have left the country from outsourcing consideration.

Who knows how much the type of efforts advocated within this chapter can be successful in derailing much of the outsourcing that is occurring. If outsourcing is viewed as a cost saving, quick-fix-type strategy for many large companies, it would appear not to exist in most cases on a solid business foundation. What will be proven over the next several years is yet to be known; however, if the profession forces large companies to recognize the accomplishments of the hundreds who are doing significant creative, valuable work the contributions of outsourcings outside of the country may be short-lived. The one thing that is certain is that most of those individuals in the less-sophisticated programming-type work are going to have to broaden their skills and move away from the commodity-type work where possible to reduce their potential vulnerability.

Using some of the concepts outlined in this chapter and networking with others regarding their experience in new job-hunting techniques can help achieve reduced job vulnerability as well as help many who have lost their jobs to outsourcing find new jobs.

13. Sample Résumés

The Objective of This Chapter

This chapter shows examples of résumés for 30 of the IT jobs that are in most demand today.

The résumé formats used illustrate the résumé components discussed in Chapter 6 and most of the sample résumés include a summary description of accomplishments/achievements. Several of the résumés relate achievements, discussing project participation and leadership aspects where significant contributions of value were provided to the employer. Whenever possible, candidates should incorporate items of this type in their résumés.

The skills summary section at the end in most of the résumés arranges skills in categories such as operating systems, programming languages, database, web, and networks, which is also recommended when possible.

Also noteworthy is the fact that most skill summaries or profiles include a listing of skills other than technical skills, which is desired today by as much as 50% of all employers job specifications. Chapter 3 summarizes the the technical skills most in demand, and Chapter 5 discusses the skills other than technical skills that are most in demand from IT employers.

It may also be to a candidate's advantage to include a listing under the heading Environment, which is included in several résumés under the individual jobs listed in the Work History summary portion. Inclusion of this type of summary could help stimulate employer interest in some cases.

The sample résumés in this chapter are correlated with the skill profile data in Chapter 3. The résumés included represent more than 90% of the IT jobs currently available within the United States and possibly a higher percentage of new (nonreplacement) jobs available. The résumés included were selected as the result of analyzing 70,000 web job-posting services listings of employer's job descriptions and those from individual companies' web sites. The results of this analysis were compared to the listings of several of the job-posting services that listed the largest number of IT jobs each month.

IT industry market research and consulting sources indicated that more than 200,000 available IT jobs were not able to be filled during 2003, which one of these sources indicated resulted primarily from the lack of required skills being available. The author is of the opinion that this has occurred because the more than 4 million estimated current IT employees in the United States have not had a good source of reference for employer skill needs. To further complicate the matter, these needs have undergone significant change and definition during the past 5 years.

As of this writing, the author is aware of *Dice.com* as the only online technical job source that currently publishes a summary of IT job skill needs regularly throughout the year. As mentioned earlier, the job skill profiles listed in Chapter 3 are consistent with the Dice data published during the past 2 years. This will undoubtedly improve, but for now IT professionals who want to better understand the possibilities and needs related to job search or additional education must put forth some significant research on their own.

The following is a listing of the primary job categories with the most IT jobs available at the time of writing and a listing of the job sample résumés included in this section.

Ryan K. Lynch
63 York Avenue
Elmhurst, IL 60201
(312) 707-5907
rklpro@aol.com

Professional Qualification Summary

IT professional knowledgeable and experienced in the development and implementation of VoIP telephony systems. Strong background working with telecommunications and data communications internet applications as well as wireless technology.

Employment History

Rockwell International   Wood Dale, IL   **2002 to present**
VoIP Engineer

Developed and implemented R&D lab network using new VoIP ACD capabilities for integration of Rockwell business net with primary vendor applications.

Motorola Corporation   Schaumburg, IL   **2000 to 2002**
Systems Engineer

Involved in engineering development work for mobile communications and wireless product software. Achieved a major design improvement and received company recognition for this accomplishment during 2001.

Internet Telephony   Portland, OR   **1999 to 2000**
Protocol Engineer

Participated on a team responsible for implementing one of the earlier VoIP installations made in the United States. Team installed voice over IP WANS for internet phone services over a voice-enabled web site.

Oregon State Department of Transportation   Salem, OR   **1998 to 2000**
Network Engineer

Participated in work group responsible for hardware and software upgrade and verification testing for the year 2000 project, which was successful in eliminating potential problems.

Technical and Other Skills Summary

Network Protocols: TCP/IP, VPN, IPsec, RIP, SNMP, DNS

VoIP Protocols: H.323, ISDN, MGCP, SCCP

Languages: Visual Basic, C, C++, Java Assembly, JavaScript, Unix Shell, TCL

Security: Cisco RSA, Check Point & PIX Firewalls

Operating Systems: Unix, Windows XP/2000/NT

Other: VoIP Gateway, VoIP Qos, VPN Solutions, IP telephony, Cisco Call Manager

Excellent team participation, communications, project management, and problem solving skills

Education

BS Degree Computer Science with Mathematics Minor
University of California Berkeley

Jason R. Richards
47 North Street
Severna Park, MD 20850
(410) 407-6855
email: jrich@yahoo.com

Summary

Eight years of network, telephone, and data communications experience. Have understanding of wireless and VoIP related technology. Am interested in a management position in an IT department interested in development and implementation of these technologies. Have high-level skills in each discipline.

Employment

Verizon   Warren, NJ   **October 2001 to July 2004**
Wireless Project Engineer

Member of a project team that developed the architecture for a Verizon wireless network. Work was primarily focused upon network and wireless protocols.

Kaiser Permanente   Walnut Creek, CA   **August 2000 to September 2001**
Network Engineer

Responsible for engineering maintenance support for voice, data, and video network systems located in Western United States.

- Successfully moved traffic from vendor network to IP network resulting in annual maintenance cost savings in excess of $400,000.

- Achieved annual savings in excess of two million dollars by moving voice network to an ATM network.

Lockheed Martin Corporation   Bethesda, MD   **November 1996 to July 2000**
Network Engineer

Primary responsibilities involved federal contract work with the Department of Defense, Air Force, and foreign governments relative to the provision of secure internet, intranet, and extranet networks. Majority of work was primarily focused upon reliable movement of engineering and parts data throughout the world.

Made significant contributions as a team member that developed and implemented the architecture of a secure network that daily moves data around the world via broadband and satellite transmission.

- Participated in receipt of vendor excellence recognition award from the Air Force.

Jason R. Richards   Page 2

Skills

Operating Systems: Windows NT, 2000, XP, Unix, Solaris, Linux

Database: Oracle 8i, 9i, SQL, MS SQL, MS Access

Protocols: TCP/IP, FTP, SMTP, AXP, SNMP, IP Suites

Wide Area: Frame Relay, ATM, SDLC, HDLC

Additional: Cisco Routers, Catalyst Switches, OSI Reference Model, Firewall, Intrusion Detection and Encryption Tools

Strong Verbal, Written, Interpersonal, and Teamwork Skills

Education

BS Computer Science Rochester Institute of Technology 1996

Certifications: CCNP, MCSE + I

Top Secret Security Clearance

Louise K. Baker
61 Sanford Street
Clifton, NJ 07013
(973) 905-6730
lkbcp@hotmail.com

Professional Experience

Database Developer with six years of experience within the Pharmaceutical Industry. Experience with the latest database development technology and capable of contributing to development of progressive industry leading systems from a value provided perspective. Excellent human relations, team building, and communications skill.

Employment History

Johnson & Johnson   New Brunswick, NY   February 2001 to present
Database Developer R&D Lab

Team leader for the design and implementation of a multi-terabyte data warehouse based upon Java using Oracle 9i database. Conducted internal systems needs survey and analysis of primary R&D users. Project is focused upon molecular biology lab workflow providing web-based application to permit users to submit and share important knowledge management data in a secured internet and intranet network, which is primarily JSP and Java Applet technology.

- Received highest level annual performance review for contributions to this system during 2002 and 2003. System is providing R&D technologists with quality data that previously was not conveniently available, which helps improve the quality and potential value of their work.

Becton Dickinson   Franklin Lakes, NJ   July 1997 to January 2001
Database Engineer New Drug Development

Involved in some of the earliest projects within the pharmaceutical industry applying the latest database technology to provide quality data mining and intelligent knowledge management tools to drug development scientists. System incorporated a comprehensive data classification system and a search engine capability that enabled scientists to locate the type of desired data rapidly.

- Received highest level performance appraisals possible for years 1999 and 2000.

Skills Summary

Programming Language: Java, J2EE, Java Swing, EJB, JSP/Servets, Java Applets, HTML, XML, XLST, C++, Cold Fusion, OOP, GUI

Database: Oracle 8i,9i, SQL 2000

Operating Systems: HP-UX, Solaris, AIX, Windows 2000

Software: PowerBuilder, Unix Shell Script, Perl, OLTP, Artificial Intelligence Software, Documentum, ATG Dynamo

Excellent interpersonal, personal relations, and communications (written, oral, and presentation) skills

Education

BS Degrees in Computer Science & Biology, Penn State University

Graduated with honors achieving a cumulative grade point average of 3.8

Have lectured at Fairleigh Dickinson University on application of computer software in the bioscience and pharmaceutical disciplines.

Michael D. Metz, Jr.
84 Birch Drive
Barrington, IL 62226
(312) 715-6343
metzmd@aol.com

Career Profile

Twelve years of database development and Oracle database administration within the medical and healthcare fields. Have comprehensive knowledge and experience working with healthcare applications. Interested in qualifying for management responsibility within a large medical enterprise with major needs for database and related applications development.

Employment

Saint Luke Medical Center   Chicago, IL   **2001 to present**
Oracle Database Administrator

Responsible for all database development within this large medical center. Primary work has involved the development and implementation of several OLTP and data warehouse databases. Developed, tested, and implemented disaster recovery and new database security software. Wrote programs for recovery and consolidation of patient records from disparate databases.

University of Utah   Salt Lake City, UT   **1998 to 2001**
Oracle Database Administrator for Huntsman Cancer Institute

Development and modification of databases used for storage of genetic analysis of cancer patient history. Developed a knowledge management type query system for retrieval of selective data. Also developed indexing type applications for inventory and control of chemicals, drugs, and genetic relevant data including DNA.

Massachusetts General Hospital   Boston, MA   **1996 to 1998**
Database Developer

Redesigned system in Oracle database for management of patient records and billing. Used PL/SQL to achieve significant improvement in the quality of and reliability associated with management report generation regarding key cost areas of hospital operations.

Battelle Institute   Cambridge, MA   **1994 to 1996**
Programmer

Worked on several government contracts that involved design modification of existing databases and development of new customized databases for internet/intranet applications.

Technical Skills

Operating Systems: Unix, Linux, HP-UX, Windows NT, 2000

Programming Languages: SQL, PL/SQL, Visual Basic, C++, Unix Shell Script, C/C#, COBOL

Software: Oracle 8i, 9i Server, Oracle Clinical, ERwin, Perl, Visio

Internet: JavaScript, PL/SQL, HTML

Other: Strong people skills, verbal and writing skills, problem solving, analytical, project management, healthcare industry hospital operations applications, and R&D processes

Education

BS Degree Computer Science, University of Massachusetts, Amherst, 1994

Stephen R. Kurtz
419 Maple Street
Richmond, VA 22042
(804) 617-4922
srkurtz@mindspring.com

Career Profile

More than ten years of data architecture and data modeling experience. Strong enterprise modeling experience supporting most functional areas within finance, government, and high-tech organizations. Detailed knowledge of federal processes.

Employment Summary

Capital One   Richmond, VA   **2001 to present**
Data Warehouse Developer

Lead developer on project to build a central data warehouse for various financial and project reports, of which many were previously completed manually. The physical model used for development consisted of Platinum ERwin & DDL, Active X, Visual Basic Script, and T-SQL.

• Resulted in reduction of annual labor costs associated with the former system by 25%.

Environment: Windows XP, Oracle 8.0, MS Access 2000, SLA/OLA, PeopleSoft, Excel 2000, T-SQL, VB Scripts, Platinum ERwin, Visio 2002, DTS packages

State of Alabama   Montgomery, AL   **1997 to 2001**
Database Engineer

Developed disaster recovery system for call centers including daily reports to department/agency management using Crystal Reports. Responsible for completion of performance monitoring and trend analysis of SQL Servers used throughout state offices.

• Results achieved reduced system downtime and error rates, which improved 40% compared to previous methods, 24/7 downtime was reduced to less than 0.5%.

Northrup/Grumman   Dayton, OH   **1990 to 1997**
Systems Programmer

Responsible for development and implementation of software network solutions/specific for several major clients. Assigned to development work for the Air Force, Army, Navy, and Marines. Development work included achieving detailed understanding of the unique requirements of each branch of the military in order for development work to achieve its objectives.

Served as team leader for four teams concurrently. Have top secret security clearance.

Environment: Oracle database, HP-UX, Unix Platforms, Windows NT, NT Server

Additional Technical Skill: DB2, MS Access, HTML, ASP, JavaScript, VB Script

Education

The Ohio State University Columbus

BS Mathematics, MS Computer Science

Alexander S. Chekoff
47 Belden Place
Livingston, NJ 07042
(973) 907-4871
Email achekoff@home.com

Summary of Qualifications

Strong software engineering skills combined with mathematical skills for complex algorithm related projects. Six years of work experience including software development work within the banking, electrical manufacturing, and transportation industries.

Employment Summary

Statement One   Lawrenceville, NJ   **2002–Present**
Software Engineer

Developed cryptographic software with algorithms for data protection application. Served as team leader for development of customer support web-based financial statement report system for analysis of transactional financial data.

Emerson Electric   St. Louis, MO   **1999–2002**
Software Engineer Product Design Department

- Project leader for the development of engineering design software used for optimization design of small electric motors.

- Team achieved reduction of motor design cost in excess of 20%, which saved a minimum of five hundred thousand dollars annually.

Federal Express   Collegeville, TN   **1997–1999**
Programmer/Analyst

Assigned project responsibility to resolve credit card processing problem that was frequently causing processing to crash on production servers. Involved significant software code revision and testing over twelve months.

- Project team solved related problems that had been causing customer service and billing adjustment problems that affected several thousand customers annually.

Technical and Other Skills

Languages: C/C++, Visual C++, Java, JavaScript, SQL Server, Embedded SQL, PL/SQL, Lisp

Data Communications Protocols: TCP/IP, IPX, Frame Relay, SNMP

Other: Assembly, XML, Unix, Solaris, Linux, ksh, EJB, JSP, ASP

Excellent interpersonal, written, and verbal communications skills

Education

BS equivalent in applied mathematics, Moscow State University

Achieved U.S. citizenship January 2004

Carol S. Pearson
142 Daniels Road
Columbus, OH 43220
(614) 270-8457
pearson@home.com

Experience Summary

Six years of software and web development work with experience for banking, retailing, healthcare, and technology environments. Expertise in the latest technology for web site, network, and database development initiatives. Strong teaming skills and working relationships with others.

Employment Summary

The Limited, Inc.   Columbus, OH   **2002 to present**
. NET Developer

Responsible for intranet, web site, and network systems support of marketing, web customer order processing and service, and inventory control, including XML web service for credit card processing.

- Received excellent performance evaluation for 2002 for contributions made for improvement of sales, marketing, inventory, and customer service efficiency.

Environment: MS.NET, SQL Database, ADO database connection, XML, TCP port, Windows 2000

Bank United,   Houston, TX   **2001**
Web Developer

Developed intranet application for maintenance of lock box operations of corporate and large private customers.

Environment: Visual Basic, C++, SQL, XML, ASP, Database Modeling

Boston Communications Group   Woburn, MA   **1998 to 2001**
Software Developer

Developed a web-based message solution and telephony platform that combined voice, fax, and telephony capabilities with wireless access to email.

Environment: Windows 2000/NT, MS.NET, Dialogic CT Media, IIS, ASP, ASP.NET, C#, C++, VB Script, HTML, XML

Self-Employed Consultant   Wellesley, MA   **1997**

Designed a web-based enterprise application and backup services for patient transfer from area hospitals to post hospital care facilities, which permitted hospital administrative staff to coordinate placement online.

System improved overall efficiency and speed of case completion 50% faster than previous method.

Environment: C#, JavaScript, HTML, XML, VB Script, Windows XP/2000, ASP.NET, SQL Server, ADO. NET, IIS

Skill Profile

Programming Language: Visual Basic, SQL, ASP, XML, VB Script, JavaScript, Java, HTML, C, C++, C#, VB.NET, ASP.NET
Database: MS SQL Server, MS Access, Oracle
Software: IIS, Rational Rose, MS Visio, .NET Server
Operating Systems: Windows 2000/NT, Unix
Application Servers: IIS, Apache web
Internet: ASP.NET, ASP, SOAP, HTML, DHTML, DOM, CSS
Other: ADO.NET, UML, RUP, Crystal Reports

Team leadership skills; interpersonal skills; written and oral presentation skills; problem solving, project management, and negotiation skills

Education

BS Degree Computer Science, Boston University 1997 with honors

Robert C. Mays
224 Aspen Road
Littleton, CO 80127
(303) 817-4500
rcmays@hotmail.com

Summary of Qualifications

Experienced developer of Java/J2EE applications. Nine years of experience with leading companies. Capable of developing sophisticated applications using the latest technology. Have good team leadership and people skills.

Employment History

PricewaterhouseCoopers   Denver, CO   **April 2003 to present**
Java/J2EE Consultant

Work in the financial services group on the web development team with responsibility for development and implementation of value-added state-of-the-art type applications.

AT&T   Boulder, CO   **October 2001 to March 2003**
Software Engineer

Involved in development work for creation of a Java/J2EE client server application for processing circuit invoices. Developed multiple user interfaces using JavaSwing applets, servlets, and server pages.

IBM   Boulder, CO   **Febuary 1999 to September 2001**
Software Engineer

Served as team leader of a group responsible for modification and maintenance of a circuit-ordering application involving coding a TCP/IP interface for communication with remote systems.

Arbitron Inc.   Philadelphia, PA   **December 1997 to January 1999**
Programmer

Developed a J2EE compliant web-based large-scale application deployed on Weblogic servers.

Skill Summary

Java Technologies: J2EE, EJB, JMS, JDBC, CMP, XML, Struts, Servlets, JSP, HTML

Operating systems: Windows NT/2000/XP, Solaris

Programming: SQL

Object-Oriented Methods: Rational Unified Process

J2EE Testing: JTEST, LoadRunner, JUNIT

Database: Oracle, DB2, BEA Weblogic

Scripting: Unix Shell Script, Shell Script

Strong problem solving, analytical, verbal, written, interpersonal, team leadership, and customer service skills

Education

BS Degree Computer Science, Lehigh University

Arnold E. Belz
84 Collins Drive
Irving, TX 78745
(817) 540-4300
arnoldeb@mindspring.com

Professional Experience

Seven years of Java and other programming experience within the telecommunications and manufacturing industries. Understand the technology associated with wireless and VoIP systems. Want to continue working with sophisticated applications development projects.

Employment Summary

Sprint Corporation   Irving, TX   **2001 to present**
Java Engineer

Primarily involved with Java web and Unix applications for customer billing information, pricing adjustment, customer reports, test scripts, and contracts revision for both front and back end processing.

Developed project forecasting software that was implemented for weekly and monthly staffing requirements planning.

Received recognition award for resolution of significant number of old systems problems.

Allison Transmission,   Indianapolis, IN   **1998 to 2001**
Programmer

Worked on numerous software development projects. The most significant was as the primary developer for a configuration management artificial intelligence application used for analysis of engineering documentation and change order processing. Perl was the primary development language used.

Received significant recognition for the application's improvements related to customer service and error resolution time reduction improvements.

General Electric   San Jose   **1994 to 1998**
Programmer/Analyst

Participated on team responsible for migration of a Windows-based client server pur purchase order, quotation, parts information, and shipping system to a struts intranet web solution.

Received superior annual performance evaluation for 1996 and 1997 for personal contributions to software modification that resolved several significant problems that had negatively effected processing speed of the new system.

Arnold E. Belz   Page 2

Skills Profile

Languages: C/C++, Visual C++, JSP, Java Beans, Java Servlets, Perl, HTML, DHTML, XML, JavaScript, SQL, PL/SQL

Technology: struts architecture, MySQL, J2EE

Operating Systems: Windows NT, Solaris, Unix

Database: Oracle, MS Access, My SQL, SQL Server

Web: HTML, XML, Cold Fusion, PHP, JavaScript

Software: Visio, ERwin, Excel

Unix Shell Script, Embedded SQL

Interpersonal, Verbal and Writing Communications, Problem Solving, Analytical, Project Management, and Team Participation Skills are strengths

Education

MS Computer Science, Rensselaer Polytechnic

BS degree in Computer Science & Mathematics, Syracuse University

Paul L. Cappozi
42 Drake Lane
Westbury, NY 11704
(516) 708-1200
plcapp@aol.com

Professional Qualifications

Strong background in J2EE applications architecture within the banking, financial, and technology industry disciplines. Significant experience in the building of network management systems and J2EE based portal development and integration within the financial industry.

Employment History

Citicorp   New York, NY   **2001–present**
J2EE Architect

Responsible for development of high-volume financial transaction applications based upon the latest technology. J2EE applications solutions architecture written in Java code using object-oriented and UML modeling.

Three related projects completed during the past two years have resulted in 30% productivity improvement in processing with a significant reduction in processing error frequency, which is now less than 1/10th of 1% of total transactions processed.

General Motors Acceptance Corporation   New York, NY   **1999–2001**
Software Consultant

Responsible for project team that developed and implemented a J2EE-based finance portal for use of banks and other financial institutions doing business with GMAC. Included the incorporation of improved network security and disaster recovery software.

Interactive   Sunnyvale, CA   **1997–1999**
Software Engineer

Team member on project to build network optimization tool for the network management system. Gained valuable software application experience for product development.

Candle Corporation   El Segundo, CA   **1995–1997**
Software Programmer

Primary responsibilities involved development of performance management solutions for use in Unix and Windows environments for web applications servers.

Paul L. Cappozi   page 2

Skill Profile Summary

Operating systems: Linux, Unix, Solaris, Windows NT, 2000

Languages: C++ server, J2EE, Java, Struts, XML

Web: EJB, CMI, JSP, Servlets, Struts, ANT, XML, HTML

Database: Oracle 8i, 9i, DB2, SQL Server

Applications servers: JBoss, BEA Weblogic

Web Servers: Apache Tomcat

Utilities: UML, ANT, Load Runner, Win Runner, Crystal Reports

Case Tools: Rational Requisite & Rose

Excellent interpersonal, verbal, written, and presentation communications skills

Education

BS Computer Engineering, California State University, Long Beach

William J. Simmons
95 East Lynn Avenue
Upper Darby, PA 19144
(215) 590-8001
wmjs@earthlink.net

Employment History

Prudential Insurance   Philadelphia, PA
Director of Information Systems   **2001 to present**

Responsible for the support of a multibillion dollar annual insurance business covering the Prudential Northeast Region. Manage organization of 150 employees with an annual budget in excess of forty million dollars.

- Systems conversion initiatives developed and implemented during 2002 and 2003 saved six million dollars during 2004.

Prudential Insurance   Jacksonville, FL   **1999 to 2001**
Business Systems Manager

- Reporting to the Director of Information Systems had responsibility for new systems development and systems operations for the Southeast Region of Prudential. Had direct responsibility for an organization of forty-five employees.

- Received recognition award from the Region Vice President for contributions for improved efficiency and cost savings achieved during the year 2000.

Pivotal Corporation   St. Paul, MN   **1997 to 1999**
Project Development Manager

Responsible for development of several initial application modules for this CRM software development company. Personally managed several of the first large client installations and participated in consulting contracts related to IT business related processes. Work provided opportunity to develop detailed understanding of client business processes within several specific industries. Staff responsibility for eight employees.

KPMG Management Consulting   Montvale, NJ   **1994 to 1997**
IT Manager Client Services Group

Responsible for client services for the audit and tax services groups serving the insurance and pharmaceutical industries. Responsibility entailed application development and project management for all approved and budgeted projects for each calendar year. Achieved excellent organization building results and was actively involved in the definition and selection of strategically significant projects. Led a group of fifteen employees.

William J. Simmons

American Express Health Services Group   Charlotte, NC   1991 to 1994
Project Manager Client Software

In charge of customization and other development and implementation of software for critical healthcare applications.

Management Skill Profile

Strong people leadership and organization building skills. Excellent interpersonal and communications skills. Have built strong skills in planning, strategy development, and knowledge of customer and client business processes. Financial skills are good in expense management and planning as well as annual operating plan preparation, financial forecasting, and budget activities. Have kept involved at the client level and have good understanding of the latest IT technologies and important client applications.

Education

BS Degree Mathematics, Duke University

Master's Degree in Computer Science Technology, MIT

Earl B. Thompson, Jr.
43 Norwood Avenue
Harrisburg, PA 19144
(717) 590-8001
email ebtjr@earthlink.net

Professional Experience

More than nine years of project management and consulting experience primarily focused upon state and federal government related projects. Have strong project management, programming, interpersonal, and team leadership skills. Have a top level security clearance for classified work. Objective is to achieve an IT organization management responsibility.

Employment Summary

State of Pennsylvania Harrisburg, PA   **2001 to present**
Project Manager for Highway Department

Head project manager for highway construction business process reengineering. Project included major software conversion focused upon engineering development software, database retention, and engineer training related components.

- Resulted in the restructuring of the department and implementation of an improved management process that has already resulted in reducing design engineering related time for a standard process by 30%.

- Early indications are annual payroll costs will be reduced by 5% and the need to hire two or three additional programmers and designers will be eliminated.

General Services Organization Alexandria, VA   **1999 to 2001**
Systems Programmer

Served as head programmer on a project that converted an expense tracking system to a web-based system. This involved the total redesign of a legacy system that had been used for years.

- Resulted in reduction of annual audit time and labor that permitted annual cost avoidance in excess of eight million dollars.

SRA International Fairfax, VA   **1997 to 1999**
Consultant

Served on teams for projects at three large financial organizations that prepared these organizations for year 2000 Y2K readiness.

Earl B. Thompson, Jr.

Self-Employed IT Consultant **1995 to 1997**

Performed programming related work on numerous projects for small- to medium-sized organizations to upgrade their software capabilities.

Skill Profile

Excellent people, team building, and verbal and written communications skills.

PMI Project Management Professional Certified, MS Project
Windows NT, 2000, Unix, Solaris, AIX, Oracle, DB2, SQL, SQL Server,
C++, HTML, XML, COBOL, Java, Unix Shell Script

Top Secret Security Clearance

Education

BS Computer Science Drexel University, Philadephia 1994

John M. Hadid
16 Country Lane
Holmdel, NJ 07031
(973) 438-3450
jmhadid@home.com

Summary of Qualifications

More than ten years of network management and engineering related experience. Have excellent understanding and have worked with the latest technology from initial network design through implementation in consulting work and directly for employers with large communications networks. Team participation, leadership, interpersonal, communications, problem solving, project management, and analytical skills are all very good.

Employment History

AT&T   Middletown, NJ   **2002 to present**
Network Engineer

Responsible for design of WAN solutions. Work involves developmental testing and validation and delivery of high-speed data packet services (Frame Relay and ATM) on Cisco WAN switches.

Kaiser Permanente   Walnut Creek, CA   **1997 to 2001**
Network Engineer Team Leader

Responsible for the design, engineering, implementation, and support for a national network for data, voice and video over public carrier and private microwave.

- Team's work saved more than two million dollars annually by moving the California voice networks to a Nortel ATM network. Consolidated SNA, DEC, and IP/IPX networks to a single Cisco IP network increasing bandwidth and related efficiency while eliminating several points of previous failures.

IT Solutions   Jacksonville, FL   **1999**
Network Consultant

Provided design support, installation, and maintenance of networks for clients using Cisco, Microsoft, VPN Solutions. Work included implementation of a 802.11b/a wireless system and application of VoIP on data networks using Qos.

John M. Hadid

Norrell Corporation (presently Spherion)   Ft. Lauderdale, FL   1995 to 1998
Network Administrator

Completed network, internet, and SQL database connections. Analyzed and fixed numerous software problems. Responsible for network problem resolution and maintenance. Established LAN WAN connections for 500 on-site users and several thousand field office users.

Skill Summary

Language: C, C++, HTML

Protocols: TCP/IP, IPX/SPX, SIP, H.323, FTP, Telnet, SNMP LANS, WANS

Frame Relay Switches, IP Network, ATM Switches

WAN Switches: Cisco BPX, AXIS, Cisco Routers, DSO, DSI, Catalyst

Security: Cisco PIS Firewall, Cisco IOS Firewall, Cisco VPN

Education

BS Degree Chemical Engineering, Virginia Polytechnical, Blacksburg, VA

Certifications: CCDP, CCNP

John R. Rasmussen
84 Summer Lane
Morristown, NJ 07036
(973) 512-6041
Email: jrrass@netzero.com

Professional Experience Summary

More than ten years of experience in various IT disciplines with significant expertise in network security engineering, quality engineering, quality process, and network engineering disciplines within the telecommunications, financial, and management consulting industries. Have consistently demonstrated the capability of improving business processes through application of the latest technology in these disciplines.

Employment History

Lucent Technologies   Holmdel, NJ   **2002–present**
Network Security Engineer

Design data and voice security solutions (firewalls, intrusion detection, encryption IPsec) internally and in consultation with sales organization for customer presentations and proposals.

Design improvements made to customer service network resulted in the reduction of 80% of the time that the sales organization was spending to resolve problems that customers and prospective customers were having in gaining access to the customer network for product engineering and technical data.

Nortel Networks,   Billerica, MA   **1999–2002**
Technical Applications Engineer

Consulted with customers on high-level network design for IP telephony, Qos, RIP, and OSPF networks. Developed and implemented tests to benchmark performance for throughput of VPNs and firewalls. Evaluated performance of security gateway equipment including router testing, IPsec functionality, firewall performance, Cisco IOS, Cisco VPN, and Nokia.

• Was selected to participate on product-planning technical advisory board as recognition for contributions made and value of work.

AT&T   Basking Ridge, NJ   **1998–1999**
Quality Engineer

Implemented the quality improvement process with the Network Engineering Business Group and provided guidance to the quality improvement process team on network engineering process improvement.

John R. Rasmussen

First Data Corporation   Englewood, CO   **1997–1998**
Network Engineer

Designed and built a secure fault tolerant network for an IRS electronic tax payment system. Implemented a secure LAN/WAN topology that passed IRS security audits and achieved 99.8 percent uptime.

KMPG Peat Marwick   New York, NY   **1994–1997**
Quality Assurance Specialist

Participated in the development and implementation of improved technology for security policies, standards and related software system was implemented in offices throughout the world.

Skill Summary

Excellent interpersonal and communications skills. Team leadership capability.

Database: LDAP, SQL, Oracle
Languages: Java, C++, C#, ASP, ASP.NET
Security: VPN, Encryption, IPsec, Firewall
Network: TCP/IP, ATM, IP, Frame Relay, RIP, Cisco Routers, DHCP, DNS, Wins
Operating Systems: Unix, Windows NT

Certification: CISSP

Education

BS Degree Computer Science, Rochester Institute of Technology
Cumulative grade point average 3.6

Tamara C. Wilson
45 Oglesby Road
College Park, GA
(404) 374-1818
tamaraw@home.com

Summary of Qualifications

Experienced Linux engineer with knowledge for operating system conversion, including wireless and IP telephony project development and implementation. Have good working knowledge of networks, the web, and their security architecture.

Employment History

State of Georgia Department of Highways   Atlanta, GA   **2003–Present**
Embedded Linux Engineer

Design development of embedded Linux systems used to control electronic highway message signs.

Citizens & Southern Bank   Atlanta, GA   **2001–2003**
Programmer Stock Trading Department

Developed Java-based financial applications for stock market trading and market analysis. Began working with Linux during 2002 performing programming work for applications on a TCP/IP network in encrypted formatting.

• Achieved a superior performance evaluation for the year 2002.

Federal Express   Colorado Springs, CO   **1999–2001**
Unix Programmer

Participated on a project team that completed development design for a shared memory server used for data retrieval from an Oracle database for application servers assisting customers to track status of shipments.

U.S. West   Englewood, CO   **1998**
Worked as college intern for communications systems.

Skill Summary

Programming Languages: C, C++, Java, Perl, Linux Red Hat, Assembly

Networks: TCP/IP, NFS, NIS, LDAP, DNS, DHCP routing

Operating Systems: Linux, Solaris, Unix

Scripting: Perl, Shell Scripts, php

Database: Oracle

Security: encryption

Additional Skills:

Communications, verbal and written, interpersonal, team work, problem solving, presentation

Experience within multiple IT disciplines

Education

BS Degree Computer Science, University of Colorado, Boulder 1998

Robert S. Gonzalez
12 West 81st Street Apt 16
New York, NY 10012
(212) 870-6105
email: rsgcp@aol.com

Professional Qualifications

Nine years of financial industry programming, database, and Unix technology experience. Have detailed understanding and work experience with primary financial industry applications. Have recent experience working with Linux and with team installing VoIP network. Have excellent verbal, written communication, and interpersonal skills. A significant leader in projects where good teamwork is important.

Employment History

Merrill Lynch   New York, NY   **1998–Present**
Unix Administrator Corporate Accounts   **2002–Present**

Current team assignment involves implementation of a VoIP system. Previous projects include implementation of a Linux open source operating system for our trading department.

- The Linux implementation will result in annual savings in excess of one million dollars on software licensing fees.
- Programmed and implemented interface software for the VoIP system that will speed up connection time by 30% when compared to our present system.

Database Analyst Bond Trading Department   **1999–2001**

Participated on a team that reconfigured the customer history database to a more intelligent system. This iniative enabled traders quicker access to better data that helped them be more professional and effective in their client sales work.

Programmer/Analyst   **1998–1999**
Performed general programming work for various departments.

Citicorp   New York, NY   **1995–1998**
Programmer
Performed entry-level programming during first year and later did file maintenance and transactional processing software writing. Work was primarily process procedural related work. My job and five additional ones were outsourced.

Skill Summary

Unix, Linux, C, C++, TCP/IP, Oracle 8i, 9i, Java, Shell Scripting, SQL, Windows NT, Windows 2000, SQL Server, JavaScript, XML

Strong team participation, interpersonal, verbal and written communications, problem solving and project participation skills

Education

BS degree in Computer Science, Polytechnic University, Brooklyn, NY, 1994

MCSE Certification

Fluent in Spanish

Stephen R. Meyers
18 West Grove Street
Northbrook, IL 62240
(312) 430-8640
stevemy@yahoo.com

Professional Profile

More than fourteen years of application development work within the heavy manufacturing, insurance, healthcare, and management consulting disciplines. Extensive knowledge of sales/marketing and manufacturing related practices, processes, and applications. An effective group leader with strong communications and motivational skills.

Employment History

Allstate Insurance   Chicago, IL   **2002 to present**
Programmer Analyst

Team leader in the development of a customer prequalification business system. System is used for assessment of potential risk associated with the qualification process for new customers, which has become more critical owing to large casualty losses in recent years within the industry. An intelligent system that analyzes and rates applicants.

Andersen Consulting   Chicago, IL   **1999 to 2002**
Programmer assigned to Financial Client Group

Developed a series of XML web services for mortgage company financial applications. ASP.NET, VB.NET, and SQL Server 2000 was used for application development. These applications were primarily used for decision analysis and future forecasting relative to money rates, inflation, demographics, income data, and other recent economic-related trends.

Bayser Consulting   Skokie, IL   **1996 to 1999**
Programmer Analyst

Worked on development of a software product used by pharmaceutical companies to monitor prescription sales activity related to specific establishments and market areas. System also included feature for sales targeting of selected physicians for contact and monitoring of this activity.

Stephen R. Meyers

Acheson Colloids Company   Port Huron, MI   **1992 to 1996**
Senior Programmer

Developed and implemented an accounting manufacturing control system, a perpetual inventory system, work-in-progress monitoring software, and a material quality control system. Completed planning for a Kanban and Just In Time material inventory system.

Ensco, Inc.   Southfield, MI   **1990 to 1992**
Programmer Analyst

Performed analysis of tariff and customs management software for General Motors.

Skill Summary

Database: Oracle, MS Access, SQL Server, T-SQL, DB2, SQL
Internet: ASP.NET, ASP, HTML, XML, JavaScript, FrontPage, IIS, XML web
Languages: VB.NET, Visual Basic, C#, C COBOL, Java
Script: VB Script
Software: JCL,SQL, DB2, Crystal Reports, Visio, IMS, EDI
Project Management, CSP
MS Access, Windows, Word

Good communications, problem solving, and group participation skills

Education

BS Degree Computer Science, Purdue University, Lafayette, IN

Eric R. Campbell
50 River Road
Bethesda, MD 20850
(301) 692-1784
erc@mindspring.com

Qualifications

Experienced in the development of sophisticated software applications for federal government primarily through employment with government contractors. Have successful experience working with development of embedded systems. Understand government procedures and regulations. Have top secret security clearance.

Experience Summary

Lockheed Martin   Reston, VA   **February 2003 to present**
Software Engineer

Developer of web applications for organizations throughout Lockheed and for external clients. Participate in all phases of the software development cycle, inception, development, testing, implementation, administration, and audit control.

SAIC   McLean, VA   **2000 to 2003**
Software Engineer

Worked on numerous government client applications. Included in these initiatives were projects for development of software systems for work station security, data mining, and web data retrieval.

Raytheon Corporation   Tewksbury, MA   **1998 to 2000**
Software Engineer

Responsible for design and implementation of an engineering department web site. Used Unix CGI Shell Script and JavaScript on Solaris. Used Java Swing for development of applications for database management by air traffic control employees.

Successfully resolved software trouble reports problems for the air traffic control system and establishment of the engineering department web site. Improved customer response to clients significantly while lowering monthly communications lines charges several thousand dollars each month.

Eric R. Campbell

Cisco Systems Corporation   Acton, MA   **1996 to 1998**
Systems Engineer

Resolved embedded web server software defects to increase the reliability of a major
product within the content server switch product line.

Skill Summary

Protocols: TCP/IP, HTTP, SOAP, RM/IIOP

Database: Oracle, MySQL, SQL Server, ERwin, Rational Data Modeler

Languages: Visual C++, C++, C#, algorithms, Java, JSP, Struts, APIs

Scripting: Perl, PHP, JavaScript, Shell Scripts

Operating Systems: Unix, Linux, Solaris, AIX, Windows

Web servers: Apace, Tomcat, IIS CIT web server

Application servers: JBoss, Weblogic, WebSphere

Good interpersonal skill including verbal and writing communication skill

Education

BS Computer Science, University of Michigan, Dearborn

Rachel L. Gomez
40 River Drive
Riverside, PA 19140
(215) 672–19040
gomezri@mindspring.com

Qualifications Summary

Experienced SAP administrator with more than ten years SAP involvement. Qualified for consideration of a SAP management position, management consultant or project manager on a large-scale project. Strong teamwork and leadership, interpersonal, communications, and project management skills.

Employment

Computer Sciences Corporation   Moorestown, NJ   **October 2003 to present**
SAP Analyst

System's configurator working on applications for sales and distribution best practices. Have primarily worked as a SAP Basic consultant at client sites performing file management structure, applications configuration, scripting structure, and Unix system Perl scripting.

Rustoleum Corporation   Vernon Hills, IL   **September 2001 to August 2003**
Project Leader

Led cross-functional team in implementation of SAP solutions for sales and distribution.

Acme Metals   Riverdale, IL   **December 1997 to August 2001**
SAP Administrator

Implemented SAP modules for sales, finance, and supply chain. Had total project responsibility and received company recognition for quality of work, resultant time savings, cost reduction, and overall efficiency improvements obtained.

Andersen Consulting   Chicago, IL   **February 1996 to November 1997**
SAP Consultant

Worked primarily with implementation team that implemented SAP applications for sales, distribution, and materials and warehouse management systems for DuPont Pharmaceutical in Mechelen, Belgium.

Skill Summary

Languages: SAP Basis, R/3, BW, APO, ABAP 4.0, Shell Script, C, C++, SQL, HTML
SAP Protocols: EDI, APPC, CPI-C, BDC, SAPcomm, ALE, OLE
Operating Systems: Windows NT, Unix, AIX
Database: Oracle, PL/SQL, SQL
Networks: TCP/IP
Testing: Load Runner
Other: SAP Solutions Manager, MS Office Suite

Excellent interpersonal, verbal, written, presentation, team building, leadership, problem solving, and project management skills

Education

BS Degrees Computer Science, Northwestern University, Evanston, IL

James H. Garza
112 Burr Street
St. Charles, MO 63301
(314) 410-1812
jhgarza@yahoo.com

Summary of Qualifications

Significant experience doing applied mathematics, algorithm, statistical, and bioscience related work with the healthcare, pharmaceutical, and financial industries. Includes significant experience working with biomedical engineering professionals within the research and development environments. Have strong project, team work, interpersonal, problem solving/analytical, and communications skills. Good conceptual and creative skill.

Professional Experience Summary

Bristol Myers Squibb   St. Louis, MO   **2003 to present**
SAS Programmer/Analyst

Designed and developed rule in SAS for establishing standards used for the analysis of chemotherapy drug administration to cancer patients. Developed computer software that identifies correlation relationships in cancer patients diagnostic and treatment histories.

University of California,   Davis   **2002**
Programmer

Developed and modified statistical algorithms and programming code on project for prevention of hoof and mouth disease.

National Institute of Health,   Rockville, MD   **2000 to 2001**
Statistician

Developed and maintained analytical and statistical report data for the Institute patient care clinical database. Responsibility included monitoring and analysis of health statistics of American Indians and Native Alaskan populations.

Wells Fargo Home Mortgage   Washington, DC   **1999 to 2000**
Statistical Programmer

Developed model for statistical analysis of client credit worthiness using SAS v.8.0. Responsible for maintenance of databases of current and potential customers for the marketing department.

Skill Profile

SAS Programming: Base, Macro, STAT, Graph and Process SQL
Software: SQL, PL/SQL, Oracle, C, C++, Pascal, FORTRAN, SPSS, MATLAB
Data Management: MS Access, SAS, Access SQL, DB2
Operating Systems: Windows XP/NT, Unix
Scripting: Perl, Korn Shell, Unix Shell CGI

Education

BS Degree Bioscience Engineering, University of Illinois

MS Statistics and Applied Mathematics, University of California, Davis

Alan J. Case
90 Ocean View Drive
San Diego, CA 91760
(619) 750-4167
ajcase@earthlink.net

Career Profile

Experienced algorithm and mathematical modeling programmer. Significant work done in pharmaceutical, drug development, medical testing, and medical diagnostic software. Strong communication skills including the ability to communicate scientific and mathematical concepts effectively to nontechnical individuals.

Employment History

Accelrys Inc.   San Diego, CA   **April 2002 to present**
R&D Scientist

Involved in algorithm and software development for structure based drug design tools. Participated on the team to develop Ligand data packages for drug discovery.

Roche Molecular Systems   Pleasanton, CA   **January 2000 to April 2002**
Clinical Database Engineer

Involved in disease diagnosis systems development. Primary responsibilities were for programming the clinical trials department database.

United Parcel Service   Timonium, MD   **November 1998 to January 2000**
Operations Research Analyst

Completed project work with internal teams and end users. Developed design architecture structure of system requirements requiring advanced mathematical modeling.

Genometrix   The Woodlands, TX   **July 1997 to November 1998**
College Intern

Involved in development of an application to automate blood DNA sequencing on a client server network written in Java and Oracle.

Skill Summary

Algorithm development
Database: Oracle Clinical, SQL, PL/SQL, eRT
Analytical Tool Kits: mathematical/molecular modeling
Languages: C, C++, Fortran, XML, XSLT, Java, JavaScript, Perl
Operating Systems: Unix, Linux, Windows NT/2000/XP
Others: MATLAB, LabView, AMP

Strong problem solving, verbal, presentation, and writing skills

Education

Master Degree Applied Mathematics, Rice University, Houston, 1998

BS Degree Computer Science, University of Houston, 1996

William T. Summers
28 Potters Farm Road
Morristown, NJ 07014
(917) 682-2590
summers@earthlink.net

Professional Experience Summary

More than twenty years experience developing and maintaining business application programs. Experience includes more than seven years of developing internet-based application solutions using Cold Fusion, JavaScript, Perl, C#, Java, and MS SQL Server for Oracle and MS Access databases.

Employment History

AT&T   Bedminster, NJ   **2002 to present**
Cold Fusion Engineer

Team leader for application development for online systems for project management, engineering content publishing and related software for project tracking status and related reports.

U.S. Department of Agriculture   Fort Collins, CO   **1996 to 2001**
Internet Engineer for Information Technology Center

Built multiple databases in Oracle, Access, and SQL Server. Primary applications were built in Cold Fusion, HTML, JavaScript, VB Script, ASP for one of nation's largest content databases.

Content was developed for supporting the U.S. Department of Agriculture and Department of Commerce data needs. Used Jacada Integrator to interface the new Oracle databases with the older legacy systems for updating them.

Write Consulting   New York , NY   **1992 to 1995**
Web Developer

Built and maintained a web-based statistical reporting system in Cold Fusion that streamlined processing for reporting monthly statistics to major vendors like HP, Cisco, and others for a large applications services provider.

Investment Data Services   New York, NY   **1990 to 1992**
Web Developer

Modified, updated, and maintained four databases containing customer history and large amounts of financial information that was sold to corporate and other financial institutions.

Earlier experience consisted of eight years as a programmer, programmer/analyst, and software engineer within technology and financial industry organizations.

William T. Summers

Skill Profile

Internet: Cold Fusion (fusebox), JSP, ASP, ASP.NET, JavaScript, HTML, XML, CSS, IIS, Apace Tomcat, VB.NET

Languages: Cold Fusion, Java, C, C++, SQL

Database: SQL Server, Oracle, MS Access

Scripting: Java Script, VB Script

Operating Systems: Solaris, Unix, Linux

Protocols: WAP, WML, HTML, XML

Tools: Jacada Integrator

Strong interpersonal, verbal and written communication, project management, analytical/problem solving, and end user/client relationship building skills.

Education

BS Degree in Computer Science & Mathematics, Virginia Polytechnic

Lee S. Takawa
12 West 94th Street
New York, NY 10128
(212) 886-4073
leepcpro@yahoo.com

Summary of Qualifications

Embedded software engineer with industry experience in the communications products, utility and information technology products industries. More than ten years experience developing embedded software solutions. Capable of leading work groups in development of embedded software for newer technologies such as smart appliances, wireless communications, digital games, and personal data assistants.

Employment History

New Jersey Power & Light   Edison, NJ   **2001 to present**
Embedded Engineer

Embedded engineer assigned responsibility for process improvement of specific applications of importance. Developed embedded software for storing data for electrical metering related applications.

Achieved metering software improvement that increased data storage capacity from three to six months of data.

Lucent Technologies   Naperville, IL   **1997 to 2001**
Software Engineer

Developed new initialization process for ATM switches. Served as project team leader for development of an ISDN project. Created automatic test scripts using Unix Shell Scripts for product tests.

Reduced time required to initialize switches by 20% using a new C++ algorithm. Received department recognition for this contribution.

Motorola Corporation   Schaumburg, IL   **1993 to 1997**
Embedded Software Engineer

Responsible for engineering research planning for integration of latest technology into mobile communications products. Responsibility also involved evaluation of various technologies associated with wireless, IP telephony, networking, and routing.

Lee S. Takawa

Skills Profile

Operating Systems: Unix, Solaris, Linux, Windows NT, 2000

Languages: C, C++, Assembly, RTOS, wireless, embedded, DSP, DSP assembly, HTML, XML, Pascal, MATLAB, Visual Basic, Java C#

Protocols: TCP/IP, FTP, Telnet, VPN, 802.11, Bluetooth

Real Time Embedded OS: DSP kernel & Linux

Hardware Platforms: DSP

Development Tools: Clearcase, ECMS

Excellent communication skills for highly technical data

Education

BS Degrees in Mathematics & Computer Science

California State Polytechnic

Carl M. Esposito
29 Pine Court
Fremont, CA 94537
(408) 271-6055
email: carlmpro@yahoo.com

Summary of Qualifications

Six years of web development experience within the financial, management consulting, and pharmaceutical businesses. Experienced and skilled in the latest web development technology with excellent interpersonal and communications skill.

Employment History

CBS Market Watch   San Francisco, CA   **2000–present**

Responsible for development of financial and portal web site for services provided Fortune 500 and equivalent clients. Developed ASP-based financial tools for online investors.

Environment: ASP, SQL, JavaScript, XML, XSLT

Booz Allen Hamilton   Crystal City, VA   **1999–2000**
Web Developer

Participated in development of web solutions for client teams throughout the United States.

Environment: Cold Fusion MX, SQL Server, Oracle, Windows 2000, ASP, JSP, PHP, .NET

Smith Kline Pharmaceutical   Iselin, NY   **1998–2000**
Wireless Web Development

Developed wireless software applications for use with vendor support system.

Environment: WML, HDML, WAP

Skills Profile

Internet; ASP, VB Script, JavaScript, HTML, CGI, XML, XSLT, Cold Fusion, Dreamweaver, ASP.NET, IIS Java Server, Perl

Programming Languages: Visual Basic, C, C++, Java

Database: SQL Server, MS Access, Oracle

Operating System: Windows NT, 2000, Unix

Team player with strong interpersonal, presentation, verbal, and written communications skills; problem solver; project management; latest technology awareness

Education

Associates Degree, Computer Technology, Stevens Institute of Technology, NJ

Brian C. Colville
104 Fourth Avenue East
Alexandria, VA 22042
(703) 246-0770
briancc@hotmail.com

Career Summary

Nine years of graphic design experience with technology companies. Have expertise in print, web, and video graphics development with past experience primarily within the marketing, engineering, and product development disciplines.

Employment Summary

Black & Decker   Towson, MD   **2002 to present**
Self-Employed Consultant

Have performed as a full-time consultant to the product development and marketing departments developing brochures, product specification sheets, and video presentations for use with large customers and trade shows. Most recently have developed an online video catalog that includes information on several hundred products.

Lockheed Martin Corporation,   Bethesda, MD   **1999 to 2002**
Graphic Designer

Worked with documentation department to develop PDF software for graphic illustrations for project management presentations to prospective customers. Also was responsible for completion of graphics for internal functional business presentations.

Fusion Systems   Rockville, MD   **1997 to 1999**
Multimedia Developer

Developed presentations for trade shows and completed an interactive training guide on disk for technical sales and technical support engineers. Worked with design engineering department to develop complex graphics for product design.

American Systems Corporation   Chantilly, VA   **1995 to 1997**
Graphics Designer

Supported marketing and sales with development of presentation and proposal graphics. Established and maintained database of several thousand content items.

Technical Skills

Software: PhotoShop, Illustrator, Power Point, Flash, Lightwave, Director, AutoCAD

Programming Language: ASP, Servlets, JavaScript Client, DHTML, XML, XSLT

Hardware Platforms: Macintosh, Windows

Education

Associates 2-year degree, Bucks County Community College, PA

Tim Van Horn
12 West Hill Drive
Cary, NC 27511
(919) 617-5345
tjvanhorn@netzero.com

Summary of Qualifications

Seven years applying the quality validation process for software, hardware, web, and client server projects from inception throughout their development cycle. Excellent analytical, problem solving, and interpersonal skills.

Employment History

Glaxo Smith Kline   Raleigh, NC   **June 2001 through November 2004**
Quality Assurance Engineer

Project participant that developed intranet portal that was the primary source for the hosting and distribution of management reports for senior management. Responsibility included work on a project team doing work on a database that consolidated research data related to research on HIV. Also participated in a work group that developed a voice application written in Perl that enabled users to search and retrieve information via voice recognition.

People Click   Raleigh, NC   **April 2000 through May 2001**
Software Quality Analyst

Worked on development and implementation of test plans for internet recruiting résumé software. Performed testing for stability assessment of new software releases.

Polaroid Corporation   Acton, MA   **November 1998 through February 2000**
Software Analyst

Developed ghost test environments to simulate actual customer product configurations for quality testing.

Hummingbird   Burlington, MA   **August 1997 to November 1998**
Quality Assurance Tester

Established a variables testing environment and performed preliminary testing for Y2K preparation.

Skill Profile

Experienced creating beta and regression testing for variable situations for client server and web applications testing

Languages: object oriented, Visual C++, C, Visual Basic, Shell Script, SQL, HTML, Assembly, ASP, HTML, Java, JavaScript, XML

Software test tools: SQA suite, QA Run, Winrunner, Test Director

Other: Front Page, MS Access, Visio, Robo Help, People Click Vision, Oracle, TOAD, Windows NT, 2000

Effective in project teams and other work group situations. Have strong communications and analytical/problem solving skills. Have ability to understand the business or customer significance of applications purpose.

Education

BS Degree Mechanical Engineering, University of Massachusetts, Amherst

Thomas B. Simpson
160 Patriots Drive
Lexington, MA 02421
(617) 422-1685
email: tsim-son@netzero.com

Professional Experience Summary

Experienced systems and network administrator within healthcare, financial, and high-technology organizations. Responsibilities have been in large organizations. Capable of total development and or management of server networks and communications systems in small- to medium-sized organizations.

Employment

Massachusetts General Hospital   Boston, MA   **2003 to present**
Systems Engineer

Responsible for server systems running IIS, SQL 2000, Windows 2000. Reconfigured numerous servers to improve functionality. Managed support of Cisco VPN, PIX Firewalls, Avaya PBX, and Audix voice mail systems at several locations.

Corning Lasertron   Bedford, MA   **2001 through 2002**
Systems Administrator

Implemented movement of users from Windows NT to Windows 2000 Professional Workstation. Worked on design of data center for new site and was responsible for implementing Windows NT/2000 and Compaq SAN mixed system for site.

Putnam Investments   Andover, MA   **2000**
Client Server Administrator

Tested, analyzed, and benchmarked new software packages; implemented wireless connections solutions for Notes mail to Palm, Blackberry, WAP phones.

SONY Electronics   San Diego, CA   **1997 through 1999**
Web Site Administrator

Coordinated upgrade of company web sites with the systems architecture and web development groups to improve the e-commerce components and overall functionality. Responsible for coordination with implementation teams throughout the United States including implementation data communication. Maintained additional responsibility for installation and coordination of hubs, switches, routers, and related cabling.

Thomas B. Simpson

Rohr Industries   San Diego, CA   **1996**
Systems Administrator

Responsible for management and support of email systems for more than 2,000
network users.

Skill Summary

Good teamwork, communications, training, project management, and problem solving
skills

Technical: Windows NT, 2000, XP, Cisco VPN/Pix, Citrix, IIS, Veritas, DB2, Active
Directory, CGI Scripts, Cold Fusion, Apache, Tomcat, SNA print servers, 3 COM hubs

Education

Associates Degree Computer Science, San Diego City College

Mary L. Jones-Smith
105 Taylor Road
Falls Church, VA 22042
(703) 235-8402
jonessmith@aol.com

Career Summary

Eight years of systems analysis and database analysis related work within the government, healthcare, telecommunications, and manufacturing industries. Have detailed understanding of the primary applications within these industries. Strong interpersonal, communications, problem solving skills, and effective in team and project team work groups. Good client relationship building skill.

Employment Summary

Department of Transportation   Washington, DC   **2002 to present**
Systems Analyst

Perform project management and quality assurance functions for integrated financial and contract management systems.

Durex Industries,   Cary, IL   **2000 through 2001**
Database Analyst

Developed business object reports for tracking all key processes associated with product development/engineering to completed manufacturing. Reports were implemented throughout four manufacturing locations.

Parklawn Hospital   Dallas, TX   **1998 through 1999**
Database/Systems Analyst

Developed intranet toolkit for application monitoring, statistical analysis, and system management using ASP.NET and SQL Server 2000.

U.S. Sprint,   Irving, TX   **1995 through 1997**
Systems Analyst

Used Java test code for object-oriented development work. Improved the process for testing by 20% which resulted in faster turnaround of products for production. Developed software for installation and maintenance charges for clients that were not being properly billed previously. This system eliminated the majority of previously lost revenues and during the first two years after installation average increases for previously nonbilled revenue were $340,000 per year.

Skill Summary

Operating Systems: Windows NT, Unix
Database: Oracle 9i, DB2
Languages: C++, SQL, PL/SQL, COBOL, Natural
Programming: Java, XML, HTML, WML, Natural, Natural with DB2, JavaScript, J2EE, JCL
Other: Crystal Reports, Rational Rose

Education

BS Computer Science San Jose State 1995

Kenneth C. Wilson
29 Myers Avenue
San Diego, CA 91750
(619) 440-1281
kcwil@yahoo.com

Qualifications Summary

Six years of help desk client server and network experience with companies in retailing, telecommunications, and IT systems work.

Work History

Arvadian Corporation   **San Diego, CA**   **October 2003 to present**
Technical Specialist

Provide technical support, problem analysis and solving, and user training for wired and wireless networks.

Verizon Data Services   **Tampa, FL**   **January 2001 to September 2003**
Help Desk Specialist

Responsible for analysis and troubleshooting technical problems in Windows, Unix, and AS 400 environments for forty different systems. Trained users on software for several hundred different software applications.

Flying J Inc.   **Ogden, UT**   **October 1999 to December 2000**
Help Desk Analyst

Responsible for problem solving and project implementation for several sites. Primary responsibility has been to keep point-of-sale installations operating trouble-free.

TEK Systems   **Roy, UT**   **July 1998 to October 1999**
Computer Technician

Installed and configured software on various computers. Trained users and troubleshot and fixed problems.

Skill Summary

Communications: OSI Model, Wi-FI, 802.11

Software: MS Office (Word, Excel, Access, Power Point), MS Outlook, Lotus Notes, Novell Group Wise, Word Perfect Office Server

Protocols: TCP/IP, VIP Network, DNS, IPX, SPX, FTP, Email

Operating Systems: Windows NT, 2000, Unix

Education

Associates Degree Computer Technical Support, ITT Technical Institute, 1998

Hillary B. Samuels
18 NW 4th Street
Fort Lauderdale, FL 33301
(954) 417-1605
Email: hbs@yahoo.com

Employment Summary

Telephone Start-Up Company   **January 2003–present**
Technical Writer

Responsible for completing all documentation, training materials, and written web content for a web dot com start-up. Personally designed and developed web-based interactive SDLC tools with links to all reference models. Included documentation of software reference data to support Unix-based telephony equipment used to monitor international calling card services.

Self-Employed Technical Writer   Jacksonville, FL   **1999–2003**

Completed documentation for engineering design work, software documentation, training materials, and web word content for several clients.

Most noteworthy was a large project for a mortgage company developing and producing online help documentation for property management software and loan customers using MS Word, PowerPoint, RoboHelp, and Adobe Acrobat help documentation produced in print PDF and online versions.

GTE Data Services   Temple Terrace, FL   **1995–1998**
Documentation Administrator

Maintained and updated documentation for a large international billing system hosted on an Interleaf publishing system.

Dade Community College   Miami, FL   **1992–1994**
Instructor

Taught writing and graphics software courses.

Skill Summary

Excellent writing, verbal communication, and presentation skills

Microsoft Word 2000, Object Oriented Design, Instructional System Design ISD, HTML, DHTML, ASP, Java, Visual Basic Script, Adobe Acrobat, Framemaker, Desk Top Publishing, Ventura, Corel Draw

Education

BA English, University of Illinois, Champaign

Have had several articles published on technical writing in business and computer publications.

Index